grand theft
2000

ALSO BY DOUGLAS KELLNER

The Postmodern Adventure, coauthored with Steven Best (Guilford, 2001)

Media and Cultural Studies: KeyWorks, coedited with Gigi Durham (Blackwell, 2001)

Herbert Marcuse toward a Critical Theory of Society, editor (Routledge, 2001)

Film, Art, and Politics: An Emile de Antonio Reader, coedited with Dan Streible (University of Minnesota Press, 2000)

Herbert Marcuse: Technology, War, and Fascism, editor (Routledge, 1998)

The Postmodern Turn, coauthored with Steven Best (Guilford and Routledge, 1997)

Articulating the Global and the Local: Globalization and Cultural Studies, coedited with Ann Cvetkovich (Westview, 1996)

Media Culture: Cultural Studies, Identity and Politics between the Modern and the Postmodern (Routledge, 1995)

The Persian Gulf TV War (Westview, 1992)

Postmodern Theory: Critical Interrogations, coauthored with Steven Best (Macmillan and Guilford, 1991)

Television and the Crisis of Democracy (Westview, 1990)

Critical Theory, Marxism, and Modernity (Polity Press and Johns Hopkins University Press, 1989)

Jean Baudrillard: From Marxism to Postmodernism and Beyond (Polity Press and Stanford University Press, 1989)

Camera Politica: The Politics and Ideology of Contemporary Hollywood Film, coauthored with Michael Ryan (Indiana University Press, 1988)

Herbert Marcuse and the Crisis of Marxism (University of California Press and Macmillan, 1984)

grand theft
2000

Media Spectacle and a Stolen Election

DOUGLAS KELLNER

ROWMAN & LITTLEFIELD PUBLISHERS, INC.
Lanham • Boulder • New York • Oxford

ROWMAN & LITTLEFIELD PUBLISHERS, INC.

Published in the United States of America
by Rowman & Littlefield Publishers, Inc.
4720 Boston Way, Lanham, Maryland 20706
www.rowmanlittlefield.com

12 Hid's Copse Road
Cumnor Hill, Oxford OX2 9JJ, England

British Library Cataloguing in Publication Information Available

Library of Congress Cataloging-in-Publication Data

Kellner, Douglas, 1943–
    Grand theft 2000 : media spectacle and a stolen election / Douglas Kellner.
        p.   cm.
    Includes bibliographical references and index.
    ISBN 0-7425-2102-8 (alk. paper)—ISBN 0-7425-2103-6 (pbk. : alk. paper)
    1. Presidents—United States—Election—2000.   2. Contested elections—United
States—History—20th century.   3. Press and politics—United States—History—
20th century.   4. Mass media—Political aspects—United States.   5. United
States—Politics and government—1993–2001.   6. Political corruption—United
States—History—20th century.   I. Title.
E889 .K45   2001
324.973'0929—dc21   2001019995

Printed in the United States of America

∞ ™ The paper used in this publication meets the minimum requirements of American
National Standard for Information Sciences—Permanence of Paper for Printed Library
Materials, ANSI/NISO Z39.48-1992.

For nothing can seem foul to those that win.

—Shakespeare, *Henry IV, Part I*

Imagine that we read of an extremely close election in the Third World in which the self-declared winner was the son of the former prime minister, a former spymaster seeking revenge and still highly active behind the scenes. Imagine that the lightly experienced son lost the popular vote by nearly half a million votes but won based on some old colonial holdover (the Electoral College) from the nation's predemocracy past. Imagine that the victory turned on disputed votes cast in a province governed by his brother.

Imagine that the poorly drafted ballots of one district led thousands of voters to vote for the wrong candidate. Imagine that members of that nation's most despised caste turned out in record numbers to vote against the son, who had executed more of them than had any other provincial official. Imagine that some members of that most despised caste were intercepted on their way to the polls at roadblocks. . . . Imagine that certain votes cannot be counted in this province unless the candidate requesting the count can somehow prove beforehand that he would win if the votes were recounted.

—E-mail widely circulated from "an unidentified Zimbabwe politician"

The election has been taken and we'll have to live with it—but please, not in harmony, not graciously, not in the full spirit of bipartisanship. Hooey.

All this back-slapping about our democracy doesn't convince me at all. This was not a democratic election. One human, one vote did not decide the outcome. The Supreme Court—which I always thought was above the fray, but is the fray, captured by the other side—gave the election to their guy.

We all know this crowning of George W. Bush stinks. . . . He did not win it fair and square. He snuck it, he wiggled it, his lawyers inveigled it, his daddy pushed it, his brother leaned on those who needed it, etc. So he has the presidency and all of its spoils.

—Anne Roiphe, feminist commentator

If, indeed, the Court, as the critics say, made a politically motivated ruling (which it unquestionably did), this is tantamount to saying, and can *only* mean, that the Court did not base its ruling on the law. And if this is so (which again, it unquestionably is), this means that these five justices *deliberately and knowingly* decided to nullify the votes of the fifty million Americans who voted for Al Gore and to steal the election for Bush. Of course, nothing could possibly be more serious in its enormous ramifications. The stark reality, and I say this with every fiber of my being, is that the institution Americans trust the most to protect their freedoms and principles committed one of the biggest and most serious crimes this nation has ever seen—pure and simple, the theft of the presidency. And by definition, the perpetrators of this crime *have* to be denominated criminals.

—Vincent Bugliosi, fabled U.S. prosecutor

CONTENTS

INTRODUCTION

The battle for the White House following the election of November 7, 2000, was arguably one of the major media spectacles in U.S. history, comparable to the Army-McCarthy hearings, the Kennedy assassination, the Watergate hearings, the Iran-Contra affair, the O. J. Simpson trial, and most recently, the Clinton sex scandals and impeachment trials. It was in many ways more contained and circumscribed than these other epochal events, taking place over thirty-six days from the uncertainty of election night to Al Gore's concession on December 13 and George W. Bush's acceptance of the mantle of president-elect. The story was highly theatrical with ups and downs, and surprises and reversals, for the candidates and the global audience, exhibiting unpredictability and uncertainty until the end. Its colorful cast of characters and melodramatic story line could hardly be bettered by the most creative Hollywood central casting.

The narrative structure of the media spectacle was conventional, with beginnings, middles, and an end, although it was a comedy with a happy ending for some and a dark tragedy for others. Of course, a contest for the presidency is more than a spectacle, and there were high political stakes in the drama. Election 2000 involved one of the most intense and important political contests in recent history, with potential for a constitutional crisis of an unprecedented proportion. During the struggle for the presidency, the U.S. machinery of voting was exposed as obsolete and dysfunctional, and U.S. institutions—from the television networks up to the Supreme Court—were radically questioned and continue to face a crisis of legitimacy.

The intense fight for the presidency is, therefore, by all standards a Big Story. But a story it is, and I propose to undertake a narrative and political analysis of the spectacle, using the methods of critical social theory, media analysis, and cultural studies to unpack and interpret Election 2000 and its stunning aftermath. I will dissect how it was produced and unfolded, what it communicated, and ultimately, what it tells us about the U.S. system of media, politics, and democracy at the turn of the new millennium.

It is clear from reflection on the period from November 7 to December 13 that television is still at the center of media culture and political contests. During both the election and the postelection combat, competing political players were most intent on manipulating the broadcasting networks. For it remains the case that people turn to television to experience key political and social events, and that television is the ultimate arbitrator of political reality. Yet the spectacle also highlighted that the United States and the global village enveloping it were entering the age of the Internet, and that more information is available to a greater number of people, more easily, and from a wider range of sources than any period in history. It was astonishing to discover the extensive array of material available, articulating every conceivable point of view on the election battle and providing news, opinion, and sources of a striking range and diversity.

Indeed, the wired world at least, and increasingly the public at large, is now in a total information environment, consisting of a broad spectrum of radio and television broadcasting networks; print media and publications; and the wired global village of the Internet, which itself contains the most varied and extensive sources of information and entertainment ever assembled that can send disparate types and sources of information and images instantly throughout the world. It is also true that thanks to media mergers of the past decade, fewer hands control the dominant media outlets, which can be utilized by powerful corporate and political interests for specific partisan ends, as I document in this study. To be sure, much of the world is not yet wired, many people do not even read, and different inhabitants in various parts of the globe receive their information and culture in very dissimilar ways through varying sources, media, and forms. Thus, the type and quality of information vary tremendously, depending on an individual's access and ability to properly interpret and contextualize it.

This study is undertaken from a specific social location, which turns out to be the very belly of the beast of the communications-spectacle industry that was crucial in the intense struggle for the presidency in November and December 2000. My focus is on how the spectacle played out on the U.S. television networks and infotainment system. I critically dissect the text of the media spectacle with sources from broadcasting to print media and the Internet. The latter often tell a different story than television, helping to provide necessary contextualization for TV's narratives and critique of its limitations.

Grand Theft 2000 follows my *Television and the Crisis of Democracy* and

The Persian Gulf TV War (1992) by applying the tools of critical social and media theory to analyze the role of the mainstream media, especially television, in U.S. politics and the ways that television has contributed to a crisis of democracy by not adequately informing, or misinforming, the public. The three books illustrate the ways the media have aggravated a crisis of democracy from the media presidency of Ronald Reagan, to the Persian Gulf TV war, and through Election 2000 and its startling conclusion. I stress, as before, the intersection of the media and politics, the means by which interested political parties manipulate the media, and the ways that various media are highly partisan and are themselves key players in political contestation. As I have long argued, the media are a contested terrain (1979, 1990, 1995), which themselves have competing interests and biases and are wooed, attacked, undermined, and used by competing political forces and interests.

Election 2000 and its aftermath acutely illustrate the crisis of democracy in the United States and the ways the media contribute to the sickness, but also suggest how democratic media can help provide the cure. More specifically, I engage what I consider a fierce confrontation over competing conceptions of democracy itself in the struggle for the White House. The spectacle projected highly resonant images of people struggling to determine the conditions and fate of their social and political life, contrasted with representations of opposing forces attempting to crush participatory democracy in favor of a more conservative concept of democracy in which elite institutions, like the U.S. Supreme Court, ultimately have sovereignty. Thus, democracy itself is at stake in the struggle that put on display the stunning limitations of democracy in the United States as well as some of its strengths.

In *Grand Theft 2000,* I also apply the model of cultural studies developed in my books *Media Culture* (1995) and *Media Spectacle* (forthcoming). In fact, a study of the 2000 election was envisaged as a dramatic opening for the latter book, or an illustrative chapter, exemplifying the ways that I saw media spectacle as increasingly central to U.S. politics and everyday life in an environment of mushrooming information and entertainment as we enter a new form of infotainment society in an emergent era of global and technocapitalism. As the battle for the White House unfolded, however, the study expanded quickly into a book-length manuscript.

While some of my recent books have engaged a postmodern turn in politics and culture in which the mediascapes of broadcasting and cyberspace have fundamentally transformed the economy, society, politics, and everyday life, the events described in this study are both a postmodern media spectacle and an old-time modern power struggle.[1] Although the Bush camp's success was in part due to the ability of Bush's handlers and the candidate's personality to construct a positive image, in the end, I argue, it was the Bush dynasty and the Republican Party's political machine that overwhelmed the Gore forces in the war for the presidency, with the media, especially certain television networks, aiding the Bush victory. Thus, while aspects of the struggle played out in cyberspace and the media, which strikingly captured some surprising and unpredictable twists and turns in the saga, it was old-fashioned power politics and the mobilization of money, lawyers, political operatives, and a disciplined and focused political organization that won the prize for Bush.

Election 2000 was indeed the most expensive in history, costing more than $3 billion, up 50 percent over 1996. According to a *Mother Jones* survey based on research of the Center for Responsive Politics, "An estimated 55 percent went to Bush and GOP candidates for Congress—and $646 million that came from corporations and wealthy executives eager to underwrite the Republicans' hands-off approach to business."[2] Bush had massive support from corporations, the Republican Party, rightwing activist groups, and allies in the media, and part of this story documents how the Bush machine mobilized support to steal an election to perpetuate its political dynasty and the economic and political interests of its supporters.

The limitations of a work of instant history are obvious. We are still immersed in the events being analyzed, and subsequent commentary and scholarship will provide more adequate perspectives and interpretations. The book was largely written during the heat of combat in which I videotaped and watched hours of television every day and downloaded stacks of information and analysis from the Internet, which now includes most mainstream newspapers and journals, as well as a wide range of political publications, Web sites, and other information sources—and an array of disinformation. In terms of material relied upon, I consulted the sites regularly on which I was increasingly depending in the Internet era, including salon.com and slate.com, as well as the main national newspapers such as the *New York Times,* the *Washington Post,* my hometown *Los Angeles Times,* and a wide range of Internet sources.[3] As is often the case in the culture of hypertext, explorations for material often take one into novel and surprising places and yield interesting material, and I have attempted to assemble the most significant of these materials for this study.

No doubt my critique will be read as a partisan text, and I readily admit to being partial toward democracy, social justice, accurate information, and good journalism. I cannot, of course, claim to tell the "truth" about the election since, as mentioned above, we are far too close to the events to completely present the whole story of the skirmish for the presidency, the factors behind the facts, or the yet-to-be-determined consequences and effects of Election 2000. I can, however, describe the unfolding of the spectacle of the Florida war for the presidency and engage issues that I believe significant—as have legions of journalists and commentators already. And I try to tell the most reliable and compelling story of the events that I can, based on sources now available.

As for my political biases, they are for radical democracy and social justice. I am not a partisan for either of the two major parties, found Election 2000 itself dispiriting, and was not enthusiastic about either major-party candidate. Both chief contending parties relied on focus groups and polls for their "issues" and "messages" and chose less than inspiring themes and foci for their campaigns. Both were financed by big corporations and represented only slightly different corporate agendas, and neither presented uplifting visions of social progress, justice, or democratic social transformation. Neither was sufficiently critical, in my view, of the U.S. military and its bloated budget and misguided priorities; neither adequately addressed the problems of globalization, of the environment, of the digital divide, and of other growing divisions between haves and have-nots.

Yet I did not agree in the least with Ralph Nader's disastrously wrong argument that there were no differences between the major political parties or candidates. The Democrats had the support of African Americans, Hispanics, gays and lesbians, and labor and working-class people; their policies were directed toward the constituencies who would be represented in a Gore White House. The Republican Party support, by contrast, was rooted in hard-core conservatives, the religious right, promarket corporate elites, and the usual upper-class constituencies thirsting for the tax cuts, deregulation, and cutting back of government that Bush had promised. Al Gore, whatever his charisma and personality deficits, was one of the most intelligent and competent politicians of his party and well qualified for the presidency. George W. Bush, by contrast, was the most underqualified candidate for the presidency during my lifetime, and he appeared to many to not have the intelligence, experience, or abilities to cope with the economic, political, and social challenges facing the United States in the new era of globalization, technological revolution, a networked society, a new cyberculture, and emerging forms of political and social unrest.

This is not, however, a book primarily about Gore and Bush, but about media and politics at the beginning of a millennium. It engages Election 2000 and its outcome in an era of spectacle politics and dissects how the drama was played out in the different stages of the struggle. A curious set of characters emerges, as does a contestation between the major U.S. political parties and players in the contemporary era, but my focus is on the often eye-catching events of the conflict and how the spectacle itself was constructed and played out. Rarely has live television ever been so raw, unedited, and direct in its immediacy, and seldom have journalistic investigations or critical commentary circulated so far and so fast. Thus, I engage the battle for the White House during an era in which politics is played out on the terrain of media spectacle—the site of my analysis.[4]

Initially, the president elect of the United States, George W. Bush, does not appear as a main protagonist in this story, although his family's formidable resources, connections, and networks play a major role in the theft of an election. George Junior himself, however, seldom appeared on stage during the Florida recount wars, preferring to let his handlers and representatives wage battle on his behalf, some say wisely. But those behind and for the conservative Republican appear front and center, and many, including myself, find the players and their actions worrisome. Bush's muted presence in this narrative suggests that George W. Bush himself is a spectacle, an actor in a ritual of image management, in which his handlers produce the script, and that the president of the United States is a puppet of powerful social forces.[5]

A change in tone and focus emerges as the book proceeds. As noted, I'd initially planned to undertake an analysis of media spectacle in Election 2000, and the opening study is a critical and analytical interpretation of the role of media and spectacle in the presidential election campaign. Like many, the drama of election night captured my interest, and initially I saw the ensuing political conflict as a great exercise in civic education that was disclosing the embarrassing flaws of the U.S. electoral system and limitations of its democracy. It also provided a revealing morality play of the foibles and follies of major political and media players within the U.S. political theater, as well as offering glimpses into how the media, political system, legal institutions, and partisan struggle work—or fail—to produce properly democratic results. Early chapters thus often dwell on the absurd and surreal elements of the contestation for the presidency and what it revealed about the current state of U.S. society. Once it was clear, however, that the Republican juggernaut for Bush was not going to concede no matter what the election results and would do anything necessary to win, the story becomes darker and my description becomes more detailed and interpretive.

Ultimately, the story becomes one of a stolen election and Republican coup d'état, and I thus focus on how this could take place, what it tells us about politics in the United States today, and the alarming consequences for democracy in the agon for the White House, as titanic a political struggle as has occurred in the United States in the modern era. The concluding studies focus on the Orwellian themes of corruption of political language in the media age and on what I consider a form of Republican Stalinism that brazenly stole the election, corrupting the U.S. Supreme Court, the political system, media, and culture in the process, thus intensifying the crisis of democracy under way for the past decades.

By "Grand Theft 2000," I mean that a crime of the highest magnitude was carried off by the Bush machine, that the presidency was stolen, that U.S. democracy was undermined, and that the hardright were able to seize control of the state apparatus and public policy. The theft of an election shows the U.S. system of democracy to be highly defective and vulnerable to takeover by societal forces that were heavily financed by corporate and rightwing groups, highly organized, and completely ruthless. The theft of Election 2000, as I attempt to demonstrate, was one of the most scandalous political crimes in American history and a demonstration of the need for radical change in the U.S. system of democracy.

Thus, while *Grand Theft 2000* presents a historical narrative of the heist of the presidency, my study also carries through a critique of the media and political system that registers a crisis of democracy in the U.S.A. today. Arguing that the media are culpable in the theft of the presidency by the House of Bush, my studies also highlight failures of voting technology and literacy, Republican manipulation of the Florida electoral process and political system in the counting of the votes, and structural problems with the system of democracy in the United States. In addition to exposing the flaws and underbelly of U.S. democracy, I also suggest some solutions to the problems revealed. A final chapter critically dissects the first 100 days of the Bush presidency, which is emerging as one of the most reactionary and contentious in U.S. history.[6]

As I unravel the story of the Florida recount wars, I argue that the theft of Election 2000 took place on three levels. First of all, before the election, Jeb Bush, Katherine Harris, and the Florida state Republican Party did everything possible to augment Republican votes and block Democratic votes, displaying gross partisanship, bordering on illegality. The Florida Republicans hired a Republican-based company, DataBase Technologies, to "cleanse" the voting lists of felons, which also eliminated thousands of legitimate voters, mostly poor and African American. The Jeb Bush gang allowed Republican political operatives to illegally fill in absentee ballot applications in Seminole and Martin Counties, breaking the law and denying Democrats equal privileges. Jeb Bush vetoed a $100,000 voter literacy bill depriving first-time voters of obviously necessary education on how to vote. The Florida Governor, brother of the Republican presidential candidate, sent out from his office absentee ballots, instructions, and a letter urging recipients to vote. Further, Florida secretary of state Katherine Harris employed Gulf War hero General Norman Schwartzkopf, a Bush supporter who frequently campaigned for George W. Bush and a close friend of his father, to participate in a get-out-and-vote TV ad campaign that was, in effect, using state funds to tell people to vote for Bush.

Second, on the day of the election, the Florida state Republican Party did everything possible to facilitate Republican votes and block Democratic ones. African American voters were harassed by police as they drove in vans to vote; largely first-time African American voters who had registered to vote found their names missing on voting lists, while many other longtime voters found that their names were purged from the voting lists and were denied their votes. There were not enough poll workers at many lower-income and predominantly Democratic Party precincts, inadequate computer lists of eligible voters, and insufficient language help for Spanish-speaking and Haitian voters. Moreover, there were a record number of undervotes that did not register because of faulty voting machines, primarily in low-income and/or heavily Democratic Party districts. In addition, there were a record number of overvotes due to faulty ballots, including the infamous butterfly ballot in Palm Beach County and a two-page ballot of presidential candidates in Duval County that contained instructions to vote for candidates on each page. Finally, there were many other voting irregularities and the manufacturing of many votes for George W. Bush and erasure of votes for Al Gore, as I will document in the course of this study.

Third, after the deadlocked election on November 7, the Bush machine and Florida Republican Party did everything possible to block the manual recount of selective counties called for by the Gore campaign. The Republicans pushed to certify Bush as president as quickly as possible, even though many thousands of votes had not been counted, attempting to seize the presidency for Bush, while blocking the counting of the votes that the Democrats demanded. In addition, the Bush camp was prepared to use the Florida legislature to name its electors, an act never before carried out that risked constitutional crisis and chaos. Finally, they ultimately called upon the U.S. Supreme Court to block the tallying of undervotes mandated by the Florida Supreme Court and in effect to give the presidency to Bush, in one of the most brazen examples of judicial activism and most controversial Supreme Court decisions in U.S. history.

I will recount the heist of the presidency as it proceeded during the Florida Recount wars, will provide documentation of the step-by-step and multifaceted theft of an election, will show how the mainstream media aided and abetted the Bush camp, and will uncover the crisis of democracy that the theft of an election reveals. It was an astounding and audacious theft, taking place in front of an audience of millions, played out on television before the wondering eyes of the world. Would the thief and his minions get away with the crime, would the President-Select (selected by the Supreme Court and not the voters) continue his reign of crime, robbing the federal treasury for his friends; undo social progress and governmental reforms of the past decade, and further subvert democracy in the United States? Or would the Presidential Pretender be unveiled, his reign cut short, his theft uncovered? The end of the story is uncertain, and the episodes in this study are thus but the beginning of what promises to be a highly eventful and unpredictable era in U.S. and global history.

This book is not, then, a swan song to American democracy, for precisely the events studied here reveal the highly contested nature of the political, legal, social, and cultural system in the contemporary era, the power of democratic forces, and the openings for a new era of radical democratic struggle. In an era of turbulent transformation, with technological revolution and the global restructuring of capitalism transforming every area of life, no one can predict what the morrow will bring. U.S. politics are especially unpredictable and indeterminate in a high-saturation media-infotainment environment in which fierce competition for audiences produces intense pressure to generate stories that will capture audience attention. Hence, as Bill Clinton discovered, the media are prepared to circulate just about anything, and in an era of frantic competition the media become the sites of intense political struggle and potential enlightenment, as well as mystification.

George W. Bush and his supporters may well learn that the loser now may later win, and the winner could become a major loser, as Richard Nixon was after his highly successful 1972 election when the Watergate scandal erupted and he became the first president in U.S. history to resign. Election 2000 could be a scandal bigger than Watergate, and it remains to be seen how the outcome of the war for the presidency will play out. As the following studies indicate, although Election 2000 leading up to voting night was relatively uneventful, with the confounding statistical dead heat erupting on election night, all hell broke loose and the seams, fissures, conflicts, and contradictions of the system burst out on the rostrum of the global village. Significant sectors of the public and media are now focused on the ongoing political confrontations, which are hardly over with Gore's concession and Bush's occupation of the White House. I tell this story after a brief setup that engages the role of the media in the 2000 election campaign—a topic that will no doubt be the subject of many articles and books.[7]

There are many people whom I would like to acknowledge for help with this project. I learned much about the Bush family during the eighteen years of 1978 through 1996 when I did with Frank Morrow *Alternative Views*, a public-access television show in Austin, Texas, and I thank our many student interns for research material into Bush senior's misdeeds during the era. Mari Shulaw encouraged me to pursue a book on Election 2000 when I first sent her my analysis of election night. Bob Antonio and Phil Agre provided useful comments on the first draft, and Agre's Red Rock Eater listserv continued to be a helpful source of information. Rhonda Hammer edited the first draft and was strongly supportive of the project, even though it forced her to endure my replaying of the tapes of the painful thirty-six days. Carl Boggs and Steve Bronner provided detailed comments and critiques of later versions of the manuscript. Steve Wrinn was highly supportive of Rowman & Littlefield's publication of the manuscript and helped through the various stages of production, as did Lynn Gemmell, Mary Carpenter, and Ginger Strader. And for excellent copyediting, I would like to thank Pat Knight. Finally, I would like to dedicate this book to the Heroes of Democracy in Florida who tried to count the votes.

Los Angeles, June 15, 2001

NOTES

1. For my studies of modern and postmodern theory, see Kellner 1989a, 1989b, 1989c, and 1995; and Best and Kellner 1991, 1997, and forthcoming.

2. See "Campaign Inflation: Industry Pumped in a Record $646 Million to Elect George W. Bush," *Mother Jones* (Mar.–Apr. 2001): 47. For a variety of sources indicating who contributed to the Bush campaign, see the Center for Responsive Politics Web site at http://www.journalism.berkeley.edu/resources/internet/crp.htm. The two presidential campaigns were restricted by law to spending $67.6 million for the general election (hard money). But the two parties were also able to raise and spend "soft money" with the Republicans raising about $211 million, 74 percent more than 1996, while the Democrats raised about $199 million, an increase of 85 percent over the

previous election. The single major cost is television ads with about one out of every five dollars raised going to TV advertising with the TV station owners taking in an estimated $600 million in revenue from political advertising in 2000, a 40 percent increase over 1996, helping broadcasters to achieve pretax profit margins that range from 25 to 50 percent (see *The Alliance for Better Campaigns*, "Gouging Democracy: How the Television Industry Profiteered on Campaign 2000," in Schechter 2001: 77–92).

The *Washington Post* reported that Republicans enjoyed a huge advantage in hard-money contributions (i.e., limiting contributions to $1,000 for candidates and $20,000 for political parties, and $5,000 political action committee [PAC] donations), amassing $447.4 million in such contributions during the 2000 election, compared with $270 million for the Democrats. But in the soft-money category (i.e., unlimited donations for issue advertising or political parties), Democrats were basically even with Republicans, pulling in $243 million compared to the Republicans' $244.4 million, leading the authors Ruth Marcus and Dan Balz to report "Democrats Have Fresh Doubts on 'Soft Money' Ban" (Mar. 5, 2001, A1). The Bush team pulled in more than $40 million from a network of Bush allies called the "Pioneers," in which those who pledged to raise at least $100,000 for Bush's campaign were put on an A-list and promised access and potential benefits for their contribution (see the list on www. counterpunch.org/pioneers.html). A more elite group, "The Republican Regents," involved 139 contributors who contributed at least $250,000 in soft money since January 1999 and were promised special access and favors; see Don van Natta and John M. Broder, "The Few, the Rich, the Rewarded Donate the Bulk of G.O.P. Gifts," *New York Times* (August 2, 2000).

3. Internet sources that were particularly useful include the daily lists of commentaries and links published by www.bushwatch.com, the commentaries and links to Internet material sources posted by Phil Agre in his Red Rock Eater News Service (RRE, now archived at http://commons.somewhere.com/rre/), and sources from http://www.counterpunch.org; http://www.alternet.org; http://www.eatthestate.org; http://www.commondreams.org; http://www.consortiumnews.com/; http://www.buzz-flash.com; http://www.americanpolitics.com/; and www.democrats.com.

4. The concept of spectacle that I am using derives from Guy Debord and the French situationists; for previous articulations of the concept of spectacle developed here, see Best and Kellner (1997 and 2001) and Kellner (forthcoming).

5. I happen to know a lot about the Bush family having published two books in which George Herbert Walker Bush plays key roles (Kellner 1990 and 1992). Moreover, I was professor of philosophy at the University of Texas at Austin from 1973 to 1998, and was thus in Austin at the time George W. Bush won his first race for governor and was then reelected. I followed his career with interest, knew some of his insiders, have heard copious stories about the person and his politics, and have read the major books on Bush junior including Ivins and Dubose (2000), Mitchell (2000), Begala (2000), Hatfield (2000), and Miller (2001). I also followed the election spectacle closely and read a lot of material, from print sources and the Internet, as the event unfolded, which I draw upon in this study.

6. The first draft of my text was written during December 2000 and January 2001, right after the events described. While editing the text and the proofs, I have been able to read a series of books that have appeared on the election. Jake Tapper, in his book *Down and Dirty: The Plot to Steal the Presidency* (2001), argues that both the Republicans and the Democrats were playing "down and dirty," attempting the heist of the presidency, and were equally unprincipled, mendacious, and ruthless. I argue, however, that the two sides cannot be symmetrized and made equivalent, that the Bush machine stole the election and was significantly more mendacious and ruthless than the Gore team, as, obviously, one side pulled off the theft and the other failed in its intention to get votes counted. A book by *Washington Times* correspondent Bill Sammon, *At Any Cost: How Al Gore Tried to Steal the Election* (2001), is ludicrously one-sided and recycles the Republican propaganda line that Bush legitimately won the presidency on election night and that Gore ruthlessly attempted to "steal" that election that Bush won. This position overlooks the simple fact that the Bush team *did* manage to seize the presidency, in a highly problematic and thuggish manner, as I attempt to show in this book, which provides the antithesis to Sammon's book and the correction to Tapper's too-easy synthesis.

Vincent Bugliosi's *The Betrayal of America: How the Supreme Court Undermined the Constitution and Chose Our President* (2001) provides a damning indictment of the role of the Supreme Court in the theft of the presidency and supplements my account. Alan Dershowitz also published an attack on the Supreme Court decision titled Supreme Injustice: How the High Court Hijacked Election 2000 (2001). Dershowitz points out how the decision for Bush against Gore contradicted the conservative justices' previous rulings, was tarnished by their partisan self-interests and motivations, and itself brought disgrace upon the Court. Since Dershowitz's book only arrived as mine was going to press, I was not able to draw upon it for my study.

I would also recommend the collection of articles found in Danny Schechter (ed.), *Mediocracy 2000: Hail to the Thief—How the Media Stole the U.S. Presidential Election* (2001). Many of the studies collected here are extremely useful, but I would disagree with the thesis in the subtitle that it was the media that "stole the U.S. Presidential Election," although I present the media as an important accessory to the crime. Jeff Greenfield's book on the media and the election (2001), however, is trivial fluff that distorts the biases of the media, generally repeats the standard Republican version of the election, and has been systematically critiqued by Bob Somerby in www.dailyhowler.com. Just as I was sending in the page proofs for my study, I received Mark Crispin Miller's provocative Benjaminian collage *The Bush Dyslexicon* (2001), a jolly good piece of Bush-bashing and theorizing that complements my critique.

On the campaign of Election 2000, reporter Dana Milbank's first-person accounts in *Smashmouth* (2001) are highly entertaining and sometimes insightful. I will also occasionally draw on the *Washington Post* instant book on the election, *Deadlock* (2001), the *New York Times* collection of articles *36 Days* (2001), and *U.S. News and World Report* correspondent Roger Simon's *Divided We Stand. How Al Gore Beat*

George Bush and Lost the Presidency (2001). The first two-thirds of Simon's book provides a lively overview of the election campaign with penetrating portraits, a lot of insider information, and perceptive analysis of Election 2000. The last third of the book, dealing with the Florida recount wars, misses the narrative and significance of the theft of the election. Simon's account dribbles into incoherence and fragments, recycles the same stories already circulated by mainstream media and published accounts, and fails to offer any original insight or reporting. All of these establishment mainstream media books are shockingly lacking in investigative reporting that unfortunately reflect the sad state of mainstream corporate media. I will argue, however, that the Internet compensates for the pathetic state of our establishment media and provide some hope that the truth about the Bush family dynasty, Election 2000, and the theft of the presidency will circulate and have appropriate consequences.

7. A word on sources and citations: I videotaped much of the battle for the White House and cite the networks viewed and the date in my analysis. I provide dates and sources for newspaper and journal citations, although since I accessed many of these from the Internet, often they do not have page number citations. I present Internet URLs for the Web sources used, but the reader is warned that these pages often disappear (which is why I also often cite source, date, and site so that readers can conduct searches). Finally, a word on nicknames. One of George W. Bush's personality quirks is the devising of nicknames for those around him so it is entirely appropriate to come up with suitable nicknames for the president, as I do throughout the text.

1

MEDIA SPECTACLE AND ELECTION 2000

When the real world changes into simple images, simple images become real beings and effective motivations of a hypnotic behavior. The spectacle has a tendency to make one see the world by means of various specialized mediations (it can no longer be grasped directly).

—Guy Debord

You've heard Al Gore say he invented the Internet. Well, if he was so smart, why do all the addresses begin with "W"?

—George W. Bush

The 2000 U.S. presidential election, one of the closest and most hotly contested ever, was from start to finish a media spectacle. Despite predictions that the Internet was on its way to replacing television as the center of the information system, TV in the 2000 election was perhaps more influential than ever. The proliferation of television channels on cable and satellite systems multiplied political discourse and images, with a large number presenting round-the-clock political news and discussion. These cable news channels were organized as forms of media spectacle, with highly partisan representatives of both sides engaging opposed positions in dramatic and combative competition. The fight for ratings intensified the entertainment factor in politics, fueling the need to generate compelling political spectacle to attract audiences.

The result was unending television discussion programs with commentators lined up for the Republicans or Democrats, as hosts pretended to be neutral, but often sided with one candidate or another. Of the twenty-four-hour cable news channels, it was clear that the Rupert Murdoch–owned Fox network was unabashedly pro-Republican, and it appeared that the NBC-owned cable networks MSNBC and CNBC were also partial toward Bush. CNN and the three major networks claimed to maintain neutrality, although major studies of television and press coverage of the election indicated that the media on the whole tended to favor Bush (see below and chapter 8).

By all initial accounts, it would be a close election, and both sides tried to furiously spin the media, getting their "message of the day" on screen or into the press. Both sides provided the usual press releases and sent out e-mail messages to the major media and their supporters, which their opponents would then attempt to counter. The competing campaigns also constructed elaborate Web sites that contained their latest "messages," video clips of the candidates, and other information on the campaigns.[1] Both sides staged frequent photo opportunities, saturated the airwaves with ads, and attempted to produce positive images of their candidates.

A HUMDRUM ELECTION CAMPAIGN

Throughout the summer, there was not much focus on the campaigns among the public at large until the political conventions took place, where both parties traditionally gathered and produced spectacles to provide positive images of their candidate and party. The Republicans met first, in Philadelphia from July 31 to August 3, filling their stage with a multicultural display of their supporters, leading pundits to remark that more people of color appeared on stage than were in the audience of the lily white conservative party that had not been friendly to minorities.

The Democrats met in Los Angeles in mid-August and created carefully planned media events to show off their stars, the Clintons and the Gores, with Al and Tipper's long kiss the most circulated image of the event. For the first time, however, major television networks declared that the political party conventions were not important news stories, but were merely partisan events, and they severely cut back on prime-time coverage allotted the spectacles. In particular, NBC and the Fox network broadcast baseball and entertainment shows rather than convention speeches during the early days of both conventions, and all networks cut back coverage to a minimum. CBS's Dan Rather, for instance, dismissed the conventions as "four-day infomercials"— advertisements for the parties and their candidates (CBS News, August 15).

Nonetheless, millions of people watched the conventions, and both candidates got their biggest polling boosts after their respective events, thus suggesting that the carefully contrived media displays were able to capture an audience and perhaps shape viewer perceptions of the candidates. After the conventions, not much attention was given to the campaigns during the rest of August and September in the period leading up to the presidential debates. The Gore campaign seemed to be steadily rising in the polls while the Bush candidacy floundered.[2]

During September, nothing seemed to go right with the Bush campaign. The hapless candidate was caught on open mike referring to a *New York Times* reporter as a "major-league asshole," with Bush's vice presidential choice, Dick Cheney, chiming in "big time." While publicly proclaiming that he would not indulge in negative campaigning, a television ad appeared attacking Gore and the Democrats that highlighted the phrase "RATS," attempting to associate the vermin with DemocRATS/bureaucRATS. Bush denied that his campaign had produced this "subliminable" message (in his creative mispronunciation) at the same time that an adman working for him was bragging about it.

Moreover, as the camps haggled about debate sites and dates, it appeared that Bush was being petulant, refusing the forums suggested by the neutral debate committee, and was perhaps afraid to get into the ring with the formidable Gore. Since the 1960s the presidential debates had been popular media spectacles that were often deemed crucial to the election. Hence, as the debates began in October, genuine suspense arose and significant sectors of the populace tuned in to the three events between the presidential candidates and single disputation between the competing vice presidents. On the whole, the debates were dull, in part because host Jim Lehrer asked unimaginative questions that simply allowed the candidates to feed back their standard positions on Social Security, education, Medicare, and other issues that they had already spoken about day after day. Neither Lehrer nor others involved in the debates probed the candidates' positions or asked challenging questions on a wide range of issues from globalization and the digital divide to poverty and corporate crime that had not been addressed in the campaign. Frank Rich described the first debate in the *New York Times* as a "flop show," while Dan Rather on CBS called it "pedantic, dull, unimaginative, lackluster, humdrum, you pick the word."

In Election 2000, commentators on the debates tended to grade the candidates more on their performance and style than on substance, and many believe that this strongly aided Bush. In the postmodern image politics of the

2000 election, style became substance as both candidates endeavored to appear likable, friendly, and attractive to voters. In the presidential debates when the candidates appeared mano a mano to the public for the first time, not only did the media commentators focus on the form and appearance of the candidates rather than the specific positions they took, but the networks frequently cut to "focus groups" of "undecided" voters who presented their stylistic evaluations. After the first debate, for instance, commentators noted that Gore looked "stiff" or "arrogant" while Bush appeared "likable." And after the second debate, Gore was criticized by commentators as too "passive," and then too "aggressive" after the third debate, while critics tended to let Bush off the hook.

It was, however, the spectacle of the three presidential debates and the media framing of these events that arguably provided the crucial edge for Bush. At the conclusion of the first Bush–Gore debate, the initial viewer polls conducted by CBS and ABC declared Gore the winner. But the television pundits seemed to score a victory for Bush. Bob Schieffer of CBS declared, "Clearly tonight, if anyone gained from this debate, it was George Bush. He seemed to have as much of a grasp of the issues" as Gore. His colleague Gloria Borger agreed, "I think Bush did gain." CNN's Candy Crowley concluded, "They held their own, they both did. . . . In the end, that has to favor Bush, at least with those who felt . . . he's not ready for prime time."³

Even more helpful to Bush was the focus on Gore's debate performance. Gore was criticized for his sighs and style (a "bully," declared ABC's Sam Donaldson) and was savaged for alleged misstatements. The Republicans immediately spun that Gore had "lied" when he told a story of a young Florida girl forced to stand in class because of a shortage of desks. The school principal of the locale in question denied this, and the media had a field day, with a Murdoch-owned *New York Post* boldface headline trumpeting "LIAR! LIAR!" Subsequent interviews indicated that the girl *did* have to stand and that there *was* a desk shortage, and testimony from her father and a picture confirmed this, but the spin was on that Gore was a "liar." Moreover, Gore had misspoken during the first debate in a story illustrating his work in making the Federal Emergency Management Administration (FEMA) more efficient, claiming that he had visited Texas with its director after a recent hurricane. As it turns out, although Gore had played a major role in improving FEMA, while he had frequently traveled with its director to crisis sites, and while he had been to Texas after the hurricane, the fact that he had not accompanied the director in the case cited accelerated claims that Gore was a "serial exaggerator," or even liar, who could not be trusted.

This Republican mantra was repeated throughout the rest of the campaign, and while the press piled on Gore every time there was a minor misstatement, Bush was able to get away with whoppers in the debate and on the campaign trail on substantial issues.[4] For example, when he claimed in a debate with Gore that he was for a "patients' bill of rights" that would allow patients to sue their HMOs for malpractice, in fact, Bush had blocked such policies in Texas and opposed a bill in Congress that would allow patients the right to sue. And few critics skewered Bush over the misstatement in the second debate, delivered with a highly inappropriate smirk, that the three racists who had brutally killed a black man in Texas were going to be executed. In fact, one had testified against the others and had been given a life sentence in exchange; moreover, because all cases were under appeal it was simply wrong for the governor to claim that they were going to be executed, since this undercut their right of appeal. The media also had given Bush a pass on the record number of executions performed under his reign in Texas, the lax review procedures, and the large number of contested executions where there were questions of mental competence, proper legal procedures, and even evidence that raised doubts about Bush's execution of specific prisoners.

After the first debate, *Saturday Night Live* heavily satirized both candidates, and Gore's handlers forced him to watch the episode. Accordingly, in the second debate Gore was highly restrained, careful not to criticize Bush too aggressively, and gave an uninspiring, if competent, performance. Now the Republicans had a field day raising questions concerning who is the real Al Gore?—a tactic that they repeated after the third debate when once again Gore was on the offensive, and when many commentators believed that Gore had decisively outshone the listless Bush (see, for example, Jake Tapper's article in *Salon*, October 18).

Gore was on the defensive for several weeks after the debates, and Bush's polls steadily rose.[5] Indeed, the tremendous amount of coverage of the polls no doubt helped Bush. While Gore had been rising in the polls from his convention up until the debates, occasionally experiencing a healthy lead, the polls were favorable to Bush from the conclusion of the first debate until the election. Almost every night, the television news opened with the polls, which usually showed Bush ahead, sometimes by 10 points or more. As the election night results would show, these polls were off the mark but they became *the* story of the election as the November 7 vote approached.

The polls were indeed one of the scandals of what would turn out to be outrageously shameful media coverage of the campaign. Arianna Huffington mentions in a November 2, 2000, column that on a CNN/USA Today/Gallup poll released at 6:23 P.M. on Friday, October 27, George W. Bush was proclaimed to hold a 13-point lead over Al Gore; in a CNN/Time poll released around two hours later that night at 8:36 P.M., Bush's lead was calculated to be 6 points. When Huffington called the CNN polling director, he declared that the wildly divergent polls were "statistically in agreement . . . given the polls' margin of sampling error." The polling director explained that with a margin of error of 3.5 percent, either candidate's support could be 3.5 percent higher or lower, indicating that a spread of as much as 20 points could qualify as "statistically in agreement," thus admitting that the polls do not really signify much of anything, as in fact election night results showed.

The polls were thus notoriously flawed during the 2000 campaign. Poll fatigue had set in with the public, and the major polling organizations admitted that they were getting a less than 50 percent response rate. Moreover, the national polls were irrelevant, because in an Electoral College system, it is the number of states won that is the key to victory, and not national polling figures. Nonetheless, network news coverage focused on the polls, or the strategies, mechanics, and ups and downs of the campaigns, rather than the key issues or the public's real concerns. With a shrinking amount of news coverage on the major network news, and soundbites in which news and information were condensed into even smaller fragments, media focus on the horse race and strategic dimension of the presidential campaigns meant that less and less time would be devoted to discussion of issues, the candidates, and the stakes of the election.

In this environment, the campaigns sought to create positive images of their candidates through daily photo opportunities and television ads, thus contributing to intensification of a superficial politics of the image. The television ads presented positive spectacles of the candidates' virtues and negative spectacles of their opponents' flaws. Contested states such as Florida were saturated with wall-to-wall advertising, and consequently Election 2000 campaign costs were the highest in history in which a record $3 billion was dispersed. The ads were closely scrutinized for distortion, exaggerations, and lies, with Internet Webzines such as *Slate* and some television networks providing regular analysis of the ads, while television networks replayed and closely analyzed the more controversial ones.[6]

Both candidates ran intense phone campaigns. Republican voters could be thrilled to get a prerecorded call from George W. Bush himself, telling them that he wanted their votes. On the Democratic side, there was a late-campaign barrage of telephone calls to black voters from Bill Clinton, while Ed Asner recorded a call to be sent to seniors in Florida warning them about Bush's

Social Security program. Of course, Hollywood celebrities and rock stars also campaigned for the candidates. Gore used his Harvard roommate Tommy Lee Jones, *West Wing* President Martin Sheen, and an array of young Hollywood stars to campaign for him, while Bush used Bo Derek and members of the Hollywood right such as Bruce Willis.

Yet it was perhaps late-night comics and *Saturday Night Live*, the longtime satirical NBC show, that most pungently exemplified the continued importance of television to electoral politics and that also made clear that contemporary U.S. politics *is* media spectacle. The comics had a field day satirizing the know-nothing smiling papa's boy "Dubya" (aka W., or Shrub, the little Bush) and AlGore, the stiff and pompous senator from Tennessee. Likewise, *Saturday Night Live* ridiculed the candidates after the debates in segments that were widely circulated and repeated frequently on nightly news as well as on a preelection special, giving rise to the claim that the *SNL* piece was the "most important political writing of the year" (MSNBC News, November 5 and November 15).[7]

The *Saturday Night Live* satire symmetrized Bush and Gore as dim lightbulbs, who were equally ludicrous. The presentations of Gore in particular were arguably inaccurate and defamatory, depicting the intelligent and articulate vice president and author as slow-talking, clichéd, and bumbling. It is true that Gore tended to dumb down his discourse for the debates and repeated certain phrases to make key points, but the satire arguably distorted his speech patterns and mannerisms, which were nowhere near as slow and lumbering as in the satire. These often-repeated satires probably went further than Republican attack ads in creating a negative public image of Gore. Their constant reiteration on the NBC news channels thus provided not only advertisements for the popular Saturday night television show, but unpaid attack ads for the Republicans.

Bush's turnaround in the polls in October after his numbers had been steadily dipping for weeks was seemingly boosted by what was perceived as his successful appearance on the debates and on popular talk shows, such as *Oprah*, where an image of the much-beloved African American talk hostess giving him a smooch was widely circulated. Some claimed that the talk shows were a natural for the more relaxed Bush, although there were debates over whether his appearance on the *David Letterman Show* hurt or helped his efforts, as he appeared giddy and was unable to effectively answer the tough questions Letterman posed.

In any case, both candidates made appearances on the major late-night talk shows, as well as other popular television venues previously off-limits to presidential candidates. In general, television spectacle helps to boost the chances of the most telegenic candidate, and according to media commentary, Bush repeatedly scored high in ratings in "the likability factor." Polls continued to present Bush as more popular than Al Gore, and most media commentators predicted that he would win the election handily.

MEDIA BIAS FOR BUSH

In the postmodern politics of promotion, candidates are packaged as commodities, marketed as a brand name, and sold as a bill of goods. In a presidential race, campaigns are dominated by image consultants, advertising mavens, spin doctors, and operatives who concoct daily photo opportunities to make the campaign look appealing, "messages" sound attractive, and "events" present the candidates in an attractive format. Such campaigns are, of course, expensive and require tremendous budgets that make competing impossible for candidates without access to the megafortunes needed to run a media politics campaign. In turn, such megaspectacles render politicians beholden to those who cough up the megabucks to pay for the extravaganzas and the vast apparatus of producers, spinners, and operatives to create them.

Bush's brand name was his family trademark, son of the former president and Bush dynasty heir apparent, with his own distinctive "compassionate conservatism." The latter phrase shows the completely bogus and spurious nature of presidential packaging, as there is little "compassion" in the record of the Texas governor who executed a record number of prison inmates, who cut welfare lists and social programs, and who promised more of the same on the national level. In the politics of presidential marketing, however, creation of image takes precedence over ideas, style replaces substance, and presentation trumps policy. With politics becoming a branch of marketing, the more marketable candidate is easier to sell. Thus, it is not surprising that Bush's image, style, and presentation trumped Gore's ideas, substance, experience, and policies with large segments of the public.

Bush had another major asset in the competition for votes and marketing of the candidates. Cultural historians make distinctions between "character," based on one's moral fiber and history of behavior, and "personality," which has to do with how one presents oneself to others (see Sussman 1984 and Gabler 1999, 197). The new culture of personality emphasizes charm, likability, attractiveness, and the ability to present oneself in positive images. Bush was clearly Mr. Personality, instantly likable, a hail-fellow-well-met and friendly glad-hander who was able to charm audiences. He was becoming a media celebrity whose record and claim to accomplishments were few, but he was able to effectively play the "presidential contender" and provide a resonant personality. Moreover, Bush was able to transmit his likable qualities to television, whereas Gore frequently had more difficulty in coming across as personable and translating his considerable intelligence and experience into easily consumable soundbites and images.

The Texas governor, who was obviously more a figure of personality than character, was also able to turn the "character issue"—with the complicity of the press—against Gore and convince audiences that he, George W. Bush, was a man of "character" as well as personality. The Bush camp used the term "character" as a code word to remind audiences of the moral lapses of Bill Clinton and of Gore's association with the president, in a sustained collapse of one into the other. The Bush campaign also systematically defamed Gore's character, and the media bought into this, as I am documenting.

Furthermore, Bush, more than the deadly serious and wonkish Gore, produced entertainment; he was amusing and affable in debates, even if weak on substance. Like Ronald Reagan, Bush looked good on the run, with a friendly smile and wave, and in general seemed able to banter and connect with his audiences better than Gore. Bush's misstatements and errors were amusing, and on late-night talk shows he poked fun at himself for his mispronunciations and gaffes; *Slate* compiled a list of "Bushisms," and they were as entertaining as David Letterman's Top Ten list and Jay Leno's nightly NBC monologue, which often made jokes about Gore and Bush.

The American public seems to like entertaining politicians and politics, and when stories broke a few days before the election that Bush had been arrested twenty years before on a drunk driving charge and had since covered this over and even lied about it, the polls did not punish him. When asked of highs and lows of the campaign on election night, Bush said with his trademark smirk that even the lows "turned out to be good for us," alluding to polls that indicate that Bush got a rise in popularity after revelations of his drunk driving charge. As with Clinton's survival of his sex scandals and the Republican impeachment campaign, it seems as if the public empathizes with the politicians' foibles and resents moral indictments of at least those with whom voters sympathize. Obviously, Clinton was a highly empathetic personality whom voters could sympathize with, and many resented the Republican moral crusade against him. Likewise, voters liked Bush and seemed to not be affected by the embarrassing disclosure of his DWI record and its longtime cover-up.

Talk radio was an important medium during the campaign, just as it was over the last decade in U.S. politics. It was the relatively new form of unrestrained talk radio that first mobilized conservatives against Bill Clinton after his election in 1992, providing a basis of indignation and anger that fueled the circulation of the details of the Clinton sex scandal and generated support for his impeachment. Of course, the very excesses of rightwing talk radio provided a backlash, and many stations chose liberals to counter the conservative hosts, so talk radio too became a contested terrain (see Boggs 2000).

Yet during Election 2000 and the ensuing struggle for the presidency, rightwing talk radio had a comeback, energizing its old audience and finding new ones, while projecting the hatred of Clinton onto Gore. The narcissistic and demagogic Rush Limbaugh, who had mercifully been taken off television because of declining ratings and who had seemed to disappear from the national mainstream media, reappeared in all his virulent unglory, frequently appearing on NBC channels, which rehabilitated the discredited demagogue to celebrity and credibility.[8] Limbaugh and other rightwing blowhards grew louder and more aggressive than ever, demonizing Gore and mobilizing conservative constituents to vote for Bush, helping as well to organize against the Democrat candidate once the postelection struggle for the presidency erupted.

Moreover, and crucially, major research studies of the nexus between media and politics revealed that both the broadcast media and the press were pro-Bush and that this bias perhaps won the Republican enough votes to ultimately wrest the election victory from Gore and the Democrats (although, of course, many maintain that the election was stolen and that Gore had won the plurality of Electoral College votes, as well as the popular vote). A study by the Pew Research Center and the Project for Excellence in Journalism (PEJ) examined 2,400 newspaper, television, and Internet stories in five different weeks between February and June 2000, and indicated that 76 percent of the coverage included one of two themes: that Gore lies and exaggerates or is marred by scandal. The most common theme about Bush, the study found, is that he is a "different kind of Republican." A follow-up PEJ report concluded:

> In the culminating weeks of the 2000 presidential race, the press coverage was strikingly negative, and Vice President Al Gore has gotten the worst of it, according to a new study released today by the Committee of Concerned Journalists.
>
> Gore's coverage was decidedly more negative, more focused on the internal politics of campaigning and had less to do with citizens than did his Republican rival.
>
> In contrast, George W. Bush was twice as likely as Gore to get coverage that was positive in tone. Coverage of the governor was also more issue-oriented and more likely to be directly connected to citizens.

These are some of the key findings of a major new study of press coverage in newspapers, television and on the Internet during key weeks in September and October.[9]

Hence, the early coding of Gore in the mainstream media was that he tended to exaggerate and even lie and was implicated in many scandals, while the media bought the Bush line that he was a different type of Republican, a "compassionate conservative," and someone who worked with Democrats and Republicans in Texas "to get things done." When the election would heat up in the fall, the Bush campaign would exploit these motifs, and the mainstream media would generally go along with this line, without serious investigation of Bush's record or his own exaggerations (see below).[10]

One of the most utilized examples of Gore the liar and "serial exaggerator" was the alleged claim that he had invented the Internet. In fact, Gore had made no such claim, although the media, the Republican spinners, and Bush himself constantly referred to this urban myth. Bush burst out in one of the debates that "his opponent" claimed to "have invented the Internet" and then smirked in contempt and during the election often repeated the joke, caught many times in news footage: "You've heard Al Gore say he invented the Internet. Well, if he was so smart, why do all the addresses begin with 'W'?"

This lie about Gore, and Bush's systematic exploitation of the myth, speaks volumes about the quality of the Bush campaign. First, it is simply untrue that Gore claimed he "invented" the Internet.[11] Second, it is interesting how Bush and his handlers utilized the "W" as a trademark to distinguish Bush from his father and how Bush became popularly identified as W., or the Texas-inflected "Dubya." Whereas JFK's initials were an apt summary of his style and achievements, and LBJ earned the gravity of his initials through many years in the Senate, culminating in becoming Senate Majority leader, then gaining the vice presidency and presidency, George W. Bush was popularly referred to as W., which is about all there is. But Bush's appeal was predicated on his being "just folks," a "good guy," like "you and me." Thus, his anti-intellectualism and lack of intellectual gravity, exhibited every time he opened his mouth and mangled the English language, helped promote voter identification. As a some-time Republican speechwriter Doug Gamble once mused, "Bush's shallow intellect perfectly reflects an increasingly dumbed-down America. To many Americans Bush is 'just like us,' a Fox-TV President for a Fox-TV society."[12]

Bush not only charmed large sectors of the American public, but was effective in schmoozing the media. Another survey released of press coverage after the conventions showed a decisive partiality for Bush. The Center for Media and Public Affairs (CMPA) study of television election news coverage before, during, and after the conventions (released on August 14) concluded, "Network evening news coverage of the GOP convention was more favorable toward George W. Bush, while Al Gore received mostly unfavorable TV references, according to a new study released by the CMPA." The study also found that "Bush has received more favorable coverage than Gore throughout the 2000 campaign, reversing a trend that favored Bill Clinton over his GOP opponents in 1992 and 1996."[13]

Surprisingly perhaps, Bush fared as well with the print media and establishment press as with television. Supporting the studies of pro-Bush bias, Charlie Peters reported in the *Washington Monthly* that according to the PEJ studies, the *New York Times* front page "carried nine anti-Gore articles and six anti-Bush; 12 pro-Gore and 21 pro-Bush" (November). Howard Kurtz, media critic of the *Washington Post,* reported: "Those who believe the media were easier on Bush will find some support in a new Project for Excellence in Journalism study. Examining television, newspaper, and Internet coverage from the last week in September through the third week in October, the report says Bush got nearly twice as many stories as Gore" (November 6, 2000). Moreover, only one in ten of the pieces analyzed the candidates' policy differences, with two-thirds focusing on the candidates' performance, strategy, or tactics. Twenty-four percent of the Bush stories were positive, compared to 13 percent for Gore, while the Bush stories focused more on issues than character or campaign strategy.

A German group, Media Tenor, also documented a persistent anti-Gore and pro-Bush bias in mainstream media presentation of the candidates (see the summary in Schechter 2001: 100f. and the Web site www.medien-tenor.de/english/). Thus three different research projects found strong media bias in the election coverage. To be sure, such "positive" and "negative" scoring of images and discourses is difficult, but I would argue that even more significant than alleged bias in new stories in the mainstream media is the preponderance of conservative punditry and, even more significant, the exclusion of wide-spread media documentation and discussion of key aspects of George W. Bush's life, record in business and government, and obvious lack of qualifications for the presidency.

In his 1992 book *Fooling America*, Robert Parry documents the pack journalism of the mainstream media in the 1980s and 1990s, arguing that the horde follows "conventional wisdom," recycling the dominant and predictable opinions, while failing to pursue stories or develop positions outside of or against the prevailing views of the day. During Campaign 2000, journalists on the whole tended to accept the line of the Bush campaign concerning Gore's purported negatives while promoting the view that the Bush camp advanced that Bush was a uniter, not a divider, a "compassionate conservative," and someone who pursued "bipartisan" politics in order "to get things done."

Clearly, media pundits tended to favor Bush over Gore. As Eric Alterman demonstrated in *Sound and Fury: The Making of the Punditocracy* (revised, 2000), conservatives had trained a cadre of media commentators, well versed in the art of soundbite and staying on message, and there were many, many more conservatives than liberals on the airwaves. The conservative punditocracy trashed Gore daily, while Bush escaped critical scrutiny of his record in Texas, his limited experience, his problematic proposals, and his almost daily misstatements. The conservative pundits, however, aggressively promoted the Republican message of the day and served as ubiquitous shock troops for the Bush machine.

It is generally acknowledged, as this chapter argues, that the media were strongly biased toward Bush. I would suggest this bias was especially visible in the network commentary after the three debates in which the pundits were more critical of Gore than Bush, often on style over substance, while journalists were quicker to pursue Gore's misstatements in the debates than Bush's. On the Fox and NBC networks the pundits were overwhelmingly conservative and favorable to Bush over Gore, while all the television networks and commentators tended to go easier on Bush than Gore on debate performance and substance.

For example, although a fierce debate over prescription drugs in the first debate led to allegations by Gore that Bush was misrepresenting his own drug plan, driving Bush to verbally assault Gore, the media did not bother to look and see that Bush *had* misrepresented his plan and that Gore was correct, despite Bush's impassioned denials, that seniors earning more than $25,000 a year would get no help from Bush's plan for four or five years. Moreover, after the third and arguably decisive presidential debate, the MSNBC commentators and punditry were heavily weighted toward pro-Bush voices. In questioning Republican vice presidential candidate Dick Cheney about the third debate, Chris Matthews lobbed an easy question to him attacking Al Gore; moments later when Democratic House Majority Leader Dick Gephardt came on, once again Matthews assailed Gore in his question! Pollster Frank Luntz presented a focus group of "undecided" voters, the majority of which had switched to Bush during the debate and who uttered primarily anti-Gore sentiments when interviewed (MSNBC forgot to mention that Luntz is a Republican pollster). Former Republican Senator Alan Simpson was allowed to throw barbs at Gore, to the delight and assent of host Brian Williams, while there was no Democrat allowed to counter the Republican in this segment. The pundits, including Matthews, former Reagan-Bush speechwriter and professional Republican ideologue Peggy Noonan, and ethically challenged plagiarist Mike Barnacle, all uttered pro-Bush messages, while the two more liberal pundits provided more balanced analysis of the pros and cons of both sides in the debate, rather than just spin for Bush.

But the bias in the mainstream media favoritism toward Bush not only came through in how the media presented and framed the two opposing candidates, but in how they failed to pursue George W. Bush's family history, scandalous business career, dubious record as governor, lack of qualifications for the presidency, and serious character flaws. None of the many newspaper, magazine, and television reports on the Bush and Gore family history mentioned the reports on the origins of the Bush dynasty fortune in a bank that financed German fascism or pursued the Bush family financial scandals that continued through Jeb, Neil, and George W. Bush.

During the Battle for the White House a story appeared in the Saragosa *Herald-Tribune Coast News* entitled "Author Links Bush Family to Nazis" (Dec. 4, 2000), which claimed that Prescott Bush (George's father and W.'s grandfather) was a principle figure in the Union Banking Corporation in the late 1930s and 1940s. The article cited a lecture by John Loftus, a former prosecutor in the Justice Department's Nazi War Crimes Unit and author of a book with Mark Aarons entitled *Unholy Trinity: The Vatican, the Nazis and the Swiss Banks* (New York: St. Martin's, 1998). Loftus noted that Prescott Bush was a director of the Union Banking Corporation, which was secretly owned by leading Nazi industrialists and helped finance the Third Reich; when the bank was liquidated in 1951, the Bushes made $1.5 million from their investment.

A Lexis-Nexis search indicated that there were no references to the origins of the Bush family fortune in Union Banking Corporation that financed national socialism until an article by Michael Kranish, "Triumphs, Troubles shape generations," *Boston Globe* (April 23, 2001), including the following:

> Prescott Bush was surely aghast at a sensational article the *New York Herald Tribune* splashed on its front page in July 1942. "Hitler's Angel Has 3 Million in US Bank" read the headline above a story reporting that Adolf Hitler's financier had stowed the fortune in Union Banking Corp, possibly to be held for "Nazi bigwigs."
>
> Bush knew all about the New York bank: He was one of its seven directors. If

the Nazi tie became known, it would be a potential "embarrassment," Bush and his partners at Brown Brothers Harriman worried, explaining to government regulators that their position was merely an unpaid courtesy for a client. The situation grew more serious when the government seized Union's assets under the Trading with the Enemy Act, the sort of action that could have ruined Bush's political dreams.

As it turned out, his involvement wasn't pursued by the press or political opponents during his Senate campaigns a decade later.

Prescott Bush's involvement in the Union National Bank had earlier been documented in a biography of George H. W. Bush (Tarpley and Chaitkin 1992, 26–44), although, unfortunately, the authors were disciples of Lyndon LeRouche and their often solid and damning scholarship was undermined by LaRouchite conspiracy theories. Hence, until Loftus no major U.S. historian or journalist has explored the connections with a Nazi bank of the Bush dynasty. Neglect of the unsavory origins of the Bush family fortune and later financial scandals of the Bush family is one of the major journalistic outrages in U.S. history. Indeed, most books and articles on the Bushes are whitewashes that repeat the same myths, and there has been little investigative study of the family by the U.S. media, political, and academic establishment.

There was also no probing of the Bush family involvement during Election 2000 in the savings and loan (S&L) scandal, arguably one of the biggest financial debacles in U.S. history, costing U.S. taxpayers over half a trillion dollars to bail out the failed S&L institutions which had gone on a spending orgy after deregulation in the early 1980s. George H. W. Bush and James Baker were instrumental in the deregulation of the industry during the Reagan administration, and their families and friends had bought up and looted S&Ls, including the Silverado S&L scandal involving Neil Bush (see Brewton 1992).

There was also little coverage of the political scandals that Bush senior had been involved in, such as the Iran-Contra scandal, the U.S. arming of Saddam Hussein, or the misdeeds of the CIA under Bush's directorship (see Kellner 1990 and 1992; Parry 1962). In addition, there was almost no reporting on George W. Bush's personal or financial history, which included reports of using favoritism to get out of military service and then going AWOL, failing to complete his military reserve service. There was little discussion of his checkered business career, including allegations that his father's friends bailed out his failing oil industry and that he then unloaded his own stock in the Harken energy company that had bailed him out, selling before revelations of a bad financial report and failing to report the sale to the Securities and Exchange Commission, giving rise to charges of "insider trading." Bush's poor record as Texas governor was also not probed, nor were his personal failings and inexperience that should have disqualified him from serving as president.

Books, articles, and easily accessible Internet sites document the entire scandalous history of George W. Bush and his dubious dynasty, but lazy and arguably corrupt functionaries of the mainstream media failed to probe this rich mine of headlines and scandals—whereas there were few embarrassments or negative aspects of Al Gore's past that were not mined and endlessly discussed on talk radio and among conservative television punditry. Likewise, there were few in-depth discussions of the record of Bush's vice-presidential choice Dick Cheney, the major role he would play in a Bush White House, and his precarious health. Cheney had one of most hardright voting records in Congress and was heavily involved in the oil industry as CEO of Halburton industries, one of the worst polluters and most ruthless corporations in an industry known for its hardball Robber Barons.[14]

Bush thus benefited significantly from media coverage of Election 2000; all studies and indicators suggest that the media were heavily prejudiced in his favor and I have argued that Bush also benefited by the domination of conservative punditry and failure to adequately investigate his history, record and qualifications, the scandals that his family has been involved in, and the record of his running mate Dick Cheney, one of the most hardright political operatives of the present era. There had been little investigative reporting on Bush and a preponderance of favorable stories for Bush and unfavorable ones for Gore, as evidenced in the CMPA, PEJ, and Media Tenor studies cited above. Likewise, television pundits seemed to favor Bush over Gore. Media critic David Corn noted that commentators such as John McLaughlin, Mary Matalin, Peggy Noonan, and many of the Sunday network talk-show hosts prophesized a sizable Bush victory and tended to favor the Texas governor (tompaine.com/news/2000/11/24). Yet the election was the closest in history, and election night and the aftermath comprised one of the most enthralling and gripping media spectacles in recent history.

NOTES

1. Unlike one-way transmission television ads, the sites of Bush and Gore in the 2000 presidential race featured interactive links for citizens to "get involved." Gore provided special links for students, African Americans, Asians, Hispanics, and gays

MEDIA SPECTACLE AND ELECTION 2000

and lesbians, all conspicuously absent on Bush's site, except for an "en español" link and a "Just For Kids!" page that likens a presidential campaign to a baseball game and contains a story about the governor's cat, Ernie. The Bush site allowed visitors to donate funds to Bush, to "Send a Letter to Your Editor," and to spread the Bush message. A Bush store sold everything from Bush baby bibs to a Bush director's chair. In an excellent overview of the role of Internet sites in Election 2000 and issues involved in online politics, see Stephen Coleman, "What Was New? Online Innovation in the 2000 Elections," in Schechter 2001: 120–33. The most controversial was a Bush satire/attack site, www.gwbush.com, which led the Bush camp to unsuccessfully sue the group, leading to bad publicity for the campaign (see the essays compiled on www.bushsuckz.com). Curiously, the Bush campaign bought up a lot of URLs, such as www.bushsucks.com, www.bushblows.com, www.bushbites.com, and similar titles which took the browser to the official Bush campaign site and today go directly to his White House site!

2. See the daily commentary on the campaign in Howard Kurtz's media columns archived at www.washingtonpost.com and Millbank 2001: 307ff.

3. See the detailed selection and analysis of pundit quotes on the debate in Howard Kurtz, *Washington Post* (Oct. 4, 2000). While there was copious discussion of Gore's sighs, there was little discussion of Bush's goofy laughs and questionable snorts. There were persistent rumors in the early stages of the presidential campaign that Bush had been a heavy drug user, including cocaine. During the campaign, however, the media, by and large, overlooked Bush's past with drugs, although his telltale snorting and uncontrollable "heh, heh" laughs in debates could be the sign of a man with a pharmaceutical problem and generating a montage on Jay Leno of Bush snorting, but there was no media discussion of this stylistic tic, as there had been of Gore's sighs and facial expressions. (The now trade-mark Bushian snort, by the way, was repeated in January 2001 in his first speech at a military base, where W. made a rousing point, then punctuated with his frequent but rarely mentioned snort, visible in the ABC news report.)

4. See the analysis of "Twenty-Five Bush Flubs in the Second Debate" and "Fifteen [Bush] Flubs in the Third Debate" at http://www.tompaine.com/news/2000/10/20/index.html. Republican pundits, however, obsessively pursued the theme that Gore was a liar. In the October 11, 2000 *Wall Street Journal*, the grossly overinflated Republican ideologue William Bennett wrote: "Albert Arnold Gore Jr. is a habitual liar. . . . The vice president lies reflexively, promiscuously, even pathologically." In fact, the alleged lies that Gore "promiscuously" promulgated were largely Republican propaganda; see the sources in notes 10 and 11 below.

5. A note on polls: The majority of the mainstream media polls on the eve of the election put Bush in the lead, sometimes as much as by 10 points during the final days of the election campaign (although the Zogby/Reuters and CBS News polls put Gore slightly ahead in the popular vote). Joan Didion reports, by contrast, that seven major

academic pollsters presenting their data at the September 2000 American Political Science Association convention all predicted a big Gore victory, ranging from 60.3 percent to 52 percent of the vote. See Didion, "In God's Country," *The New York Review of Books* (Nov. 2, 2000). Academic pollsters tend to use rational-choice models and base their results on economic indicators and in-depth interviews; they seem, however, to downplay moral values, issues of character, the role of media spectacle, and the fluctuating events of the election campaigns. Indeed, the academic pollsters argue that the electorate is basically fixed one or two months before the election. Arguably, however, U.S. politics is more volatile and unpredictable and swayed by the contingencies of media spectacle, as Election 2000 and its aftermath dramatically demonstrate.

A story in the *Washington Post* (Feb. 9, 2001) by Robert G. Kaiser, "Experts Offer Mea Culpas for Predicting Gore Win," presents interviews with major political scientists who had predicted a strong win for Gore based on their mathematical models and data collected months before election day, seeing Gore winning from 52.8 to 60.3 percent of the national votes. One professor admitted that the "election outcome left a bit of egg on the faces of the academic forecasters," whereas others blamed a poor Gore campaign, "Clinton fatigue," and an unexpectedly strong showing by Ralph Nader. One defiant forecaster said that the election was simply weird, "on the fringe of our known world, a stochastic [random] shock."

6. Slate.com had a Web site available during the election campaign on the television political ads, CBS had an "ad watch" Web site at http://cbsnews.com/now/story/0,1597,143267-412,00.shtml, as did ABC (http://dailynews,yahoo.com/h/abc/20010326/pl/floridafelonvote_010321_1.html). The *Washington Post* also ran a regular "ad watch" feature, archived at http://www.washingtonpost.com/wp-srv/politics/campaigns/adwatch2000.htm. Political ads, however, were not only broadcast by the major parties, but special interest group ads also saturated the airwaves; see Milbank 2001, 359ff and the study of television advertising by the Alliance for Better Campaigns, in Schechter 2001: 77–92. In an illuminating study of ads in Election 2000, Lynda Lee Kaid argues that Bush's TV ads established eye contact with viewers in 26 percent of his spots compared to only 6 percent for Gore. Bush was three times as likely to be shown with a smiling expression than Gore; and Bush was shown in close-up or tight shots in 41 percent of his ads compared to 24 percent for Gore, thus using video imagery to sell Bush's "personality" to voters. See "Videostyle and Technological Distortions in the 2000 Political Spots," International Communications Association Convention, Washington, D.C., May 2001.

7. For discussion of the *Saturday Night Live* effect, see *Suck* (Nov. 16, 2000), and on comedy and the media, see Marshall Sella, "The Stiff Guy vs. the Dumb Guy," *New York Times* (Sept. 24, 2000).

8. Highlighting the reborn importance of Rush Limbaugh after the election, Matt Druge gushed that Limbaugh had become "the highest paid info-broadcaster in history," clocking in with $30 million this year, more than the network anchors combined (http://www.drudgereport.com/rr.htm). Once again, we see that in the United States

today, narcissism, celebrity, and brute aggression continue to sell and pay, as Limbaugh symbolizes these traits. He rose to media prominence during a period when Homer Simpson, Beavis and Butt-Head, and other aggressive narcissists were popular figures in the American imaginary. Limbaugh and these other cartoon figures embodied the bigotry and resentment of angry white males, who began collecting together to hear Limbaugh's daily radio show. They were soon known as "dittoheads," which meant that they parroted Rush, shared his bigotry and hardrightwingnuttery, and were mad as hell and not going to take it anymore. Like Homer Simpson, Limbaugh's white male rage made him endearing to mass audiences that were also entertained by his buffoonery.

9. For the PEJ report, see http://www.journalism.org/publ._research/campaign1.-html. For a good overview of the PEJ findings and critique of mainstream media news coverage of the election, see Bill Kovach and Tom Rosenstiel, "Campaign Lite: Why Reporters Won't Tell Us What We Need to Know," *Washington Monthly* (Jan.–Feb. 2001).

10. For a wealth of studies of the media and politics of Election 2000, see the Project for Excellence in Journalism (http://www.journalism.org/) and the studies in Schechter 2001. In a *Columbia Journalism Review* article, "Gore Media Coverage—Playing Hardball," Jane Hall systematically analyzes negative and often misleading coverage of Gore, contrasted to soft and generally uncritical coverage of Bush (September/October 2000). For analyses of distortion of Gore's record and refutations of Republican mantras about his "lying," see Robert Parry's studies "Al Gore v. the Media" (February 1, 2000, www.consortium.com) and in the April 2000 *Washington Monthly;* the compilation of Bob Somerby's critiques of false Bush campaign claims and the media buying into these at www.dailyhowler.com; Sean Wilentz, "Will Pseudo-Scandals Decide the Election?" *The American Prospect,* Vol. 11, Issue 21 (September 24, 2000); Eric Boehlert, "Gore's too-willing executioners," *Salon,* October 27, 2000; Mollie Dickenson, "Who's Lying? Gore or the Media?" www.tompaine.com, October 18, 2000; and Susan Douglas, "Bush's Fifth Column," in *In These Times* (December 25, 2000). The prize for most inept media criticism goes to Camille Paglia who declared "the only thing worse than the candidates this year is the shockingly biased liberal press" (*Salon,* Dec. 6, 2000), a judgment rendered without one example of liberal bias and in the face of stacks of studies documenting conservative and pro-Bush bias.

11. For convincing demolitions of the allegation that Gore claimed to "invent" the Internet, see "The Red Herring Interview: E-Gore" (*Red Herring,* October 30, 2000). A story in *Wired* falsely reported that Gore asserted that he "invented" the Internet, whereas in fact he had simply stated that "I took the initiative in Congress" to help "create" the Internet, a completely accurate statement that key members of the high-tech community involved in producing the Internet confirmed. The Republicans continued to spread the false smear about Gore, including George W. Bush who baited Gore in a debate with the lie and repeated it constantly in his stump speech. This is

an example of Republican use of the "Big Lie" technique, where a falsehood is stated over and over as if it were a truth, which would come to characterize "Bushspeak" during the Battle for the White House and Bush presidency (see chapter 9).

12. Doug Gamble, cited in Martin A. Lee, www.sfbg.com/reality/12.html. See also Jake Tapper's discussion of Bush's "Dumb Chic," *Salon*, Nov. 2, 2000, and Miller's probing analysis (2001).

13. Cited in www.cmpa.com/pressrel/electpr2.htm. The Center for Media and Public Affairs (CMPA) is run by Robert Lichter, who has generally been perceived as a conservative critic of the media's liberal bias (although he claims to be a neutral social scientist), so it is interesting that his organization found a bias in favor of Bush. Later CMPA findings indicate that Gore's positive network news coverage went up sharply after the Democratic convention, as did Gore's ratings (Sept. 5, 2000). But a study released by CMPA on October 18 indicated that "network news coverage of Al Gore turned sharply negative after the first presidential debate." It appears that CMPA's positive/negative network news codings of the candidates correlate remarkably with the candidates' rise and fall in the polls, although since polls themselves came under dramatic attack in the election, it is obviously not clear what exact impact positive and negative presentations of candidates on television news and in print have on voters. See also the discussion of positive/negative coding and the work of the German group Media Tenor in Markus Rettich, "Into the White House through the Television Screen," in Schechter 2001: 100–102.

14. For books on George W. Bush that document the allegations made above, see Introduction, note 3; websites that document the history of Bush family scandals and George W. Bush's history include www.moldea.com; www.bushwatch.com; http:/prorev.com/bush3.htm; and www.gwbush.com/. For a useful overview of Cheney's health, history, voting record, and hardright credentials, see Begala 2001: 126–36.

②

THE LONGEST NIGHT

If you're disgusted with us, frankly, I don't blame you.

—Dan Rather, CBS

. . . we don't entirely trust all the data we have.

—Judy Woodruff, CNN

As usual on election night, the television networks assembled their top anchors and commentators and their political analyst teams and prepared to present election results to the public, in highly competitive conditions. As usual, each network trumpeted its ability to present fast and accurate results, with Dan Rather of CBS declaiming early on election night that "if we say somebody's carried the state, you can take that to the bank."

After the first polls closed at 7:00 P.M., EST, on the East Coast the networks started calling states, and initial predictions suggested an upset victory for Gore, as the networks called the crucial and heavily contested state votes in Michigan, Pennsylvania, and Florida for Gore. These three states rich in electoral votes were hotly contested, and when at 7:50 P.M. the networks called Florida for Gore, it seemed that a victory was in the making. In an unprecedented election night event, Bush campaign officials invited reporters into Bush's office in the Texas governor's mansion, allowing Bush, surrounded by his parents, wife, and the Cheneys, to claim that their polling data for Florida and Pennsylvania suggested that they could win these states and were still in the race.

Initially, when Bush campaign officials and then Bush himself indicated that they had polling results for Pennsylvania and Florida that led them to believe they would prevail, it appeared that this was mere bravado (and indeed Bush's media adviser Mark McKinnon acknowledged later in the evening when the three key states of Pennsylvania, Michigan, and Florida "went south," the Bush camp somberly faced the prospect of defeat). CBS commentator Dan Rather declared that Bush's prospects of winning were "shakier than cafeteria Jell-O." Moreover, the array of gloomy Republican supporters and gleeful Democratic supporters over the next couple of hours interviewed on the television networks made it appear that Gore would be the next president.

One of the more ominous notes of the evening was struck by former Republican presidential candidate and Viagra salesman Bob Dole, who dolefully whined that for the first time in U.S. history it appeared that one candidate (Gore) was going to win the Electoral College (the majority of state votes), while another candidate (Bush) was going to win the popular vote. Dole threatened that the American people wouldn't stand for this, sending out a chilling message that the Bush forces would challenge the legitimacy of the election if they won the popular vote and lost the electoral vote—a possibility earlier suggested by Bush officials in a *New York Daily News* story, later reported in *Newsweek*.[1] Such an appeal to the primacy of the popular vote in the face of U.S. electoral laws would be, of course, highly ironic in the light of later events in which Gore won the popular vote by more than 500,000 votes while the Bush forces desperately struggled to win the Florida vote and thus prevail with a squeaker in the Electoral College.

To the shock of the nation, to the horror of the Gore supporters, and to the joy of the Bush camp, the networks confessed around 10:00 P.M. that their earlier call for Florida to go to Gore was based on "faulty data" and the state was now "too close to call." Dan Rather now declared that "this presidential race . . . is crackling like a hickory fire." There were six states where the winner could not yet be determined from the voting and exit poll data upon which the election turned. As Bush received the Arizona votes but Wisconsin, Iowa, Oregon, and Washington were still too close to call, CBS's Rather enthused, "The presidential race is still hotter than a Laredo parking lot, 246–242."

It was declared around 11:00 P.M., EST, that the Republicans had won the House, maintaining control of its agenda and chairmanships, but the Senate was heading for a tie as Democrats picked up key seats. But Bush appeared to be gaining momentum, winning a string of states and surging ahead of Gore in the crucial electoral vote, as well as maintaining a lead in the popular vote, inspiring Rather to conclude, "Al Gore's situation is he's basically got his back to the wall, his shirttail on fire, and a bill collector's at the door, but he's not yet finished."

Yet Gore hung in, and as November 7 faded and the early morning hours of November 8 unfolded, it was clear that whoever won Florida would win the election. Shortly after 2 A.M., the television networks announced, portentously and wrongly, that Bush had won Florida and thus the presidency—the second predictive error of the night. The strongly pro-Bush Fox network, owned by Rupert Murdoch, was the first to call it for Bush at 2:16 A.M., EST, followed by NBC, CNN, and the other networks moments later (*Los Angeles Times*, November 9). An overcaffeinated Dan Rather of CBS intoned, "Sip it, savor it, cup it, photostat it, underline it in red, press it in a book, put it in an album, hang it on the wall. George W. Bush is the next president of the United States."

In an astonishing aftermath, it came out that it was Bush's cousin, John Ellis, working for Fox who had helped make the call for the Republican. Moreover, the network polling consortium, initially blamed for the miscall, claimed that it did not have the data to make this prediction. It was also revealed that Bush's cousin had been phoning and perhaps leaking proprietary polling information to his cousins Jeb, the governor of Florida, and George, the Republican presidential candidate, the entire evening.[2]

Initial reports had it that the Voters News Service (VNS), which provided polling data to all the networks, was responsible for the error in the call during the middle of the night that Bush had won. But it turns out that the Fox network made the call for Bush without the VNS polling data, and the beleaguered polling company insisted that it had not called Florida for Bush. There was then a flurry of media attention on Bush's cousin, John Ellis, who had encouraged Fox to make the call for Bush based on Florida data. Ellis himself wrote a highly revealing description of his activities at Fox during election night, which included accounts of his phone conversations with his cousins George and Jeb Bush, as well as a report of his initial briefing of Fox owner Rupert Murdoch and the former Republican operative and now president of Fox News, Roger Ailes, in their executive suite (see www.inside.com). Immediately after Fox's call for Bush at 2:16 A.M., Murdoch's *New York Post* produced a red-bannered headline reading BUSH WINS! which the network proudly displayed, until the turnaround, at which time other networks used the headline as an icon of the rush to judgment in the calling of the election.

For the next hour or so, the networks showed images of joyous Bush supporters in Austin, Texas, waiting for the victory speech, contrasted with the dejection of Gore supporters in Nashville, waiting for the Democrat to give a concession speech. In retrospect, the networks' premature call for Bush created the presumption that the Republican candidate had won the presidency and that Gore was engaging in delay tactics and desperate maneuvering to snatch the election from the Republicans. In fact, it was a highly questionable call by the Fox network, prompted by Bush's cousin, and the ensuing network rush toward coronation that created the false impression that Bush had legitimately won the election by capturing Florida, creating the presumption that Gore was challenging a presidential victory won by Bush. In fact, the election was a statistical deadheat and required a careful process of accurately recounting the ballots—a constitutional procedure that the Bush team attempted to block and demean from the beginning.

Meanwhile, there was great commotion within the Gore campaign as new results from Florida revealed that Gore was rapidly closing the gap and that the concession call to Bush was a mistake. Minutes before making his concession speech, and after he had already phoned Bush to congratulate him and concede, Gore received a cell-phone message informing him that new results in Florida made the state too close to call, that they were easily within the percentage in which a recount was automatic, and that Gore should not concede. After quick deliberation, Gore telephoned Bush to retract the concession, and Gore's campaign released to the public that he was not yet conceding. At the same time, the networks announced that the Florida vote was "too close to call," that a recount was inevitable, and that the election was not yet decided.[3]

The stalemate was ratified with a dramatic appearance by William Daley, Gore's campaign manager, brother of the Chicago mayor and son of the notorious Chicago politician Richard Daley. Daley's father, the fabled "boss" of Chicago, was rumored to have illegally manufactured Kennedy's election victory in Illinois in 1960, and he was at the center of controversy in the 1968 Democratic convention in Chicago. Looking every bit the tough Chicago ward boss himself, Daley strode up to the podium in Nashville, Tennessee, and told rain-soaked young Gore supporters, who had thought their candidate had lost, that the Florida election was "too close to call," that a recount was mandated, and that the campaign was roaring ahead to its next challenge, as the assembly broke into cheers.

Crowds had been waiting for hours in front of the Texas State Capitol in Austin, thinking that their candidate had won and expecting a victory speech and celebration. The Bush supporters were forced to settle for a brief statement from Bush's campaign manager, Don Evans, that a recount of the votes in Florida was necessary, that they expected to win, but that the election was on hold. The dejected congregation departed, and official events of the evening were over.

In the succeeding hours of election night, Gore picked up a few electoral votes and surged ahead narrowly in the popular vote, and the populace, many of whom had gone to bed thinking that Bush was going to be president, awoke to hear that the election was a dead heat, that Gore was now ahead in both the popular vote and the Electoral College, that a recount of the vote in Florida was in the cards, and that it would thus be some days before the election results were final. The media also reported that Congress appeared split, with the Republicans holding on to a narrow lead, and that the U.S. Senate was also split, with the possibility of a 50–50 tie, depending on the outcome of a close Senate race in the state of Washington (that would eventually go to the Democrat and thus produce a tie in the Senate).

Bush's electoral strategy had been to play the spectacle to its partisan advantage. His political adviser, Karl Rove, felt that many voters were undecided, that they would make up their mind at the last minute, that a "bandwagon effect" would ensue to go with the winner, and that therefore Bush campaign officials should manipulate the media spectacle to make their candidate appear a winner.[4] Accordingly, the Bush camp highlighted polls that indicated it was on its way to victory, and traveled to states such as California during the crucial final days that it had no chance of winning but that guaranteed media spectacle in the sunshine and celebrity state. Consequently, during the last days of the campaign, the Bushites cultivated the appearance of being confident of success, with Bush strutting about looking primed for victory. On election eve, Rove and the Bush camp predicted that Bush would "win in a walk," and their candidate exuded smirky and self-satisfied aplomb.

Of course, when election results showed no clear decision, other Republicans severely criticized Bush campaign officials for overconfidence and not campaigning hard enough in the key swing states during the final days. Pundits had a field day explaining the election, and the legal wrangle and political struggle. Relentless media coverage accelerated with the recount, with both sides posturing and putting their spin on the dramatic and rapidly shifting events. Election 2000 had thus become media spectacle of the highest order, a mediathon that would bedazzle the populace for weeks to come.

Election results showed that the United States was deeply divided along gender, race, class, regional, religious, and ideological lines. Initial reports indicated that 57 percent of the women voters opted for Gore, while 57 percent of the male voters went for Bush (the Voters News Service, however, gave a 53 percent majority for men and women voters to Bush and Gore, respectively) (*Newsweek*, November 13). Ninety-four percent of African Americans voted for Gore, while 65 to 67 percent of Latinos voted for Gore and 60 percent of white men voted for Bush. Seventy-nine percent of Jews voted for Gore, while 65 percent of Protestants went for Bush; city dwellers chose Gore with 61 percent while rural people voted 59 percent for Bush and the suburbs split; seniors went slightly for Bush and young people also split.[5]

In other words, the country was divided between northerners and southerners, those living in the city and those living in the country, pro-choicers and pro-lifers, straights and gays, gun owners and advocates of gun control, secular folks and religious folks, people of color and whites, the wealthy and the poor, and those who want government to address social problems and those who want less government, reflecting as well the growing division between the haves and the have-nots. The color-coded maps used by the television networks displayed the political division in the country. Gore states were pictured in blue encompassing the entire Northeast (except New Hampshire), spanning upper Midwestern states, and covering the entire West Coast and New Mexico, and the rest of the country was pictured in red for Bush.

Of course, without more finely textured interviews and survey research, one could not adequately grasp the significance of the divisions between the voting constituencies who chose the two candidates. Almost half of the country failed to vote, and of the half that split down the middle between Gore and Bush, it was not clear how many voters were hard-core liberals or conservatives. The passionate aftermath of the election with fierce partnership for both sides did suggest, however, a continuation of the cultural wars of the 1960s with significant divisions along ideological lines. It was clear that Bush had a strong conservative base, while the Democrats needed to depend on growing multiculturalism, unionism, urbanism, and education to gain a majority of the changing and polarizing electorate to sell their programs and candidates. It also appeared that Bush appealed to an anti-intellectual tradition in U.S. culture that responded to his good-old-boy, backslapping banter and was not put off by his mangling of the English language or lack of political knowledge and experience.

In any case, Election 2000 and the ensuing battle for the White House suggested that the new millennium would exhibit proliferating divisions and fragmentations, new party realignments, and continued political and ideological war, with the media and Internet serving as wild cards that could promote, and then undo, either side, adding a potentially explosive mixture to an already turbulent and unpredictable situation. The highly conflicted and volatile state of U.S. politics was visible during the thirty-six days following the election that featured one of the most bitterly partisan and intense struggles and media spectacles in U.S. history.

Other dramatic events in the 2000 elections included the decisive victory in the New York Senate race by Hillary Clinton, the controversial wife of the U.S.

president and who had never lived in the state of New York, and the victory in the Missouri Senate race of a deceased candidate. Governor Mel Carnahan, who was killed in a plane crash three weeks before the election, remained on the ballot and defeated Republican opponent and hardright conservative John Ashcroft, who had led the impeachment charge against Bill Clinton and who Bush would later name his designate for attorney general. In addition, millionaire Jon Corzine won in New Jersey, after spending over $60 million of his own money to help purchase his election, and Maria Cantwell, a woman computer-industry executive who also spent multimillions of her own money on the campaign, beat the Microsoft-supported Republican in the state of Washington. An unusual number of incumbents in the Senate were defeated, resulting in a tie in the U.S. Senate, with the Republicans holding a small majority in the House of Representatives.

The spectacle of the dead-heat presidential election and ensuing struggle for the presidency dramatized the importance of politics in the life of the country, and the significance of each individual vote in close elections. For decades the trend had been toward declining voter turnout, apathy, and cynicism in U.S. politics, partly because of corporate control of the political system and partly because the populace was besotted on entertainment and spectacle and viewed politics merely as a diversion and not as a serious civic duty (see Boggs 2000). But the closeness of the 2000 election dramatized that there were serious issues at stake, that the country was divided over important concerns, and that voters should be informed and vote responsibly to preserve the fragile democracy and make the will of the people heard in response to the powerful political and corporate forces that were increasingly dominating the economy, polity, media, and everyday life.

In the days that followed, the media, legal, and political clash over the election became an engrossing political passion play, enthralling the nation and the world in a highly suspenseful story with daily twists and turns. The political theater following Election 2000 was at once highly entertaining and in its own ways educational, as well as dispiriting, ultimately revealing a massive crisis of democracy in the United States that allowed what in effect was a Republican coup d'état. The intense thirty-six days of agon for the presidency disclosed to many the complexity of how the U.S. political system works, of its serious problems and limitations, and of the deep partisan divisions in the country. It also exposed how Republican power politics was able to overwhelm law and democracy. Lessons included the importance of each individual vote; the need to be competent and informed as a responsible voter; the urgent obligation to obtain new voting technology and a more effective way of voting, bringing the electoral process into the new millennium. In addition, Election 2000 demonstrates the necessity of devising an electoral system that is not susceptible to inefficiency, corruption, and mischievous partisan manipulation, allowing the theft of the presidency (see chapter 10).

Chapters 1 and 2 have just confronted campaign 2000 and election night, focusing on the bias and mishaps of the mainstream media in their favoritism toward Bush and their botching of election night coverage. The following six chapters will tell the story of the Florida recount wars through the heist of the presidency via the Supreme Court decision. After a blow-by-blow narrative account of Grand Theft 2000, I will provide more in-depth analysis and critique of the crisis of democracy disclosed in the events and will propose some solutions. But now, on with the show . . .

NOTES

1. Jonathan Alter claimed in the November 13, 2000, *Newsweek* that a Bush aide had said that if Gore won the electoral vote while Bush won the popular vote: " 'The one thing we don't do is roll over,' a Bush aide told the *New York Daily News*. In that event, the aide said, the Bush forces planned a huge talk-radio and TV ad campaign to delegitimize Gore: 'Even papers that supported Gore might turn against him because the will of the people will have been thwarted.' "

2. See the article in the *New Yorker* (Nov. 13, 2000) and follow-up in *Salon* (Nov. 15). See also Seth Mnookin, "It Happened One Night," who provides another revealing account of how the networks used the Voters News Service (VNS) polling data and how the flaws in the data all night long compromised their calls and analyses (*Brill's Content Online*, www.brillscontent.com/2001feb/features/mnookin.shtml).

3. Florida mandated that election results of less than one-tenth of a percent could be subject to recount, and obviously the Gore forces were going to take that option— which they did, opening the way to tangled legal controversies and conflicts. For lively accounts of the behind-the-scenes maneuvering for the Florida recount, see Tapper 2000.

4. On the Rove strategy, see *Feed Daily* (Nov. 14, 2000). Bush's campaign strategy was severely criticized by other Republicans when the deadlock appeared the day after the election. See Richard Berke, "Some G.O.P. Leaders Question Bush's Campaign," *New York Times* (Nov. 13, 2000). Such are the contingencies of U.S. politics that the Bush team "victory" elevated Rove to status of political guru and genius, fawned over by an obsequious press. If Gore had prevailed, by contrast, Rove would no doubt be dismissed as a failure and false prophet.

5. Another postelection analysis of voting patterns also exhibited significant divisions; see Thomas B. Edsall, "Analysis: Bush Cut into Democratic Coalition," *Wash-*

ington Post (Nov. 8, 2000). The study confirmed that Gore had won strong support from African Americans, union workers, working women, and older voters. But it indicated that Bush had gained among moderate voters and made inroads in the three target groups of Catholics, suburbanites, and Hispanics, who in past elections had given stronger support to Democratic Party candidates. For another account of the division of the country in Election 2000, see Simon 2001; I return to this theme in chapter 10.

INDECISION 2000

The votes have been counted once, twice, and in some cases three and four times. . . . The manual recounts are arbitrary, subjective, and allow mischief.

—James Baker, Bush team manager

With close elections come recounts, come challenges, come all these things. . . . I have a totally different take on this than the whole pundit bloviating class: I think this is a good thing.

—James Carville, media strategist for Clinton campaign and Gore supporter

The spectacle of the aftermath of Indecision 2000 involved the country in a more intense conflict than during the lackluster election campaign itself. Florida votes were recounted and contested, with fierce struggles over individual ballots. New Mexico suddenly swung to Bush by four votes, and then flipped back to Gore. Likewise, in Oregon Bush was initially ahead but Gore eventually won the state. In particular, Florida was ground zero for the recount wars that would determine the presidency. As the recount began in Florida on November 8, the media circus was fully under way with demonstrations, press conferences, and spin by both sides in the contested Florida counties. Hordes of media from throughout the world provided round-the-clock coverage of the events, as the television networks supplied an unending blabathon about the election and the minutiae of the campaign, now resting on manual recounts, legal decisions, and high-powered political maneuvering.

It was revealed on November 8 that many usually Democratic Party voters in Palm Beach County, Florida, had accidentally voted for ultra-rightwing candidate Pat Buchanan because of the confusing, and allegedly illegal, "butterfly" ballot that listed the candidates side by side with arrows pointing to the holes to be punched. Hence, Florida Jews, who had lost relatives in the Holocaust and in some cases were survivors, learned to their horror that they had voted for the most anti-Semitic figure in American politics, a man who had long defended Nazis and in a recent book had argued that the United States should not have gone to war against Germany in World War II!

Soon after, it was reported that more than 19,000 ballots had also been disqualified in Palm Beach County because voters had punched in two presidential candidates, and there were allegations that the ballots were misaligned and that voting machines were not working properly. Moreover, some people claimed that throughout Florida there were irregularities in the voting, intimidation of African American voters throughout the state on election day, and an inaccurate vote that needed recounting.

The most spectacular "irregularities" stories involved allegations that "up to 17,000 ballot papers in the Miami area had been tampered with in what they described as 'organized corruption' " (*The London Times*, November 13). Another story, "The Disappearing Ballots of Duval County," alleged: "More than 22,000 were tossed out in this Republican stronghold, but most of them were cast in minority, Democratic neighborhoods, and the Gore camp is crying foul" (*Salon*, November 13). It appears that the tossed-out votes in Duval County were due largely to a two-page presidential ballot in which voters punched candidates on both pages, thus nullifying their votes. Stories of irregularities by both sides continued to circulate. One of the most striking concerned irregularities in Seminole County, in which Republican workers were allowed "to fill in 4,700 incomplete GOP ballots while rejecting incomplete Democratic absentee ballot requests.[1] While some newspapers pursued these stories, the Democrats focused on counting uncounted ballots in four counties, and the other irregularities and potential crimes were barely mentioned in the mainstream media. In late November, when a Republican mob prevented the court-ordered recount in Miami–Dade (see below), Democrats should have begun to take more seriously claims about the organized Republican irregularities and make this an issue, as Republicans had done earlier in aggressive claims of Democrat fraud and corruption in the election. As detailed below, the Seminole and Martin County cases went to court in early December, but systematic Republican irregularities and illegalities were never seriously pursued by the mainstream media or the Democratic Party.

By early morning on November 8, pictures of the infamous Palm Beach butterfly ballot were circulating and representative Robert Wexler (D-Fla.) was on television telling the sad stories of his district's voters making mistakes because of the confusing ballots. Jesse Jackson appeared early in the morning on CNN, noting that he was about to leave for Florida where stories were multiplying that African Americans had been harassed at voting sites, prevented from voting, and thus subjected to civil rights violations.

The first pronouncements from Bush campaign officials were confident assertions that they had won the election, that most votes were counted, and that the absentee ballots in Florida were certain to favor the Republicans, as had absentee ballots, many from overseas military, in recent elections. Midday, Governor Bush and Dick Cheney strolled out of the governor's mansion in Austin to meet with reporters. His chest held high, Bush exuded confidence and good cheer, telling reporters that former secretary of state and Bush family friend James Baker had been sent to Florida to oversee Republican operations and that Bush campaign officials expected a quick recount that would confirm their victory.[2] Moments later, footage was released of the Bushes and Cheneys at lunch in the mansion, where Bush lightly bantered with reporters. However, he would not be seen so relaxed and cheerful during the rest of the war for the presidency, which would take stomach-churning and unexpected turns for both sides.

The Gore team also sent groups of lawyers and staff to Florida to help supervise the recount and investigate irregularities. The Gore forces would be headed by William Daley, scion of the Chicago Daley family, the campaign manager, and Clinton's secretary of commerce. He was accompanied by Warren Christopher, former secretary of state and well-respected éminence grise of Democratic Party politics. Al Gore appeared on television, surrounded by flags, and intoned how democracy demanded that every vote be counted and that people respect the results of the election. Interestingly, in light of the principles through which the election would eventually be settled, Gore insisted that democratic sovereignty comes from "the consent of the governed" and that voting is the measure of the consent.

Reports from Florida as to when the recounting would start, how it would proceed, and when it would be over were confusing. First indications were that the recount would be finished by Thursday afternoon, but later bulletins indicated that it would take longer and that absentee ballots were allowed, if postmarked by November 7, up to ten days after the election. Stories circulated about a mysterious ballot box found in a Miami elementary school that had been a polling site, and there were countless other rumors of irregularities and problems with the voting.

This was the first national election during an era of proliferating media that focused on the small details of the voting process. The unusual close scrutiny of every aspect of the electoral procedure in Florida revealed sloppiness, confusion, and partisan and possibly criminal corruption. The obsolescence of U.S. voting technology and the highly problematic voting process, usually concealed, were now in the open with a high stakes outcome.

The media spin cycle was intense: The Bush side claimed that the disputed votes in Palm Beach County were in a "Buchanan stronghold" and that the "reform" party candidate had not received an unusually high number of votes—a claim quickly ridiculed by Democrats and denied by Buchanan and his sister as well. Republicans claimed that an equal amount of mutilated, or rejected, ballots had appeared in the same counties during the last election, and later investigations revealed that indeed many of the machines were highly flawed, especially in African American and poorer voting districts.[3]

Continuing the Karl Rove "bandwagon" strategy, Bush and his team acted as if they had sowed up the presidency in the days following the suspenseful election night. On November 8 they provided the press with photo opportunities of cabinet members of the future Bush administration, projecting the strong presumption that they had won. All Republicans who appeared on television had been prepped by the Bush team and were "on message" that the election was all but over, that Bush had won, and that the new Bush administration was beginning to choose its cabinet members.

The Democrats came out on November 9 with another narrative. Gore Campaign Manager William Daley and Warren Christopher held a tense press conference, claiming that there were "serious and substantial irregularities" and that the election was not yet over. The Democrats requested that four disputed counties have mutual recounting procedures and that the country not "rush to judgment," but allow the "process" to work itself out, thus ensuring a first-rate media spectacle.

To counter the Gore press conference in what would become a daily war of the opposing camp's political operatives, the Bush campaign sent its spin meisters to meet the press on November 9. The nation was thus introduced to three of the major players in the Bush campaign in a televised press conference that afternoon. First to speak was Don Evans, Bush's campaign manager, who would later be rewarded for his efforts with the office of commerce secretary, assuring his Texas good-old-boy buddies a largesse of political and economic spoils as the Bush machine divided up the U.S. Treasury among its supporters. Evans could barely read the large-print text, mispronouncing words, misplacing verbal emphasis, and botching an attempted attack on the head of the Gore campaign, William Daley.

Next, the global village was treated to a presentation by Bush's campaign "guru," Karl Rove, who had arrogantly predicted the night before the election that Bush would "win in a walk," carrying more than 320 electoral votes. Rove cited statistics that indicated that results were extremely close in New Mexico, Wisconsin, and Iowa, insinuating that the Republicans could call for recounts in these states if the Gore forces pressed too hard in Florida.[4] Rove also insisted that the 20,000-plus misvotes in Palm Beach were not an anomaly, but that 15,000 voters had double-voted in 1996 in the same county and had their ballots eliminated (it would be revealed later in the day that Rove inflated the number). Then with a triumphant smirk, Rove presented a ballot for judicial elections in Cook County, Illinois, William Daley's home, which also apparently used the infamous butterfly ballot. Rove was somewhat deflated when he was forced to admit that he wasn't sure if this form of ballot was used in presidential elections in Illinois and was further deflated when it was later revealed that it was not. In any case, since Bush "guru" Rove had revealed himself to be a consistent abuser of "fuzzy math" and fallacious argument, one had to wonder: "If this guy is a 'genius,' who are the idiots in the Bush camp?"

As their next gift to the world, Bush campaign officials offered their inimitable communications director, Karen Hughes, who had already alienated many reporters following the Bush campaign. Hughes would distinguish herself in the battle for the White House by daily spinning with enormous aggressiveness one of the great sets of political lies in history. She began by stating that the Bush campaign had sent James Baker, "a man of unquestioned integrity," to Florida to oversee the vote recount, and by repeatedly linking Baker with integrity in her remarks she raised questions as to whether "integrity" was indeed an accurate word to use in relation to the hardfisted political operative Baker, who in the course of the combat would become inextricably associated with its opposite.

Hughes's task for the day, though, was to attack the Gore campaign for its "shrillness" (this coming from one of the more shrill spinners in memory) and then to launch a personal attack on Daley and the Gore campaign for allegedly attacking the Bush campaign, making the recount "personal," rather than acting calmly and dispassionately like the Bushites. Screwing up her face, her lips pursed together in an expression of disapproval often seen by students in Texas classrooms, Hughes spewed forth venomous assaults on the villainous Democrats, previewing what they could expect from the Bush campaign in days to come. Neutral observers could only ask what wonders of history and nature had produced this masterwork of political Americana, who would soon become a fixture of the Bushian bestiary.

Upping the ante, on November 10 after Associated Press (AP) sources indicated that following the first machine recounting Bush was still ahead by 327 votes, the Bush forces were suggesting that Gore should concede, even though the absentee ballots had not been counted, and would not be for at least a week. The television morning of November 10 began with an informal news conference with Karen Hughes, who insisted that Bush had won the recount, was expected to win the Florida absentee ballot tally, and that the process was all but over. We are, Hughes insisted, "a nation of laws" and of "rules," and out of "respect for the integrity of the process," the Gore camp should realize that it has lost and give up further challenges and legal "wrangling" (this would be the buzzword of the day). Hughes's cynical bluster covered over that precisely the "laws" and "rules" that the Republicans were invoking allowed for a manual recount in disputed cases, that this was common in close elections, and that never in history had there been such a close presidential vote or more at stake than in the Florida recounts for the presidential election.

Later in the day, around noon, James Baker appeared on television with the same message, mixing lies and bluster in an astonishing concoction of Realpolitik and spin that would characterize his performances for the duration. On this day, the velvet hammer was more brutal than smooth, beginning with the Republican mantra that the counting was over, that Bush had won the election and the recount, that the Republicans expected to win the absentee ballots, and that the Democrats should realize that the process was reaching "closure" (another buzzword of the day). When a reporter confronted Baker with the fact that the absentee ballots had not yet been counted and that the Gore forces had the right for a manual recount in disputed cases, Baker evoked the "mischief" (buzz) that could result in continued recounting of the votes, the "mess" that tying the election up in courts could produce, and the "threats to the national interest" that prolonging the process could produce. There was a hint of desperation in Baker's responses, as though he knew that if the ballots were actually counted and closely inspected, Bush would probably lose and perhaps irregularities would be uncovered that would send Republicans to jail.

In addition, following Rove's comments of the day before, the Bush camp was threatening legal action that would contest close elections in Wisconsin and Iowa, as well as Oregon, which had not yet been called, although Gore was slightly ahead. And although New Mexico had been awarded to Gore, the vote count was narrowing among allegations of irregularities and perhaps illegalities. Hence, while the Republicans desperately wanted the process to come to a close, with Bush declared winner, in fact the situation was becoming increasingly complex and unpredictable, leading both sides to organize their troops for protracted melee.

Meanwhile, after sometimes contentious deliberations, three counties in Florida had agreed to a manual recounting of the votes, a laborious process that would take days. Thereafter, the world would be treated to the spectacle of the recount in Broward, Palm Beach, and Volusia Counties, soon to be joined by Miami–Dade. Each site would be subject to political and legal contestation and media overload, and would offer insights into the messy processes of U.S. local politics and the complexities of voting machines, local canvassing boards, and the relations among local, state, and federal legal machinery. Nothing less than the presidency was at stake, and for the next few weeks the highly contested Florida recount would be the focus of intense scrutiny and debate, as the manual recounting would begin, be halted by legal injunctions or political decisions, and would start up again after another cycle of legal and political maneuvering, providing some of the fiercest war zones in the Florida combat for votes.

Intensifying the suspense, media commentators noted that court action and redress for voting grievances were "uncharted territory." Continuing confusion and growing chaos were creating a global spectacle, with foreign commentators having a field day pronouncing ironical judgments on the foibles of democracy in the United States. One Italian newspaper declared that "the first election of the new millennium has brought America into the realm of the surreal," and one reported on another "day as a Banana Republic." European Union officials declared that the confused outcome of the American election shows that the U.S. Constitution is outmoded and needs a makeover. A Russian official proclaimed that the U.S. constitutional system "needs modernizing" so that it can "catch up with Russia" (November 10, MSNBC.com/news).

Both parties obviously disagreed on how to resolve the complex issues, and by November 10, commentators were admitting that the "election outcome could take weeks." The same day, the Associated Press awarded "too-close-to-call" Oregon to Gore, but also announced that Gore's margin of victory had shrunk to 206 votes in New Mexico and that Republicans charged election irregularities there as well as in Wisconsin, which Gore had also narrowly won. And although the Bush campaign was calling for Gore to concede and arguing that the Democrats should not call in the courts and get the election process entangled in legal wrangling, the next day when the manual voting recount began in three counties in Florida, the Bush campaign put in a legal injunction against the recount, escalating a legal and political war that would eventually end up in the U.S. Supreme Court.

Hence, while on Friday, November 10, the Republicans argued that an election should not be settled in the legal arena, on Saturday they began intervention in the courts with an appeal to a U.S. federal court to block the manual recount on what appeared to be extremely shaky grounds. There had been, to be sure, several local court challenges, such as with the Palm Beach ballot, by local Democratic Party forces, but the Gore campaign had not formally intervened in the courts, thus the later Republican charge that the Democratic Party was the first party to try to resolve an election in the courts was simply not true.

During the weekend of November 11–12, Gore seemed to have the initiative, with the majority of people polled approving of counting the ballots, while recounts were slowly but surely amassing votes for Gore and closing the gap. The Republicans screamed about the "subjective" nature of manual vote counting, but the public seemed sympathetic to vote counting, and the media showed the people in various precincts in Florida counting the votes and doing the hard work of democracy.

THE KATHERINE HARRIS SPECTACLE

On Monday, November 13, a federal court ruled against the Bush camp's demand to stop the recount, but the Florida secretary of state, Katherine Harris, announced earlier in the day that she was going to require that all election results be certified the next day, guaranteeing another legal confrontation, since the manual recounts could not be completed by that date. The "permanent campaign" intensified as the two sides hardened their positions, the drama escalated, and the high stakes were obvious. Thousands of lawyers and campaign workers from both parties descended on Florida.

Bush-family consigliere James Baker, who emerged as one of the central and most controversial players in the war for the presidency, led the Bush efforts. Although the Bush campaign had made a leitmotiv of its efforts the claim that Bush and the Republicans trusted the people while the Democrats trusted the government, the Republicans went to court on November 11 to stop the manual recounts, and to allow the Republican Florida secretary of state to certify the election. The Republicans' mantra was that only machines could be trusted to count votes and that people should be removed from the process; this provided some interesting philosophical debate on the relative merits of humans and machines. Their flip-flop from their campaign rhetoric gave rise to charges of "disingenuousness" and "hypocrisy squared" for the Republicans, who now only trusted machines and the courts (until the latter ruled against them).[5]

Bush partisans held rallies with signs that read "No more hand jobs" and "God made Bush president." On Tuesday, November 14, Katherine Harris, the Republican secretary of state of Florida, cochair of the campaign election team in Florida, and a close friend of the Bushes, brazenly declared that she would certify the Florida electoral votes on Saturday and that she would not accept the recount votes. In effect, Harris was proclaiming that she would pronounce Bush president if he stayed ahead in the "official" election tally once the absentee ballots came in that were expected to break for Bush, as they had done for Republican candidates in the past.

Harris quickly became one of the most visible and controversial characters in the saga. A fourth-generation Floridian with family ties to the citrus and cattle interests, Harris had campaigned heavily for Bush, including a well-photographed trip to New Hampshire. With a flamboyant hair-do and excessive make-up, Harris quickly became a butt of satire and gossip. The media reported that she had used state funds for television spots urging high voter turnout, featuring Gulf War hero H. Norman Schwarzkopf, who had passionately campaigned for Bush and viciously attacked Gore late in the campaign, thus making the public-service announcements in effect television ads for Bush. Denounced for her partisanship, Harris would continue to carry out bold, and to some disgraceful, uses of her office for Bush; moreover, it was soon reported that her office had also engaged in questionable partisanship for Bush before and during the election as well as afterward.[6]

For instance, once the manual recounts began, Harris's office sent out a memo to Florida counties arguing that the hand recounts were illegal, and demanding that the counties halt the procedure—a false claim that stalled the Palm Beach recount for some days, but was overturned in the courts. It had also been reported that before the election, Harris's office had instructed local officials to allow Republicans to fill in the Republican absentee ballots that were to be sent out to their voters and that were missing crucial voter IDs. This blatantly illegal ballot tampering was soon to be at the heart of the Seminole and Martin lawsuits initiated by local Democrats over the absentee ballots. It was also later revealed that Harris had commissioned a Republican-connected firm to "cleanse" voter lists of felons, and in so doing had wiped off around 100,000 legitimate voters, mostly African American and poor voters who tended to vote Democrat (see below and chapter 10, note 11).[7] Harris's phone bill indicated that during election night her cell phone was used twice to call George W. Bush in Austin (although she claimed someone else had made the calls with her phone).

It was thus manifestly clear that Harris was doing everything possible to use her office to help Bush get elected, and the Democrats were claiming that she was systematically abusing her office to promote her fellow Republican. Later, Harris would be the center of controversy and legal chastisement by the Florida Supreme Court for refusing to certify already-counted manual ballots when Palm Beach County was late. She had also advised the Nassau County supervisor to throw out the legally mandated machine recount and revert to the original count, thus costing Gore fifty-two votes. In short, Harris had done everything possible to halt, or ignore, ballot recounts to rush to certify Bush as the winner of Florida's decisive electoral votes.

On November 14, the Gore camp got a boost when it was announced that David Boies was going to work with its legal team. Boies had been named Lawyer of the Year in 1999 by the *National Law Journal,* which referred to him as "the Michael Jordan of the courtroom." The high-powered lawyer had gained renown for leading the successful government effort against Microsoft, and he had successfully defended IBM, CBS, media personality Don Imus, comedian Garry Shandling, and New York Yankees owner George Steinbrenner. Boies also had won impressive victories against Penzoil and Texaco, Christie's and Sotheby's, and Bridgestone–Firestone tires, and was currently representing Napster against the U.S. music industry.

In a dramatic press conference on November 14, Warren Christopher and Boies attacked Katherine Harris's attempts to block the manual recount and declare Bush the winner, and they argued that state law mandated that every vote be counted, that the will of the people be heard, and that all votes be recounted. The Gore team explained that the machines did not count all votes, that the failure rate of punch-card machines was as high as 5 percent, and that manual recounts were normal in Florida, as well as Texas and other parts of the country.

The Bush–Harris preemptive strike did not come off well with the major media commentators.[8] But conservative pundits upped their attacks on Gore. Conservative activist and former Republican secretary of education William Bennett threatened on CNN that the election would be "illegitimate" if won by Gore, whom he accused of "trying to steal this election. . . . This may be the worst thing I have ever seen." Former Reagan and Bush speechwriter Peggy "Thousand Points of Light" Noonan also accused Gore of "stealing the election" (*Wall Street Journal,* November 15), and George Will fumed that the recount was "slow-motion larceny" and the Gore troops calling for the recount were "people incapable of embarrassment" (November 14, syndicated column)—the Republican ideologues and hypocrites were furiously projecting onto the Democrats exactly their own actions and character traits.[9]

November 15 unfolded another dramatic day in which the fortunes of the two competing camps ebbed and flowed. In the morning, Judge Jorge la Barga ruled that the local canvassing boards had their "discretion" to discern the intent of the voter, meaning that they could set their own rules to determine standards to count votes. This discretion was regularly provided to Florida canvassing boards, as the state had a variety of voting machines, ballots, and local conditions that mandated local control and decision making.

Soon after, Broward County decided on a full manual recount, and the presumption was that Gore could gain hundreds of votes from the process. The Bush camp went all-out in the courts to stop the recounting and maintained a constant media blitz, decrying the "subjective" and "partisan" nature of the recount. A federal appeals court in Atlanta agreed to hear the Bush camp plea, and Bush's lawyers rushed to prepare documents for the next morning. In one of the most dramatic events of the postelection crusade, Katherine Harris appeared on national television at 9:10 P.M., EST, to declare that she was exercising "discretion" given to her by a local judge who had ruled that she could determine whether to accept the manual recounts. She announced that she would not accept the manual recount numbers, that the local canvassing boards' arguments were "insufficient," and that she would certify the election on Saturday, upon completion of the absentee balloting on Friday night, the deadline for overseas ballots to arrive and be counted. George W. Bush, in his first appearance in days, followed Harris's intervention with a short speech in which he refused Al Gore's offer earlier in the day to meet personally, to decide on a range of agreed-upon manual recounts, and to accept the results without more legal wrangling. Bush affirmed the correctness of Harris's decision, attacked the manual recounts, and made it clear he expected the election to be over by the end of the week with himself in the saddle to the White House.

There was an immediate uproar following Harris's bombshell. The Gore side claimed that this decision was completely arbitrary, went against the ruling that she had cited to allow "discretion," and contravened state law. On *Rivera Live* famed lawyer Gerry Spence declared Harris a "terrorist" who would spawn an "illegitimate president," if indeed she was to declare for Bush on Saturday once the absentee ballots were counted and without including the manual recounts. It was certain that the Gore side would contest Harris's ploy in the Florida Supreme Court, and the suspense of the legal and political warfare was accelerating rapidly.

The battle for the White House continued to dominate the news twenty-four hours a day, with media pundits and coverage creating an enthralling and all-consuming spectacle that gripped the nation and entertained the globe.[10]

The London *Guardian* published a humorous article that the queen of England had declared they had better take back their colony, while a Chinese commentator wondered whether the hand count represented a return to the Stone Age. A Zimbabwean diplomat suggested that Africa send international observers to help arbitrate the process. But an *Irish Times* editorial sympathized with the Yanks who must "endure the banality, ignorance, arrogance and presumptuousness of Europeans" and others discussing the complex U.S. electoral process.

November 16 was another theatrical and topsy-turvy day from dawn to dusk and into the night. In the morning, a local Florida court ruled that Katherine Harris had acted within her discretion and could certify the election results on Saturday as she had boldly declared. Bush camp officials in Austin were slapping high fives and exuberantly pumping their fists in the air, while rumors circulated about a victory celebration for the weekend. But later in the day, the Florida Supreme Court ruled unanimously that hand counts of the disputed punch-card ballots in Palm Beach County should proceed, and within hours, workers in the pro-Democratic district began a manual recounting of more than 460,000 votes.

The flip-flopping of Florida fortune continued on Friday, November 17. In the morning, a Tallahassee judge cleared the way for Katherine Harris's vote certification on Saturday, concluding that Harris had exercised "reasoned judgment" in making her decision. Momentum suddenly accelerated for Gore later in the day when the Florida Supreme Court overturned the lower court's decision, ruling that Harris could *not* certify the election until the manual counting was concluded, that the recounting should go on, and that the Florida Supreme Court would rule on a series of issues confronting the court on Monday. The Bush side appeared to gain a victory when in another Florida court, a judge refused to require that hand recounts be included in the final result. But shortly thereafter, a district federal court ruled against the Bush request that the manual counting of the untallied votes be halted, rejecting again on the federal level the Bush arguments to stop the manual counting process.[11]

The weekend of November 18–19 was one of spin, rumors, and fierce partisan warfare. As the absentee ballots came in, both sides called foul, with Democrats criticizing the Republicans for filling in incomplete absentee ballots when lacking crucial information, allowing them to be counted, while Republicans protested as further absentee ballots were invalidated for missing postmarks or other requirements. The ever-active Katherine Harris, however, announced that the tallying of the overseas absentee ballots had boosted

Bush's lead to 930 votes—although this number would immediately be contested by Democrats.[12]

RECOUNTS, CHADS, AND LEGAL WRANGLING

Throughout the weekend, Democrats complained that Republican observers were slowing down the manual recount efforts, whereas the Bushites argued that the very process was illegitimate. Previously, allegations swirled around possible Republican corrupt electoral practices, but over the weekend, charges were directed against alleged Democratic Party wrongdoing. In an all-out media offensive, Republicans accused Democrats of stealing votes, targeting military absentee ballots for disallowal on technicalities, and, most bizarrely, eating chads (i.e., illicitly punching out the holes of ballots for their candidate and eating the evidence; see the Associated Press and *New York Times* reports, November 19).

The chad had become part of the mythology of the postelection spectacle and a potent ideological weapon for the Republicans. Print and broadcast media reproduced countless images and descriptions of punched-out, hanging, dimpled, and pregnant chads, and the media told of how the various canvassing boards were treating the ballots to determine "the intent of the voter," as Florida law mandated. The media endlessly repeated images of Judge Burton of Palm Beach County holding up ballots to discern the intent of the voter and Broward County Republican Judge Rosenberg using a magnifying glass to scrutinize the ballots.

It later came out during a Tallahassee trial over the contest that the ancient voting machines were often overstuffed with ballots and chads, which blocked the punching out of the chads that were stuck in the paper ballots, which were then rejected by the voting machines—this problem occurred especially at the top of the ballot, which contained the presidential votes. It was therefore a complex issue to determine how conditions of the chad might signify a vote. At first, strict interpretations of punch-machine ballots required a hole in the ballot that allowed light to shine through to be counted as a vote, an image memorialized by countless replay. Certain counties, such as Broward, adopted more "liberal" interpretations for determining intent of the voter; this involved scrutinizing the entire ballot and allowing dimples to count as votes, if the entire ballot suggested a Democratic Party voter via the rest of the votes—a procedure that aroused Republican ire and arguments that the Democrats were stealing the election.

Hence, the conflict over chads displaced discussions of the scandal that many poorer districts had outmoded voting machines, that these districts deserved the extra effort to determine their votes, and that it was precisely the task of democracy to engage such difficult problems. Republicans, however, effectively took up the issue of the conflicting standards and allegedly "mystical" attempts to discern the intent of the voter by the various canvassing boards—even though many other states, including Texas, allowed the liberal interpretation utilized in some of the counties that were attempting to count ballots that the machines had been unable to tabulate because of blocked, or hanging, chads. Obviously, the old hand-punch voting machines that required the punching out of chads were technologically obsolete and had been replaced in the mostly wealthier and affluent (and Republican) Florida counties by more advanced optical-scan machines. The Republicans exploited the complexity necessitated by the chad situation and manipulated public confusion and legitimate concern over the chad interpretations to their public relations benefit.

At this stage in the skirmish, the Republicans were taking no chances that they would lose, warring in the courts, in the media, on the battlefield of public opinion, and, if necessary, in the political institutions that they dominated. The *Washington Post* reported on November 18 that the Florida legislature was contemplating choosing a slate of electors for the Electoral College. The Associated Press noted the previous day that congressional Republicans were examining legal precedents to see if Congress could determine the Florida electors, thus raising questions as to who would and should decide the election. More ominously, *On-Line Journalism* noted on November 17 that if the election did not go Bush's way, rightwing extremists were calling out their goon squads. Talk show host Hal Turner, who broadcasts via shortwave and the Web, said, "As a result of all this election fraud, Bush supporters are convinced that Gore, with Clinton's help, is stealing the U.S. presidential election. Bush supporters are going to gun stores and pistol ranges in large numbers. They are buying large amounts of ammunition for their guns and brushing-up on their aim. Many are openly saying they will not allow Al Gore to steal the election and are calling those who support Gore 'the enemy.' "

Once the media began to spotlight the legal confrontation in the Florida Supreme Court on Monday, November 20, attention was focused upon the opposing lawyers. David Boies led the Democratic legal team and was appearing daily in the media to plead the Democrats' case. The Republican legal players included none other than Ted Olson, one of independent counsel Ken Starr's friends who had run the Arkansas Project—a multimillion-dollar investigation into the life of Bill Clinton funded by rightwing billionaire Richard Mellon Scaife, a major force behind the Clinton impeachment mediathon (see the dossier of articles collected in *Salon*). Olson was a longtime Republican activist, representing Ronald Reagan during the Iran-Contra scandal and defending policemen in the Rodney King case. Olson had participated as well in the University of Texas case that undermined affirmative action and the failed attempt to keep the Virginia Military Institute all male (see *Salon*, November 19).

Ultimately, the Republicans would save Olson for battle in the federal courts and in particular the U.S. Supreme Court, where he would face off against Boies in the final conflict. In Florida, the Republicans scoured the state to purchase the best lawyers for their legal wars, including silver-haired Barry Richards, a well-respected Florida lawyer reputed to be a Democrat, as well as members of James Baker's Houston-based law firm and another legal eagle, Phil Beck, who looked like movie star Kevin Spacey.

The dramatic judicial proceeding in the Florida Supreme Court on Monday, November 20, was televised live, and the earnest justices interrupted the lawyers on both sides frequently, asking probing questions. After an intense two-hour hearing in which both sides made their case, the court adjourned and the world awaited their decision, which could decide the presidency. A CBS news survey showed that 59 percent of Americans favored continued manual counts of the uncounted votes, demonstrating widespread public patience with the complex procedure and desire to get an accurate and fair vote count. So far, Republican arguments that prolonging the election was generating crisis and chaos were not being bought by large segments of the populace, which viewed the procedures with mixtures of serious attention, detachment, amusement, and intense partisan response.

Protestors amassed in Tallahassee on November 21 in expectation of the Florida Supreme Court ruling as weary canvassing boards in Broward, Palm Beach, and Volusia Counties labored to count the votes and Miami–Dade prepared for the task, awaiting instruction from the Florida Supreme Court. The ensuing mediation was interrupted around 10:30 P.M., EST, and the results of the court deliberations were announced to denizens of the global television village who were tuned in to the election drama. The Florida Supreme Court ruled that manual hand counts were legal and that the counting should continue in the three counties and begin in Miami–Dade. It also ruled that Florida secretary of state Katherine Harris had overstepped her authority when she imposed her deadline and that the secretary was required to certify election results, which would include hand counts, by Sunday night at 5:00 P.M., or Monday morning if her office was closed, as it usually is, on Sunday.

The ruling strongly rebuked Katherine Harris and seemed to open the door for counting the "dimpled" chads in that the process was left to each local election commission, apparently producing a stunning victory for the Gore team. Shortly thereafter, Gore appeared on national television, looking extremely presidential, and his triumphant lawyer David Boies then appeared, highly approving of the decision.

Within minutes, Bush's chief warlord, James Baker, came on, defiantly accusing the Florida Supreme Court of "usurping" the power of the legislature to set state election statutes and of the state executive branch to certify the election. In effect, he made clear that Team Bush would do everything possible to overturn the decision, and he threatened that the Florida legislature may well oppose the court and take steps to ensure that state statutes are being followed. This was an ominous development, since the Florida state legislature had been discussing holding a special session to certify its own electors and since such a procedure would clearly produce constitutional crisis.

NOTES

1. For a thorough documentation of the potential fraud and crimes, see the article by an investigative reporter, author, and retired commissioned officer in the Public Health Service, David E. Scheim, "Absentee Ballot Fraud in Seminole County" (www.campaignwatch.org).

2. Baker had managed George H. W. Bush's early congressional campaigns and his unsuccessful 1992 bid for reelection against Clinton. Baker had also served as Bush's secretary of state, and although he had run five Republican campaigns (winning three) and served as Reagan's chief of staff, he was generally regarded as the Bush family "garbage-man," brought in to solve their political and legal problems and to clean up their messes (see the story in salon.com, Nov. 9, 2000). A November 17, 2000, *Slate* article by David Plotz, "James Baker: The Bush Family Janitor," presents Baker as the Bush handler and janitor (http://slate.msn.com/Assessment/00-11-17/Assessment.asp).

3. Carl Bernstein, one of the Watergate reporters, discovered an uncanny similarity between the 1988 Senate contest in which Democratic candidate Buddy McKay was declared winner early in the evening based on exit-polling data and early returns, while later in the evening Republican Connie Mack pulled ahead and eventually won. Voting machines in the same districts that failed to count ballots in the 2000 presidential election—heavily Democratic strongholds—eliminated between 10 and 30 percent of

the ballots, pointing either to highly flawed equipment or perhaps to machines subject to tampering and mischief; see http://election.voter.com/f/326/2049/10m/www.voter.-com/home/news/article/0,1175,2-16556-00.html.

Shortly after the publication of the Bernstein report, attention was called to a book by the Collier brothers, now deceased. Published in 1992, *Votescam* detailed the fraud in the 1988 election, noting that many ballots were double-punched and thus the votes were not counted, erasing a large number of Democratic Party votes—a similar phenomenon that happened in the 2000 presidential election. The 1988 allegations were sent to the Justice Department for prosecution, but the "case was allegedly stuffed by someone Bush later appointed to the U.S. Supreme Court. His name is Antonio Scalia" (www.bushwatch. com, Dec. 12, 2000).

4. For a revealing overview of Rove, see Louis Dubose, "Bush's Hit Man," *The Nation* (Mar. 5, 2001), which describes Rove's history of dirty tricks and smear campaigns in Texas politics, his whispering campaign against John McCain in the Republican primaries, his deep-seated conservative beliefs, and his key role in the Bush administration, which I discuss in chapter 11. In later chapters, I suggest how Rove was influenced by Nixon dirty tricksters Murray Chotiner and Lee Atwater and refined the technique of the Big Lie developed by Hitler and Goebbels. On the Bush–Rove Nixonian connection, see also Miller 2001: 43ff., who follows Hatfield (2000) in stressing the centrality of George W. Bush in the dirty tricks against Dukakis in the 1988 election, pointing to a mean and vicious streak beneath W.'s smiling exterior.

5. The Republicans seemed unembarrassed when the media noted that Governor Bush had signed a law in Texas mandating manual recounts when elections were contested and that the Texas ruling Bush signed onto had indicated that manual recounts were the best way to resolve disputes over ballots. They were also unfazed when they later demanded a manual recount in areas of New Mexico as the tallies went back and forth from Bush to Gore in which was, like Florida, a statistical dead heat. Republican spin simply disregarded facts and contradictions, collapsing political language into doublespeak and lies, as documented throughout this study.

6. Harris had been caught up in one major political scandal, receiving over $20,000 in illegal contributions from Riscorp Insurance Company, and offering a bill in the Florida legislative that the company wanted passed, leading Alan Dershowitz to call her "corrupt" and a "crook" (see Tapper 2001: 157–58). In the comical mode, it was reported that in an earlier incarnation, Katherine Harris acted in a Sarasota nightclub. According to the *New York Daily News* (Nov. 17, 2000), "Harris was second banana in a musical revue there; she would exhort audience members to jump from their seats and dance like chickens." Harris was reportedly hired "to be like Vanna White . . . and bring out guests and give them prizes." But her main task onstage "was to lead the audience in a chicken dance and get everyone to flap their arms."

In the more salacious mode, a *New York Observer* story (Dec. 4, 2000) by Ron Rosenbaum, noted journalist and author, discussed the "Harris Rumor" that the Florida secretary of state was Jeb Bush's mistress and that the *New York Times* and other major media were looking into the story. This story would be interesting because Harris had involved herself in questionable actions to rush to certify Bush before all of the votes had been counted and had involved herself in countless potentially illegal and highly contested uses of her office as state official in charge of elections to aid George W. Bush.

Jake Tapper recounts that a "high-ranking Gore adviser," whom he baptized "Strep Throat," called him with the rumor that "everyone" is talking about, namely "that Katherine Harris and Jeb Bush had, or are having, an affair." Tapper claims that he discussed the story with others in the media, who had also been contacted by the Gore team, that there was no evidence to the story which Tapper dismissed as "vile and despicable stuff, completely untrue, and it comes from a senior adviser to Vice President Al Gore" (Tapper 2001: 160–61). While the "rumor" might be disinformation planted by the Gore team, it is also possible that the Gorebies, like many others, heard the story and wanted a scandal-crazed media to pursue and confirm it. In any case, there have been countless reports that tabloids were going to break the story, but so far there is no credible documentation and the story remains a rumor; in May 2001, rumors circulated that Jeb Bush was having an affair with another state employee, Cynthia Henderson, leading to speculation that he was not going to run again as Governor of Florida, but he denied the rumors and announced in June 2001 that he was planning to run again for Governor.

7. Tapper provides a useful account of both the Seminole and Martin County trials and the purging of the voting rolls by Database Technologies (2001: 220ff.).

8. In unusually harsh criticism, editorialists intoned on November 15 that "Bush Shows His Bully Side" (Joe Conanson); Bob Herbert protested in the *Washington Post* that "the GOP is attempting to Hijack the Presidency"; and the *New York Times* complained in an editorial that Katherine Harris failed to understand the legal issues involved.

9. Conservative columnist George Will had earlier whined about Gore's "serial mendacity" and spied a "corrupting hunger for power" (syndicated column, Nov. 11)—another projection of Republican traits onto the Democrats. See the critique of out-of-control conservative commentary by Eric Boehlert in *Salon* (Dec. 1, 2000); Bob Somerby's *Daily Howler* delighted in attacking the lies and mendacity of conservative punditry (see the *Daily Howler* archive at www.dailyhowler.com). During the heated media war, many pundits and commentators lost credibility for their intemperate and off-target commentary and rhetoric. My winner in the off-the-wall conservative commentary sweepstakes is the December 4, 2000, *Weekly Standard,* whose cover story compared Al Gore to Aaron Burr, the infamous nineteenth-century politician who tried to steal the presidency from Thomas Jefferson, twice tried to create breakaway countries and install himself as their ruler, killed Alexander Hamilton in a duel, and was the subject of a novel by Gore Vidal. These conservative pundits were claiming that, like Burr, Gore was megalomaniacal, brutal, and cunning, exploiting a constitutional crisis for his personal advantage.

10. A CNN/USA Today poll of November 11–12 revealed that 87 percent of the viewers polled rated the vote recount the media story that the public most carefully followed, followed by 85 percent who had avidly watched coverage of Princess Diana's death and funeral, 84 percent who had regularly viewed the Gulf War coverage and air strikes in Kosovo, and 83 percent who had followed the Clinton sex scandals and impeachment trial. Clearly, the battle for the White House was one of the major media spectacles of its time.

11. Editorials on Saturday, November 18, in the major newspapers tended to applaud the Florida Supreme Court decision, expressing relief that the courts were intervening to attempt to put some rationality, objectivity, and legality into the vote-counting procedures. See, for example, the following November 18 editorials: *Mercury News* stated, "At last the courts are pulling the right levers"; the *New York Times* was relieved that "Florida's High Court Steps In"; the *Boston Globe* warned Bush "Not so Fast"; and the *Washington Post* advised about the need for "legitimacy."

12. After the election, in his book *Down & Dirty: The Plot to Steal the Presidency*, Jake Tapper (2001) claims that "a conference call was held among Bush politicos, on or around November 11, in which a strategy was discussed to have GOP operatives seek out Republican members of the military who hadn't voted and encouraged them to do so. If this plan was followed through, any votes that were counted as a result could have made the difference in who won Florida, and in turn the presidency of the United States" (Mar. 2, 2001, PR memo). If this is true, the stink that the Republicans spewed forth for the next week about Democrats blocking the counting of military ballots and the Florida court appearance by Bush machine lawyers to demand that absentee ballots be counted, even if they did not have required postmarks, dates, and signatures, was a smoke screen to cover malodorous Republican illegalities. On November 25, Gore legal adviser Ron Klain, in fact, claimed on CNN that the Bushites were "stuffing the ballot" box with late and illegal absentee ballots, and Bush legal advisor Ben Ginsberg dismissed the claim as "outrageous." As far as I know, the charge was not repeated by the Gore team nor discussed in the media. For the more complete story of the alleged military absentee ballot scandal and the Republican "Thanksgiving stuffing" when absentee ballots were illicitly counted, giving Bush a critical boost, see Tapper 2001: 204ff. As I indicate in chapter 11, a *Washington Post* (June 1, 2001) inspection of the ballots found that many military absentee ballots were counted that were mailed after the required November 7 election date; the *Post* even found a sailor who admitted mailing his ballot a week after the election whose vote was found to be tallied in the Duval County results.

4

OUT OF CONTROL

The winner isn't clear, the recount is a cliffhanger, the networks look terrible, the system's very legitimacy is under withering assault, and the reaction among bone-weary journalists is nearly unanimous: it doesn't get any better than this!

—Howard Kurtz, *Washington Post* media critic

[It is] spinning even further out of control. . . . It's hard, day to day, to see how the situation could get worse—and then it does.

—*Washington Post* editorial

The battle was intensifying, and both sides were in the full court press mode, struggling mightily for victory. In Florida, more than a thousand citizens were enlisted to examine more than 1.7 million paper ballots in the full view of the media—a spectacle of the intimate workings of democracy never before seen in such excruciating detail. This work of democracy was obviously laborious, and it was inspiring to see hardworking citizens doing their best to achieve a fair and accurate count. Endless debates over how to interpret chads, and pictures of election officials and party representatives carefully scrutinizing the ballots and debating the results, created images that could be—and were—interpreted in conflicting ways. On the one hand, Republicans exploited the obvious difficulties in determining "the intent of the voter" to make the argument that the counting process was necessarily subjective and partisan and could not yield a reliable result. The Democrats countered that this difficult process was the best possible under the circumstances and the only fair way to determine the election according to the rules and processes of U.S. democracy.

Bush officials were involved in the complex multiple strategy of doing everything possible to stop the vote counting in the courts, to marshal public opinion against the process, and to make sure that their observers and operatives were involved in the counting, either to disrupt and inhibit it, or to make sure it benefited their candidate. The Bush attack on the Florida Supreme Court was fierce, and Bush officials intensified their threats to use the Florida legislature to choose their electors. One of Gore's Florida lawyers declared that the Bush team was "rejecting rule of law" by refusing to respect the judgment of the Florida Supreme Court, and the next morning *New York Times* editor R. W. Apple wrote that "the nation might be heading for political Armageddon" (November 22).

Republicans across the nation screamed about the Florida Supreme Court giving "the election to Gore" (Senator Orrin Hatch, R-Utah) and accused the Gore team of "stealing the election." Ann Coulter accused the Democrats of being "delusional nutcases" and called the Florida Supreme Court a "kangaroo court" with "power mad lunatics." Florida voters were "stupid" and "feeble-minded jackasses," while the Democrats had crossed the "fine line" between "typical Democrat lies and demonstrably psychotic behavior."[1]

Throughout the spectacle, Republicans regularly projected their own worst sins and limitations onto the Democrats. The process involves "projecting" one's own internal aggression, rage, resentment, and other psychological turbulence onto objects of the other, of "the enemy." The conservative politics of resentment and rightwing paranoia had been focused upon Bill Clinton, who it imagined was guilty of everything from sexual indiscretion (he was) to crimes in the Whitewater investigations and even murder of associates (never proven). When the hardright was unable to unseat Clinton, its rage was projected upon the Gore candidacy, which it saw as a continuation and redemption of Clinton, and it opposed the Democratic candidate tooth and nail.

In the complex combat for votes in Florida, rightwing hostility and paranoia were projected onto Gore and the Democrats, who were seen as thieves of the election. The fanaticism for (the scarcely deserving) Bush and against Gore illustrated what historian Richard Hofstadter called "the paranoid style in American politics" (1996), in which conservatives projected traits of evil, often grounded in their own rage and resentment, onto political opponents.[2] Examples of rightwing rage and detachment from reality of Bush supporters are copious.

A Republican sign displayed the weekend of November 18–19 read "Al Gore, Liar and Thief." Such rhetoric demonized the Democrats, hyperbolized their behavior, and arguably projected exactly what the Republicans were doing onto the Democrats (i.e., lying about the votes being recounted and Democrats stealing votes, while trying to block the manual recount of the uncounted votes). On the behavior of the conservative troops in the trenches, reporter David Corn describes typical attitudes of Bush supporters in Austin awaiting a victory speech on election eve. When the Bush victory was snatched away as Florida was determined "too close to call," one Bush supporter, a retired business analyst for NASA's space shuttle program, declared, "It's the unions who are mixed up with some of the mafia." Another Bush supporter said, "I don't want any more of this lying stuff. And look at Gore's eyes. He's doing coke."

Such irrational projection and rage were evident in Florida amid those demonstrating for Bush–Cheney and against Gore, who they were convinced was doing the devil's work in stealing the election. One frequently saw signs proclaiming that "God had chosen Bush to be president." A woman called a CNN phone-in show the day after the election, reporting how a Christian Coalition worker had approached her the day of the election and whispered into her ear, "God wants you to vote for Bush." The woman then handed out a Christian Coalition list of approved candidates to the would-be voter, which, if true, would be an illegal act, since campaigning inside voting precincts is forbidden on election day. Even more disturbing, one of Bush's supporters at the Miami–Dade vote-counting site took a reporter to his car, opened his trunk, and pointed to a semiautomatic rifle, explaining, "You never know, if things hit the fan." Popping the chamber, he said, "The minutemen had their muskets, and I have my FN [assault rifle]."[3] Scary people.

Some of the more ludicrous projections gushed forth daily from conservative demagogue Rush Limbaugh, who was arguing that the Democrats were fighting harder and dirtier than Republicans and that if the Republicans expected to win, they needed to use the same hardball tactics and ruthlessness of the Democrats. Limbaugh pushed this line on his radio show, which was repeated frequently on the NBC and Fox networks and was the focus of many discussion programs on both radio and television that day. Ironically, however, just when Limbaugh and his crew were calling for tougher tactics, the Republicans were orchestrating some of the most ruthless political hardballing in recent years.[4] From the beginning, the Republican Party and Bush organization had indeed engaged in practices that were as down and dirty as any seen in contemporary U.S. politics, while stretching and probably breaching bounds of legality in so doing.

NOVEMBER 22

The day after the Florida Supreme Court ruling, November 22, the anniversary of the John F. Kennedy assassination, included momentous ups and downs for both parties in the roller-coaster ride for the election prize. A Republican mob stormed the Miami–Dade County federal building where the manual recount was suspected to yield a rich harvest of votes for Gore, demanding, "Stop the count! Stop the fraud! Cheaters! Cheaters! Let us in!" In a staggering reversal of their decision to undertake a counting of the uncounted votes, the Miami–Dade County election board voted to halt the process, saying that concluding its work before the Sunday deadline imposed by the Florida Supreme Court was impossible to meet.

ABC News reported on November 23 that some of the mob were out-of-town Republicans, bused in for demonstrations and perhaps mischief. A CNN commentator noted that he had seen some of the same trouble-makers present at the Elian Gonzalez demonstrations in Miami some months before; rumors were circulating of a mob of a thousand Cuban Americans on their way to the site. The November 27 *Wall Street Journal* reported that many of the "protesters" were Republican Capitol Hill staffers flown down by the Bush campaign and organized by ultra-rightist Tom DeLay (R-Tex.). This was admitted by Paul Gigot, who in the *WSJ* described his own participation in what he called a "bourgeois riot." According to the same article, both Bush and Cheney personally called the demonstrators at a celebration they were holding at a Fort Lauderdale hotel, joking about the day's events as singer Wayne Newton crooned the song "Danke Schoen." Later, in appealing the Miami–Dade decision not to recount, the Gore lawyers cited "organized intimidation" that made it difficult to proceed with the recount.

George W. Bush returned briefly to the spotlight that day to reassure his supporters that he was still around and to play his scripted role in the intense battle. Bush had been largely invisible since the crisis had begun. He had been holed up at his rural Texas ranch, appearing the weekend after the election with a red nose, splotchy cheeks, and a large bandage on his face that his handlers said was an infected boil; the *New York Times* commented that he looked "dazed, confused, and not sure where he was" (November 10). Subsequently, Bush had limited his comments to carefully scripted remarks read on a teleprompter before he hurriedly retreated to his ranch.

But with his old confidence seemingly back, W. reappeared in Austin and breezily attacked the Florida Supreme Court, repeating his camp's spin that the court had "used the bench to change Florida's election laws and usurp the authority of Florida's election officials," explaining: "It's the legislature's job to write law; it's the executive branch's job to interpret law" (November 22). A minute or so later, he ad-libbed, "As I just said, it's the executive's job to write law; it's the legislature's job to interpret law," reversing the order and managing to mangle further his knowledge of the U.S. balance of powers. In both cases, Bush left out the crucial role of the judiciary, which is to interpret the laws—*not* the role of the executive or legislature as the hapless Bush commented, thus flunking American Politics 101. In addition, the language of courts "usurping" state power used by Bush and Baker echoed the segregationist rhetoric of Governor Orval Faubus of Arkansas and George Wallace, governor of Alabama, when they refused court orders to integrate schools in 1957 and 1963, respectively.

The spectacle thus revealed the unveiling of a presidential candidate ignorant of the U.S. Constitution who did not understand the basic principle of separation of powers. The same day, in another escalation of the spectacle, Bush's running mate for vice president, Dick Cheney, had a heart attack and underwent emergency surgery. Bush was evidently not informed by his handlers concerning the seriousness of Cheney's condition, denying in his press conference that Cheney had suffered a heart attack when, in fact, the operation was already under way, thus making Bush appear out of the loop when the doctors explained the procedure in a press conference, juxtaposed with Bush's denial.

Also on November 22, a federal circuit court agreed to hear Bush campaign objections to the manual recount, and a Miami–Dade County judge was preparing to deliver an opinion in Palm Beach County as to whether dimpled chads could be counted as votes (the ruling left it to the individual election boards). But most spectacularly in a day of dizzying spectacle, as noted above, mayhem erupted in Miami–Dade as a group of Republican partisans stormed the offices of the local canvassing board after it had announced that to meet the Florida Supreme Court deadline it would start counting immediately the 10,750 "undervotes" that had been rejected by the voting machines and for which no presidential vote had been tallied. Shortly thereafter, the Miami–Dade canvassing board shocked the world by stopping all recounts, declaring that it could not finish its work by the deadline on Sunday—evoking rampant speculation on what happened behind the scenes to persuade the canvassing board to change its mind, which many felt would cost Gore the election.

This was a potentially fatal blow for the Gore campaign, and Gore's lawyers immediately appealed the Miami–Dade decision and demanded a manual counting of the never tallied ballots that the Florida Supreme Court had ordered. The Bush camp, meanwhile, approved submission of a U.S. Supreme Court appeal of the Florida Supreme Court decision on the recount, and also petitioned the highest U.S. court to count the contested military ballots that had been disqualified for lacking postmarks, signatures, or other requirements. It was clear that the Gore–Bush deadlock was inexorably moving toward the U.S. Supreme Court for resolution of the surreal Florida situation.

The night of November 21, after the Florida Supreme Court mandated the manual recount and ordered that the tallies be included in the official certification, Gore lawyer David Boies categorically stated, in response to a question, that the U.S. Supreme Court would "never" receive and act upon the Bush petition. Moreover, the next day, almost every legal authority interviewed on television doubted whether the U.S. Supreme Court would accept the Bush request on the grounds that there was no real federal issue, that the Florida Supreme Court was the legitimate site for adjudication of state election disputes, and that there would not be enough time for the U.S. Supreme Court to deliberate and adequately assess the issues involved. The day that the Bush camp petitioned the court, however, was the most chaotic yet. Following the aftermath of the Florida Supreme Court bombshell, there was a riot at Miami–Dade that shut down the manual recount. Court cases mushroomed throughout the state, serious disputes erupted about dimpled chads and absentee ballots, Republican anger escalated with claims that the election was being stolen, and threats of Florida legislature or U.S. Congress intervention by hardright supporters of the Bush clique circulated, making it clear that the Republicans were not going to allow the recounts to continue and would do anything necessary to seize the election prize.

It was also becoming apparent that if by chance Gore won enough manual recount votes to put him ahead of Bush, and thus win the election, the Bush machine would go to the Florida legislature, controlled by George's brother Jeb and the Republicans, to reject the manual recount mandated by the Florida Supreme Court and to name a set of its own electors for the crucial December 19 Electoral College vote. If this failed, it was threatened that Republican forces in Congress would choose which Florida delegation would vote in the Electoral College, thus potentially sparking a constitutional crisis and a highly unpredictable situation.

And so the Gore forces, which had appeared to be gaining strong momentum the night before, were reeling from the Bush blitzkrieg. Such was the magnitude and daring of the Bush machine effort to win the Florida votes and the presidency at any cost that Republican supporters across the country were mobilized to demonstrate against the Florida Supreme Court ruling, to protest in the media, and to shriek to whoever would listen that the Democrats were "stealing the election," and that the outrage "would not stand" (Bush senior's ultimatum to Saddam Hussein at the beginning of the 1990 crisis in the Persian Gulf). Moderate commentators marveled that the Bush forces were carrying out an assault on the legitimacy of the judiciary, assailing "lawyers" and "judges" in ferocious terms, suggesting that they were prepared to do anything to win the prize, including provoking constitutional crisis.[5]

KATHERINE HARRIS'S CERTIFICATION

As the spectacle-saturated country took a break for the Thanksgiving holiday on November 23, the Gore and Bush forces prepared for a flurry of legal skirmishes on the local, state, and national level. Both sides concocted a public relations spin for their positions, and they devised strategies for the battle that was intensifying on all fronts. Dick Cheney had a turkey dinner at the George Washington University Hospital, while President Clinton dined with family and friends at the presidential retreat in Camp David, Maryland, and urged the public to be patient as the hand counts and legal maneuvering proceeded.

On Friday, November 24, the U.S. Supreme Court agreed to hear the Bush camp contestation of the Florida recount, and the Democrats made clear that they were going to contest any count that was certified by Katherine Harris that did not include the vote counting mandated by the Florida Supreme Court. Democrats began to criticize the growing number of irregularities, including the Republican mob that had helped to block the counting of the Miami–Dade ballots never tallied because the voting machine rejected them. The same day, ABC reported on its evening news that the demonstrators had been bused in and were paid Republican Party operatives.

Over the weekend the Republican bus headed north to Broward and Palm Beach Counties, where the manual recount was proceeding. Recounts and demonstrations by both sides provided a spectacle of the partisan struggle. Accompanied by a highly aggressive Bob Dole, the Republican operatives continued to harass recounters and accost the media with their signs and slogans, making it clear that the Republicans were not going to accept an Al Gore presidency. Democratic vice presidential candidate Joseph Lieberman protested that the Republican mob was out of control, and he begged Governor Bush personally to "call off his attack dogs." One of the many unsettling Republican tactics included a demonstration in front of Lieberman's home on the Sabbath, with Democratic supporters begging the Republicans to respect his religious holy day, while the demonstrators retorted with "liberal slander!" Throughout the agon, there were also daily demonstrations in front of Al Gore's home in Washington, D.C., some of which were very loud and unruly, upsetting his family.

On Sunday, November 26, Broward County had finished its recount, awarding 557 votes to Gore and closing the gap between the candidates to a few hundred. The canvassing board in Palm Beach County worked feverishly to finish its recount, and in the late afternoon petitioned Katherine Harris for a few hours more to complete its work after the 5:00 P.M. deadline. She refused, but the Palm Beach board sent the results it had concluded and resolved to finish the count and release the final figures later. In a spirited press conference, Gore's chief Florida lawyer, David Boies, outlined the reasons the Gore team was contesting the count, and tension rose as the nation awaited Harris's certification.

Shortly after the 5:00 P.M. deadline, dressed in a bright red power dress, Harris announced that she was not accepting the Palm Beach recount, since the canvassing board had missed the deadline, and that George W. Bush had won the Florida electoral votes by 537. Thus, Harris certified Bush as winner, and the cover of the next day's *Newsweek* featured Harris's winning number "537," while *Time*'s cover read "537 Votes." The contrast between the images of the hardworking Florida citizens doing their best to count the votes and the haughty Harris announcing a highly arbitrary number in the regal setting of the Florida Capitol cabinet room revealed the way that the Bush forces were using state power and the political institutions they controlled to enforce their political will over the will of the people—as they would continue to do.

Moments after Harris's certification, a triumphant James Baker appeared on television to announce the Bush victory, to declare it as final, and to argue that an American election had never been determined in the courts (in retrospect, a highly ironic pronouncement), as announcements flashed on the screen that Bush would speak three hours later. At 9:30 P.M. Bush strode up to a podium in Austin and, in the heavily sedated and teleprompter mode, repeated the platitudes of his campaign, pledged that he would "work to unite our great land," begged the Gore campaign to "reconsider" its legal challenges to the Florida recount, announced his transition team, headed by Dick Cheney, and said that Cheney would "work with President Clinton's administration to open a transition office in Washington," in effect asking the Clinton administration to give him the keys to federal buildings and federal funds so that he could plan his inauguration.[6]

The Republicans now fiercely attacked Gore's right to contest Harris's premature certification. A snide James Baker sneered: "Now the Gore campaign lawyers want to shift from recounts to contesting the election outcome." His puppet, George W. Bush, shortly thereafter read from his teleprompter: "Until Florida's votes were certified, the vice president was working to represent the interest of those who supported him." But now "that they're certified, we enter a different phase. If the vice president chooses to go forward, he is filing a contest to the outcome of the election. And that is not the best route for America."

The Baker–Bush assault on Gore's right to contest the certification was especially hypocritical since Katherine Harris had justified her speedy certification on the grounds that "the time for filing an election contest commences upon certification. . . . To delay certification affects the ability to have an election contest heard and possibly appealed and to implement whatever remedy the court might fashion." James Baker and the Bushites had repeatedly asserted this same argument to justify the legal and political positions taken, but now were hypocritically denying Gore the right to contest what many considered a highly partisan, unfair, and illegal certification of the Florida election before thousands of ballots had been counted.

Within minutes of Bush's speech, an extremely angry but forceful Democratic vice presidential candidate Joseph Lieberman protested Harris's refusal to include the Palm Beach votes, denounced "what by any reasonable standard is an incomplete and inaccurate count," and concluded that the Gore campaign had "no choice but to contest their actions," noting that Gore himself would soon address the nation and explain their position. The pundits jabbered into the night with their partisan spin, and the following day the hype continued on both sides. The media strategy of both antagonists was now well established in the war mode, with the campaigns providing media spokespeople, putting their own spin on events, and establishing a line of the day, sent out early in the morning to all supporters and repeated endlessly in the media—until the next spin cycle rendered the previous day's line "inoperative."

On November 27, Democratic Party leaders of the House and Senate held a press conference to affirm their support for the Gore campaign's call for court action, and the transcript and video of an ensuing conference call with Gore and Lieberman was released to the media, attempting to confirm the Democratic Party spin that the party was strongly behind Gore's legal maneuvers. Al Gore appeared on television at 5:55 P.M., EST, to defend his call for contestation of the Florida vote. Earlier in the day the *New York Times* had published an oft-cited article indicating that Gore believed he was certain he had won the Florida vote and thus the election, and he was determined to fight what he saw as an injustice. In any case, surrounded by American flags and with flashbulbs popping during his entire five-minute speech, Gore made his plea for patience and his argument that every vote in a democracy counted and needed to be accurately calculated and included in the tally.

Gore's battle would be uphill. A *Washington Post*/ABC News poll taken just after Katherine Harris's certification of Bush's victory on Sunday indicated that 60 percent of the public believed Gore should concede.[7] Yet Gore campaign officials insisted that were the votes properly counted they would win Florida, with the numbers of their victory margin predicted to rise from 9 to 1,248 as the day went on. The Gore side insisted that many votes, including more than 10,000 Miami–Dade votes, had never been counted, and that democracy required that every vote matter and be counted.[8] No one could predict, however, how the Florida courts and U.S. Supreme Court would factor into the drama.

The spectacle of the battle for the White House had intensified, and it was uncertain what would happen next in this remarkable saga. In Washington, Bush camp officials created the impression that they had won the election, and Dick Cheney, clearly the key Republican player on the political front, seemed to have recovered from his heart attack. At a news conference, Cheney outlined his plans for the Republican transition team, surrounded by fourteen American flags, two more than Gore the night before (persistent rumors circulated, however, that Cheney's condition was serious and that he would, or should, soon resign; see the op-ed in the *Los Angeles Times,* November 25).

The Democrats were resolved to pursue the Florida election results in the court, and if the judiciary allowed recounts or made decisions that would give the Florida electors to Gore, the Republican-dominated Florida state legislature was prepared to send its own electors, an action never before undertaken that would surely be struck down by the Florida Supreme Court, thus throwing the election decision to the U.S. Congress in Washington, D.C. The Republican-dominated House of Representatives would probably narrowly vote for the Bush Florida electors, but the Senate was now split 50–50 between Democrats and Republicans, and the tie-breaking vote would be cast by the current head of the Senate—Vice President Al Gore. However—the plot thickens—according to some pundits, a tie in the vote between the House and the Senate would be decided by the Florida state governor—Jeb Bush![9]

But lurking behind these bizarre, although plausible, scenarios was the U.S. Supreme Court, whose decisions were expected later in the week and perhaps further into the contest if it continued to escalate. This, of course, made for a great story, the around-the-clock news channels were getting their highest ratings ever, and the mediathon mavens were in bloviating heaven. Lawyers on both sides presented their briefs in local and state Florida courts, as well as the U.S. Supreme Court, and legal commentators attempted to explain the complex issues to the public. Both sides used the media to spin their version of what was occurring, with an NBC poll finding that 49 percent of the public believed Gore should concede, while 49 percent believed he should not.

On November 28, the Republican spin of the day was an assault on the "myths" that the Gore team was using to undo the Florida-state certified election results. The Republicans insisted that all votes had been counted and recounted, but the Gore camp replied that there were more than 10,000 ballots from Miami–Dade alone that had never been counted. In fact, the situation was more complex and messy than either side acknowledged—nationwide more than two million votes had not been properly counted by the voting machines, and the punch-ballot machines were much more likely to produce errors; there were also claims that more than 180,000 votes in Florida had been rejected by voting machines and not counted either because of double voting, no discernible choice, or mechanical error (punch-ballot machines were especially prone to clogging; see the Associated Press, November 28). It was also reported that it was precisely the African American and poorer communities, which usually vote Democratic, that had the most ballots thrown out by the machine counting and thus had not been tallied (*New York Times*, November 29). Other accounts revealed that many Republican counties in Florida *had* undertaken a manual recount of votes rejected by machines, yielding a rich harvest of votes for Bush (see *Salon*, November 28). Thus, it was simply not true that all votes had been counted in Florida, although a dirty little secret of the outdated U.S. election system revealed that a large number of votes were regularly not included because of problematic voting machines, mostly in poorer and African American districts.

It was evident, however, that a certain pattern for the "contest" period of the postelection clash had emerged. In fact, the Republican rush to certify covered over the two designated phases of the postelection period in which a candidate could first "protest" the initial election counts and then "contest" certified results. As the complex legal skirmishes moved through the courts, the candidates' camps would daily attack the opposing side, providing media events to spin their candidates' line of the day, using various spokespeople to make the point. On November 27, the Republican line was that although it must have been painful for Gore to lose, it was now time to bow to political reality and concede. The next day the Bush camp assaulted once again the "myths" of the uncounted ballots and continued to declare the election over as the Republicans put together a transition team and began leaking their cabinet appointments.

Gore now began appearing in public on a regular basis to make his case. After his rather formal November 27 evening plea for patience and to count every vote, a confident and smiling vice president emerged before the television cameras on November 28, calling for a quick recount of the contested votes, or the entire state, if the Bush camp agreed. Gore also proposed a meeting between the candidates, and the dropping of all legal procedures to resolve the issue as quickly as possible. The Bush camp rejected the overture and intensified its rhetoric that the election was over and that the Gore side was prolonging the ordeal.

Bush, meanwhile, had disappeared from sight, leaving his office in Austin to wave at crowds on the way to three-hour workout sessions, or leaving Austin for his ranch in Crawford, Texas, in the Waco area, to cut wood, work on home improvements, and make telephone calls to his operatives. As Maureen Dowd commented in the *New York Times*, "During the campaign, W. had a swagger, a John Wayne gunslinger pose. But when he comes out to face the cameras he blinks and shrinks, looking tremulous and frightened, dwarfed by American flags. He struggles to exude authority. He furrows his brow, trying to look more sagacious, but he ends up looking as if he has indigestion" (November 29). In an article that suggested Dick Cheney was taking over the Bush campaign while Bush retreated from the spotlight, Joan Walsh commented, "W. is scaring people, maybe including himself. While Gore has been everywhere the last few days making his case, however woodenly, from his driveway in D.C. to NBC's *Today* show, Bush has been hiding in Texas. His speech Sunday night claiming victory was alarming. He looked frightened and a little simian, blinking wildly, appearing to shrink down into the collar of his shirt as he spoke" (*Salon*, November 29). Resurrecting a metaphor previously used for Bush senior's Veep Dan Quayle, David Nyhan in the *Boston Globe* referred to Bush as "Mr. Deer-in-the-Headlights" (November 29). Indeed, late-night comics had a field day with the dim-witted President-to-Be, Dan Quayle redux—the first time as national farce, the second as global tragedy.

NOTES

1. Film critic Roger Ebert collected these pungent phrases. In a fine postelection analysis, Ebert argued that Republican mantras and propaganda lines—such as "the

Democrats are stealing the election" and "The Florida Supreme Court is partisan"—
planted "memes" in the collective public mind that helped mobilize support for the
unsupportable Republican cause of stopping the ballot counting (www.suntimes.com/
output/eb-feature/ebert14.html). Pundits, like Ann Coulter, aided the Bush campaign
by repeating their line-of-the-day, puffed-up with pungent sound-bites. Coulter is one
of a squad of Republican women, often young and blonde, to whom the NBC, Fox,
and other network shows liked to give airtime. Coulter became a familiar part of the
punditocracy during the Clinton sex scandals and impeachment trial. Her eyes would
widen as she shrieked the Republican line of the day, and if contradicted she would
heighten the decibel level and yell non sequiturs, marking a disturbing decline on conservative discourse and rationality. On a February 26, 2001, *Politically Incorrect*,
Coulter, not a poster girl for feminism, stated that she thinks "women are too stupid
to vote." See the transcript at http://abc.go.com/primetime/politicallyincorrect/pi_ho-
me.html.

2. Hofstadter's *The Paranoid Style in American Politics and Other Essays* (reprint
1996) had become a classic. His later *Anti-Intellectualism in American Life* (1966)
could also usefully be rewritten in reflections on the Bush phenomenon. T. W. Adorno
produced even more penetrating analyses of conservative rage, resentment, paranoia,
and projection in his writings; see, especially, Adorno et al., *The Authoritarian Personality* (1950) and the essays collected in *The Stars Down to Earth and Other Essays on
the Irrational in Culture* (1994).

3. See David Corn, "The Loyal Opposition: One Night, Two Different Elections"
(tompaine.com.news/2000/11/10/3.html); and David Grann, "Bush Rides the Tiger,
Quiet Riot," *New Republic* (Dec. 25, 2000).

4. Rightwing rage, hysteria, and projection regularly oozed forth on the *Washington Post* op-ed page. On November 22, in response to the Florida Supreme Court
ruling, Michael Kelly penned a screed "Send in the Thugs," attacking Democratic
Party lawyers, politicos, and pundits for allegedly bringing thuggery into the sacred
electoral process on the very day that young Republicans were engaging in widely
deplored hooliganry in Miami–Dade. Kelly attacked Paul Begala, whom he quoted out
of context, as an example of mad-dog Democrats, but in context it is Kelly who appears
canine and out-of-control.

Also on November 22, another *Washington Post* op-ed piece by George Will,
"Ferocity Gap," repeated Rush Limbaugh's line that Democrats are more "ferocious"
than Republicans. Will added that Democrats are driven by "material greed" for the
spoils of government, and are unrelenting in their struggle for the prize of federal jobs
and booty. This argument, however, overlooks the fact that it was the Cheney–Bush
team that had received the largest amount of corporate contributions in electoral history and that the Republican administration was promising billions of dollars of tax
and regulatory relief, as well as contracts and other spoils to its contributors, payoffs
brazenly evident the first weeks of Bush's reign. Thus Will and his ilk exploded with
rage and egregiously projected the worst features of Republicans onto their enemies.

5. The fierceness of the Republican onslaught shocked editorial commentators: a November 23 *New York Times* piece deplored "Reckless Republican Rhetoric," while a *Boston Globe* editorial called Bush's assault on the Florida court "ludicrous" and lamented that the talk of Florida state Republicans "had the scent of a banana republic to it."

6. Bush's speech elicited strong media criticism on November 27, with the *New York Times* citing his attempt "to leapfrog the nation past the important pending legal challenges to . . . [Florida's] incompletely counted vote." *USA Today* complained that Bush's speech "amplifies the arrogant tone he and Republicans generally have set since the election" and rejected Harris's rush "to certify an outdated count" in Florida. The *Boston Globe* criticized Harris's "regrettable act" to "deny *all* of the Palm Beach manual recounts," which "flies in the face of the [Florida Supreme Court's] entire ruling, which blocked her authority to precipitously certify the vote in the first place." *U.S. News and World Report* noted how Bush had "displayed an off-putting bit of insecurity" and "a smug arrogance and a sense of entitlement about the presidency." The *Washington Post* noted that the General Services Administration rejected Bush's request for a transition office and funds "with a terse reply: no money or keys to the offices until the challenges to the election are resolved."

7. Of course, it is astonishing that a poll taken of a small sample of the public immediately after the certification, when most people were watching football or enjoying the last day of their Thanksgiving holiday, was taken so seriously, repeated constantly by talking heads, journalists, and Republican spinners; one would think that a result of the Indecision 2000 fiasco would be skepticism toward polls that were especially high for Bush and thus unreliable indicators during the last two weeks of the campaign. But Republican spinners cited polls day after day that indicated that the majority of the public thought Gore should concede. Such faith in poll numbers is belied by the fact that more and more people are refusing to even respond to telephone polls which are becoming ever more misleading and inaccurate.

8. Gore's speech received mixed editorial responses. On November 28, the *New York Times* supported Gore's "plea for patience" as "a matter of law and fairness." The *Washington Post* worried that "Mr. Gore has already had many bites at the apple" and "three weeks to overtake his rival and [has] been unable to do so." The *Boston Globe* insisted that "legitimacy counts" and thus "the best way to avoid such a national embarrassment is still—as it has been since Nov. 8—to count as many votes as possible." An article in the *Miami Herald* (Dec. 2), based on a statistical study by an Arizona State University social scientist, Stephen Doig, claimed that if all uncounted ballots were counted, Gore would win by a hefty 23,000 votes. Republicans, predictably, denounced the study as "voodoo mathematics."

9. Tom "The Hatchet" DeLay (R-Tex.) created a "doomsday scenario" in which even if the Florida Senate did not send Bush electors, the Republican House is preparing to block a Gore Electoral College victory." It is not clear, however, on what legal basis it could proceed. See the discussion by John Dean, Nixon's lawyer in the Watergate scandal, "Tyranny of the Majority" (www.msnbc.com/news/49405.asp).

5

LEGAL WRANGLING
AND POLITICAL
SPECTACLE

Confusion now hath made its masterpiece.

—Shakespeare, *Macbeth*

*Essential American institutions—the presidency, the courts,
the press, the electoral process—have each sustained damage,
and that damage will linger beneath the placid surface long
after the country as a whole has moved on.*

—Jonathan Alter, *Newsweek* commentator

By Tuesday, November 28, legal proceedings were unfolding on sixteen
different fronts, with the major focus on proceedings in a county courtroom in the backwater Florida state capital of Tallahassee. The Gore camp
was contesting the circumvention of the manual recount that had been ordered
by the Florida Supreme Court and short-circuited by Miami–Dade County's
on-and-off efforts to count the uncounted ballots. The Democrats were also
contesting the certification of election results by Katherine Harris before Palm
Beach County had completed its recount, as well as Nassau County's reversion
to the original count before the state-mandated machine recount, which had
added 262 votes to Bush's tally.

THE WAR IN THE COURTS

We're all legal experts now. Not just the journalists, who are trying to guide readers and viewers through the legal maze that Indecision 2000 has become, but

the country as a whole, which seems increasingly engrossed by the lawsuits, the allegations and the constitutional arguments that are keeping a small army of attorneys happily employed. —Howard Kurtz, *Washington Post* media critic

Judge N. Sander Sauls, selected by rotation, was appropriately ambiguous for the job, described as a Democrat who had shifted his political allegiance to the Republicans and then returned to the Democrats; in a previous conflict with the Florida Supreme Court he had resigned as chief judge of the 2nd Judicial Circuit, although he stayed on as a trial judge. Sauls began by posing as a folksy country judge, and he readily agreed to a request to have the disputed ballots sent to Tallahassee—although he was never to actually look at them, a fact that angered the Gore team.

Judge Sauls's courtroom proceedings were televised live, and overheated media commentators hyped the drama as decisive for the "battle for the White House," as the struggle was now labeled by the television networks. On November 29, the Bush lawyers asked Sauls if the entire lot of 1.1 million ballots could be hauled up from Palm Beach and Miami–Dade Counties, instead of limiting the ballots to the never counted undervotes requested by the Gore team. Sauls nonchalantly agreed to the Bush team request, denounced by Gore's lawyers as a stalling tactic and publicity stunt to ridicule the entire proceedings.

While Sauls allowed the ballots from Palm Beach and Miami–Dade Counties to be packed to ship to Tallahassee for possible inspection and recounting, he delayed the trial to Saturday morning, thus losing what the Gore side saw as valuable time. Moreover, Sauls refused to allow the ballot counting until the contested legal issues were resolved. The Democrats were exceedingly frustrated, and the Republicans organized another campaign to pressure Gore to concede. Earlier in the week, their spin of the moment was that while everyone understood Gore's pain in losing, he had to face reality and for the good of the country concede. Upping the rhetoric, the GOP began using Web sites, e-mail, phone banks, and other instruments to try to influence the media, public, and especially Democratic regulars that Gore *must* concede for the good of the country.

On November 29, Dick Cheney held a press briefing at a Mayflower Hotel ballroom in Washington to announce the formal opening of a Bush–Cheney transition office. The operation would be privately funded and would be housed in an office building near Cheney's home in McLean, Virginia. Meanwhile, Gore went on a television blitz, appearing on network morning shows and prime-time newscasts, insisting that he had a "50–50" chance of winning.

He also visited Bill Clinton, marking the first time that they had been together for more than a month (this must have been an interesting meeting, since Democratic Party operatives had been whispering that Gore's failure to make more use of President Clinton in the election campaign had cost him an easy win, while many in the Gore camp blamed Clinton's scandals for depriving Gore a decisive victory).

The newsday of November 30 was dominated by the spectacle of a yellow Ryder truck filled with ballots snaking across the state of Florida. Television news helicopters provided live aerial photographs reminiscent of O. J. Simpson's Bronco ride.[1] Meanwhile, back at the ranch in Crawford, Texas, Bush and Cheney received Gulf War hero Colin Powell with great media fanfare, leading to speculation that the "Dumb Son's ingathering of Daddy's Legion of Doom" might mean that unsettled business with Saddam Hussein could be at the top of the new Bush administration's agenda (*Suck,* November 30).

On Friday, December 1, the U.S. Supreme Court held a hearing. Following their longtime procedure of banning television cameras from the court, the justices held proceedings in chamber, but immediately after the ninety-minute hearing, in which both sides presented their cases and the justices questioned the parties, audiotapes were released, and the media commentators strained for meanings. Once again, as in the O. J. Simpson trial and the Clinton impeachment trial, large publics became involved in complex legal and political proceedings with significant implications.

The same day and throughout the weekend, Judge Sauls's courtroom proceedings in Tallahassee, televised live, educated the nation in voting machines, statistics, recounts, and high-powered legal shenanigans as both sides spun to the maximum, making their candidates' case to the public. It was a field day for lawyers and legal commentators, who, as in the O. J. Simpson trial, became media celebrities with the audience hanging on their every word, while pundits attempted to read the tea leaves of the complex political and legal maneuvering.

The hearing in Tallahassee continued all day Saturday, December 2, before Judge Sauls. In a nine-hour televised marathon session, attorneys for Bush and Gore squabbled before a bored and seemingly disengaged judge. The weary lawyers haggled over which ballots should be counted, how the process should proceed, and what standards should be used. The legal wrangling continued on Sunday morning when Sauls heard testimony from seven Bush camp witnesses about the technicalities of Florida ballots and voting processes, though he did not seem particularly interested. Gore trial lawyer Dexter Douglass pleaded with Sauls to give a ruling that would allow the ballots in question, now in Tallahassee, to be counted, stressing the crucial time issue. But Sauls curtly refused the request, bringing the hearing to a close around 10:45 P.M. and promising to issue his ruling the next morning.

The U.S. Supreme Court decision, announced on Monday, December 4, shortly before the Sauls ruling was to be declared, appeared to be ominous for Gore. In a somewhat Hamletesque decision, the high court "vacated" the Florida court judgment that had mandated the recount, required the Florida court to clarify its reasoning, and reserved later judgment. Both sides declared themselves satisfied with the unanimous ruling that many commentators claimed hid a probable five-to-four division, replicating the partisanship and deep schism of the rest of the country.

There had been (futile) hope among many that somehow the U.S. Supreme Court would rise above the fray and come up with a Solomonic edict that would resolve the conflict (a pious respect for the wisdom of the Supreme Court that would henceforth be undermined by the highly partisan later decision for Bush that awarded him the presidency). The questions revealed the usual split among partisan lines, with the conservative wing led by Bush appointee Antonin Scalia and Chief Justice William Rehnquist. These justices seemed to have foisted a ruling on the court that dodged the partisan issues over the recount in favor of a rarely cited principle of the U.S. Constitution (Article II, Section 1) that enabled state legislatures to appoint the electors and that downplayed popular sovereignty. (I discuss the selective use of the U.S. Constitution by the Supreme Court in analysis of the Court's final and decisive ruling in chapter 7.) The U.S. Supreme Court ruling on December 4 suggested that the Florida Supreme Court had erred by basing its decision on the sovereignty of the voter and the right for votes to be counted (also principles in the Florida state constitution and statutes of the Florida state legislature). A few commentators remarked that not only did this ruling decenter voters' rights and privilege state legislatures over judiciaries, but it also provided a legal basis for the Florida state legislature to appoint its own electors, sending out a chilling message that the U.S. Supreme Court was clearly in Bush's camp (and perhaps advising Gore to pack it in and signaling the Florida Supreme Court not to bother to rule in Gore's favor).

The ruling also pointed to serious flaws in the U.S. Electoral College voting system and put in question the concept of the sovereignty of the people in elections. Most media commentators were too embarrassed to point out the extremism and partisanship of the Supreme Court's ruling. In fact, adulators of the Supreme Court continued to believe that it would ultimately provide a fair and reasonable solution. The initial ruling did provide an occasion for

Rehnquist critics to recycle an old story that the chief justice had his start in a Republican project in Phoenix in 1964, called "Operation Eagle Eye," in which Rehnquist and other Republicans harassed (mostly minority and pre-sumed Democratic) voters, challenging their qualifications to vote—a system-atic intimidation remarkably similar to the Republican efforts that helped stopped the Miami–Dade recount.[2] In his 1971 Supreme Court hearings, Rehnquist denied that he had personally intimidated voters, although over the years several witnesses, including a deputy U.S. attorney, signed affidavits indi-cating that they had witnessed his participation in this activity (for details on Rehnquist's checkered career, see Bugulosi 2001: 25f.).

Sauls postponed his decision in order to study the seven-page Supreme Court ruling, to make his own decision conform to the high court thinking, and in a dramatic courtroom appearance in mid-afternoon knocked out every contestation of the Gore side, ruling decisively in favor of the Bush forces.[3] Pundits declared the election all but over, and pressures on Gore to concede mounted, but the Gore team immediately appealed to the Florida Supreme Court, prolonging the spectacle with more high-stakes legal conflicts.

In the intense focus on the judicial proceedings, an important *Washington Post* study had been overlooked. On December 3, the *Post* reported that in many African American precincts as many as one in five, or even one in three, ballots were thrown out and not counted, either because of faulty machinery, voting error, or irregularities. On the whole, about three out of a thousand ballots were rejected and not counted in the Florida optical-scan systems, and about fifteen out of a thousand were thrown out in the hand-punch systems with the infamous chads, as in the counties in question. The *New York Times* (December 5) also covered the story, as did some of the television networks, but African American leaders were furious that more attention had not been given to this scandal and that the U.S. Justice Department had been slow in investigating; some people also criticized the Gore camp for not making this issue more important in its offensive.

On Tuesday, December 5, the Florida Supreme Court agreed to hear Gore's appeal of Judge Sauls's ruling for Bush and gave the two sides one day to file their legal briefs in a one-hour hearing. A federal appeals court in Atlanta rejected the Bush camp claim that it was unconstitutional and a viola-tion of the "equal protection" clause to hand-count the ballots in selected Florida counties. At the same time, in other parts of Florida, court proceedings were beginning that gave the Gore camp some hope. In Seminole and Martin Counties, Democratic Party activists launched lawsuits claiming that election supervisors colluded with the state Republican Party to fill in blanks in flawed absentee ballot applications in the two Florida counties, while denying Democrats similar access to absentee ballots. Plaintiffs claimed that the Republican operatives and the local election boards had violated election law by allowing the operatives to fill in voter identification numbers on Republican Party absentee ballot applications in the county office in Seminole, and even to take the applications off the premises in Martin County to fill in missing data. The Democrats alleged that this was part of a pattern of irregularities by the state Republican Party, while Republicans dismissed the charges as "technicalities."

Televised trials on the absentee ballot issue took place on December 6 and 7, and if the disputed ballots were to be thrown out, Al Gore could attain a net gain of almost 8,000 votes. This possibility perhaps inspired the Florida state legislature on December 6 to announce the long-awaited "special session" to choose their own electors in case Gore was declared the winner in Florida. Such an event was unparalleled and appeared to open the door to constitutional crisis, giving rise to copious speculation on the possibility of two opposing sets of electors from Florida emerging from the vote counting (Gore) and the Florida legislature (Bush).

The Seminole and Martin County lawsuits played out in the courts of (Terry) Lewis and (Nikki) Clark, the former a soft-spoken young judge who doubled as a published mystery author, and the latter a serious African American woman whom the Republicans evidently feared and tried to have removed. Governor Jeb Bush had passed her over for a promotion, and Republicans dreaded she would retaliate. Although the Gore campaign was not officially involved in the cases, in an off-moment of banter with the press, Gore disclosed his detailed knowledge of and interest in the case. Republicans then accused the Gore camp of hypocrisy, since the Democrats claimed that their recount efforts were driven by the principle of counting every vote, while the Seminole and Martin County cases would remove allegedly illegal votes for Bush, to Gore's potential favor.

On December 7, the Florida Supreme Court heard Gore's appeal of the Sauls ruling, commentators indicated that this was his last chance, and television networks ran banners at the bottom of the television screen proclaiming that Gore had announced he would concede if he lost the Florida Supreme Court appeal to resume the manual ballot counting. In a televised hearing, both sides presented their cases in a concise one-hour format. Once again, media commentators and spin doctors appeared in the talking-heads format, interrupted by live broadcasting of the concluding arguments of the Seminole and Martin County cases where the major Bush team lawyers took on local Democratic Party attorneys trying to pull off a long-shot victory for Gore.

Adopting the crisis-mode terminology used for hostage situations, television networks and newspapers declared the moment Day 30 of the battle for the White House. The Associated Press reported that the fortieth execution of the year had taken place in Texas, a dubious national record. Reports were hidden in back news pages that George H. W. Bush was recovering from hip replacement surgery at Minnesota's Mayo Clinic and contemplating his next bungee jump; his son "said a little prayer" for his father and planned to call him later in the day. The Bushes were not, however, asked to respond to a newspaper story circulating through the Internet that the Bush family fortune was partly derived from affiliation with Nazi banks."[4]

Another explosive story alleged that the Florida secretary of state had removed 173,000 names from state voter rolls during the year leading up to the election, based on a list of supposedly ineligible voters provided by a private firm with strong Republican ties; an examination of the list showed that many eligible voters, mostly African American, had been wrongly eliminated from the voting rolls and not allowed to vote.[5] Evidently, the state of Florida had hired a company, Database Technologies (DBT), with strong Republican connections, to cross-check state voter rolls to eliminate felons who were not allowed to vote in Florida elections. The company, however, illicitly eliminated thousands of eligible voters who found themselves crossed off the voting lists on election day and were in many cases denied their vote.

The broadcast media, however, were solely focused on the battles in the Florida courts, and the cable television news networks hyped the announced (Judges) Lewis and Clark rulings with florid "countdown" signs; the initial 12:00 ruling time was postponed until 2:15 P.M., EST, and the tension mounted. Amid flashing cameras, a court official read the ruling, which in both the Lewis and Clark decisions came out on Bush's side: two nails in Gore's election coffin with a ruling expected in the Florida Supreme Court anytime that could end the agon (and the agony for those involved). But, no! Hours later in a stunning decision, the Florida Supreme Court overruled Judge Sauls by a thin four-to-three margin and ordered manual recounts of all the "undervotes"—ballots on which no vote for president was picked up by machines during the mechanical counting—and throughout Florida! The Florida court argued that Sauls had errored in principle and in fact, and had trapped the Gore side in a Catch-22 dilemma where they could only prove that the uncounted ballots would yield a significant change in their favor if the ballots were actually counted, and then ruled against the counting, never examining the crucial evidence. In addition, the Florida Supreme Court awarded Gore Palm Beach County's tardy 215 votes and Miami–Dade's 168 uncertified votes from the partial manual count, winnowing down Bush's 537-vote lead to 154 votes. The race for votes was now on and in earnest![6]

SPECTACLE OF DEMOCRACY IN THE STATE OF FLORIDA

Democracy is sometimes difficult. —Senator Barbara Boxer (D-Calif.)

Just another day in Election 2000. —Pam Iorio, Hillsborough County, election supervisor

The Florida Supreme Court decision sent shockwaves through the country and unleashed a sweet and very short day of democracy in Florida. Hence, on December 8, Day 31 of the Florida war for the presidency, the anniversary of the assassination of John Lennon, and the day after the Pearl Harbor anniversary, the nuclear bomb of recounts fell on the Bushites, just as they thought victory was in their grasp. The Republicans went ballistic. Raising its artillery on the Gore candidacy, the Florida legislature was now prepared to go full steam ahead to name its own electors, a result guaranteed to produce constitutional crisis. Hoping to torpedo the Gore advance, the Bush machine assembled its groggy lawyers for more legal combat to try to halt the recount. Republicans pulled together their troops for the big fight, and their e-mail, faxes, and telephone pools leaped into overtime. Republican snipers began appearing in the media, stammering their objections, trying to assemble a critical mass of anger that could go nuclear against Gore.

The gleeful Democrats were able to take the high road of principle, maintaining that all they had ever wanted was a full and fair count of the votes, and they would accept the results without further legal appeals. William Daley, speaking for the Gore campaign, was obviously elated, proclaiming a victory, not for Al Gore, but for "fairness, accountability, and our democracy itself." On the Democratic fourth down, with the elusive goal rapidly receding from view, the turnover produced a first and goal, with the target finally in sight.

The monumental epic quickly unfolded the night of December 7. A county clerk appeared on the television networks and indicated that the Florida courts were ready to begin the manual recount of the undervotes and that Judge Terry Lewis would supervise the process. Earlier, the court had floated a rumor that the humiliated Judge Sauls, whose ruling had been overturned on principle and fact, was going to recuse himself. In marked contrast to his previous hysterical reaction to the unfavorable Florida Supreme Court ruling, a measured but bristling James Baker appeared to indicate the Bush camp's unhappiness with the ruling and indicated that it was appealing to the U.S. Supreme Court. Baker used Florida Chief Justice Charles Wells's dissent to make the Bush camp's point that the Florida court decision would produce "an unprecedented and unnecessary constitutional crisis"—the spin strategy that the Bush machine would use in the days to come, using Judge Wells's dissent to argue its position.[7]

ABC's Peter Jennings described the Florida ruling as an "earthquake" that was generating shockwaves throughout the nation and creating a "mess" of legal and political complexities. On PBS, historians and political analysts calmly discussed and analyzed the issues, stressing the great pedagogy of the event—that this was teaching the world the complexity of democracy and that calm and thoughtfulness was needed, rather than "the antics of Chris Matthews and his ilk," a reference to the verbose MSNBC commentator who was becoming the poster boy of hyperchatter. On MSNBC the frequently hysterical Matthews was, as was often the case, way over the top. With his face sweating and his hair hanging over his forehead, he shrieked whatever inane thoughts appeared in his mind or on his teleprompter. His first guest was a livid Senator Orrin Hatch (R-Utah), who ranted and raved against the great atrocities being committed by the activist "Democratic [Party]" Florida Supreme Court. The high-volume, high-intensity spin cycle was under way.

Republican congressmen went off the froth meter, spewing invective. Former bug exterminator Tom DeLay fumed that "this judicial aggression must not stand" and plotted to defeat those pesky liberal judges and bothersome people who wanted a vote counting. DeLay had earlier helped organize the trip to Miami–Dade of Republican operatives who helped stop the manual count of never-counted ballots rejected by the voting machines, which some opined threw the election to Bush by intimidating the group ordered to do the manual counting. Meanwhile the (heavily Republican-biased) Fox network flashed a large pulsating and red "Election Alert!" graphic on its screens, perhaps sending a not-too-subliminal message to the party faithful to get off their reclining backsides and get ready to hit the streets, or at least the computer, to militate for their now threatened candidate.

On the MSNBC December 7 evening news, Brian Williams opened by marveling that "after a near-death experience, Al Gore has returned to life." Internet Webzines were also posting their analyses. In *Salon*, Jake Tapper enthused, "In a shocking, even unbelievable turn of events Friday afternoon, the Florida Supreme Court delivered Vice President Al Gore the best news he's heard since Tipper accepted his marriage proposal." Tapper noted that none of the legal authorities in Florida whom he had interviewed thought that the Florida court would rule in Gore's favor and that the decision was highly surprising.

The same evening, an Associated Press report indicated that, as Gore and his family huddled in his library to watch a small television set, "what seemed a miracle was delivered by Florida's Supreme Court": "Just as a court spokesman announced on live television that Gore's near-dead hopes for a recount would be revived by court order, fairy lights on the Christmas tree outside his home flickered to life ('It comes on automatically,' a uniformed Secret Service officer assured bystanders dazzled by the mystical timing)." The AP noted that since the "high court delivered its shocker a breath before sundown," Gore's running mate, Senator Joseph Lieberman, an Orthodox Jew, was able to watch the ruling on television: "He and his wife, Hadassah, who observe the weekly Sabbath by not operating machinery such as cars or televisions, then walked in twilight from their Georgetown home to the vice presidential mansion on Embassy Row." Television images showed excited groups gathering around the vice president's mansion, and parades of honking cars circled the house with salutations.

Things were not as holiday cheery in the Bush camp. The AP's Tom Raum reported, "Bush glum over Florida court ruling." "Even before the decision was turned down, Bush was more muted than he has been in days," said Raum (yet the *New York Times* reported that Bush was "chuckling" through an earlier photo opportunity, as he chatted with reporters about the staff members he was about to appoint for his new administration). After the Florida Supreme Court decision, however, the Bush staff in Austin stated that "we've run out of reaction" as groups of pro-Gore demonstrators congregated outside the governor's mansion honking horns and shouting at the Bush–Cheney supporters, who were expecting a victory celebration that night. Cheney, according to Raum, snuck out of the McLean, Virginia, transition headquarters "without telling his press aides, who normally alert a pool of network television crews camped out on the building's first floor so they can film Cheney walking to his car."

On the macro- and microlevel the two camps intensified their trench warfare. Supplementing the Bush campaign's appeal to the U.S. Supreme Court to stay the order to count the undervotes, the Republicans appealed to the 11th Circuit Court in Atlanta to stop the count of undervotes immediately.

The Bush side filed papers with the Florida Supreme Court as well, demanding the halt of tallying never-counted or inspected undervotes rejected by the machine. Rumors floated that some Florida counties would refuse to undertake the mandated manual count of the undervotes, unleashing the specter of anarchy in the Sunshine State. In fact, the next day some counties were indeed unable to proceed, either because of lack of will or of technology. But after Sauls recused himself, Judge Terry Lewis, who had just adjudicated the complex Martin County absentee case, was assigned to preside over the proceeding and he called a hearing, calmly stating that he had read the Florida court's four-to-three ruling mandating the statewide counting of the undervotes, "and I intend to follow it."

The great adventure of democracy set sail for uncharted waters in the Tallahassee courtroom as the weary legal heavies from the Bush and Gore teams assembled to give Judge Lewis advice on how to proceed. After a couple of hours of legal wrangling, telecast live, Lewis adjourned. He returned about midnight and attempted to set forth some guidelines to proceed with the recount the next morning, which he scheduled to begin early, wanting it to be completed by Sunday at 2:00 P.M. Judge Lewis ruled that the supervisors of each county's tallying of the undervotes could interpret the high court's voter-intent standard on their own, without detailed instructions on dimples or indentation, and that he would not tolerate delays in the counting.

Awaking in Los Angeles with excitement at 5:00 A.M., PST, to see if the Evil Magi of the U.S. Supreme Court had yet enacted the Will of the Father (i.e., the Bush who had appointed some of them) and brought the tallying of the undervotes to a halt, I was excited to see the Heroes of Democracy in Florida already hard at work, assembling to separate and collect the undervotes, to count and register the tally, and to engage in the humble and difficult work of democracy throughout Florida. Judge Lewis had decided that Florida judges would be in charge of overseeing the count, that each political party could have observers at the local canvassing sites, and that the proceedings would be open to the media. Lewis had appointed a group of judges to count the contested Miami–Dade ballots that had been the target of the Republican "bourgeois riot," and this group dutifully set to work.

Democracy was unfolding again in all its messy glory with its solid citizens gathering in small and larger Florida towns to undertake their civic duty. The world watched with amazement, the chattering classes chatted on, and the political camps devised on the run their strategy and tactics for the political war now under way. The Gore camp was ecstatic, but the Bush forces clearly had many big guns still to fire as the U.S. Supreme Court and federal circuit court in Atlanta deliberated their response to the legal bombshell delivered by the Florida Supreme Court. Republican legislators in Florida intensified their plotting to devise their own slate of Bush electors in case Gore should win the tally, and DeLay and his merry band of Republican congressmen charted their strategy to assassinate Gore's candidacy in Washington should he survive the formidable legal and political machinery aimed at his campaign.

On Friday night and early Saturday morning, political operatives from both camps chartered planes and bought tickets to send their troops to Florida to do battle in the proceedings. The separation and tallying of the undervotes began in an orderly fashion as local canvassing boards debated voting procedures, standards, and schedules and in some cases sought software to help with the ballot-sorting preliminary to the count. Diligent groups of citizens began their work, and television cameras cut from one Florida county to another to show the local people undertaking their civic responsibilities.

Groups for Gore and Bush appeared at recount sites to observe the proceedings and demonstrate for their candidates, and political celebrities from the entire country began appearing to spin their side's positions. California Democratic senator Barbara Boxer, who admitted the night before crying when she heard that the votes were to be tabulated, flew to Florida to support the counting; when queried as to the varying standards being used to count the votes, Boxer conceded that "democracy was messy," but said that the serious efforts under way were as fair as possible. Republicans shouted, "Traitor!" and worse at Boxer, who was forced to cut short her speech and escape from the unruly Republican mob.

The attempt at the tallying of the uncounted votes throughout Florida and passionate partisan response to the event produced a dazzling spectacle of people's democracy unfolding in full view of the television cameras. Unlike recounts in previous elections, which had proceeded in secrecy, subject to who-knows-what funny games and vote tampering, this time, it was a public affair, subject to scrutiny by all. As the morning went the way of all mornings, intensity and tension mounted. While public servants in some parts of Florida calmly counted never-tallied undervote ballots, in other parts, such as Jacksonville, there were fierce arguments over the rules and procedures, and it took hours to get the process going. One saw ordinary men and women of all ages and colors working together to determine the outcome of the election. Democrats, Republicans, election officials, and judges were attempting to produce a fair and accurate counting of votes never tallied due to failures of the voting machines. Outside the various tabulation sites, demonstrators shouted their slogans, and the media blowhards blathered on, while the Bush legal team mounted local-, regional-, and national-level assaults on the process.

The multiple legal fronts escalated suspense as to whether a local Florida judge, the 11th Circuit Court of Atlanta, or the U.S. Supreme Court would stop the tabulation of the undervotes. The cable news networks cut from Florida images of people engaged in the counting process, to correspondents in front of the respective courts, to legal or political commentators, to demonstrators and representatives of the two warring camps, attempting to spin the complex proceedings. Not surprisingly, the Florida Supreme Court rejected the Bush request to halt the counting, but reports circulated that the U.S. Supreme Court justices were engaged in polling to determine whether, or how, they would act.

Around 2:30 P.M., EST, the Gore camp was encouraged when it was announced that the 11th Circuit Court of Atlanta had rejected the Bush demand for a halt to voting eleven-to-four, but the court also mandated that election results could not be certified until rulings by the U.S. Supreme Court, or its own body, reviewed the vote counting.[8] A few minutes later, however, the U.S. Supreme Court issued an order by a close five-to-four ruling to halt the hand recount. The decision, along the usual partisan lines, dealt a crushing blow to the spectacle of democracy. Opponents of the Bush machine saw the ruling as the heavy hand of oligarchy, conservatism, and partisanship, bringing the remarkable experiment of the undervote counting to a halt, while Republicans saw it as the triumph of reason and order (or at least of their guy).

Some of those involved in the Florida recount shouted with anguish on camera, or were reduced to stunned silence, while Bush supporters cheered. CNN showed a poignant split-screen image of hardworking groups of citizens inspecting ballots in Florida as the correspondent in Washington reported on the Supreme Court decision to halt the counting. CNN had focused in on preparations for the recounts in Hillsborough County and captured the confused, unhappy, and/or gleeful faces of the citizens at work when told of the Supreme Court stay of the process. Head of the local canvassing board Pam Iorio described with a smile the elaborate procedures and futile work as "just another day in Election 2000," but pledged to be ready to go if counting were to recommence.

The Gore supporters were "shocked" and "outraged" by what they saw as the blatant partisanship of the U.S. Supreme Court, and both sides prepared for the hearings called for Monday at 11:00 A.M. that could produce the end of the most bizarre election in U.S. history—or just another interlude in a disputed campaign. The spectacle of democracy—of ordinary people trying to determine the will of the people in a complex and extremely close electoral process in which handfuls of votes could decide the fate of the future—gave way again to the panorama of spin as the media pundits returned to the center of the image.

At 3:36 P.M., EST, the networks showed a radiant Dick and Lynne Cheney returning to the Bush transition team headquarters that they had snuck away from the night before. At 3:48, the omnipresent James Baker emerged to say how pleased the Bush side was with the Supreme Court ruling and that they were preparing to prevail in the hearing on Monday. At 4:06, Ron Klain, Gore campaign legal adviser, appeared to register his side's disappointment, to claim that they were gaining votes in the counting of the undervotes, and to express "optimism" that they would prevail in the Supreme Court hearing on Monday. He was accompanied by David Boies, Gore chief legal counsel, who indicated how they were extremely pleased that the Florida Supreme Court and 11th Circuit Court had refused the Bush team request for halting the undervote count, and how disappointed they were that a five-to-four Supreme Court decision had closed down the process. Taking several digs at Antonin Scalia, the ultra-right justice who helped shape the deadly U.S. Supreme Court decision, Boies set forth three sets of arguments as to why the Florida Supreme Court was correct to call for the undervote counting, which would provide some of the basis for the Gore campaign appeal before the Supreme Court.

The CNN commentators discussed the rapidly shifting "political distress level" and "whiplash" as the opposing sides' fortunes dramatically shifted moment by moment. Leading Republicans held press conferences to attack the "judicial activism" and illegality of the Florida Supreme Court decision and to praise the U.S. Supreme Court. The Republican strategy was to follow James Baker in using the harsh dissent by Florida Chief Justice Charles Wells from the Florida Supreme Court decision to count the undervotes to attack the Florida court ruling, and then to defend the U.S. Supreme Court intervention.

NOTES

1. O. J. Simpson, in response to a call from the Associated Press, declared the images "boring" and stated that his own Bronco chase by police was more "intriguing," since the outcome was not known in advance. The following week, the Ryder truck was put up for sale on e-bay. Compounding the historic irony and semiotics of the situation, Timothy McVeigh had used a Ryder van in the 1995 Oklahoma City

bombing, and no doubt the Ryder company donated its truck to carry the ballots to create a more positive iconography for its corporate brand.

2. See Dennis Roddy, "Just Our Bill," in the December 2, 2000, www.common-dreams.org site. Later, *The Nation* published the pertinent 1986 testimony in the hearings of the Senate Judiciary Committee on Rehnquist's nomination for chief justice of the United States; www.thenation.com/special/20010101rehnquist.mhtml; see also Bugliosi 2001: 25 and 77ff.

3. There was much critical commentary on Sauls's decision, which had overlooked more salient relevant cases and more recent Florida law. The *New York Times* bluntly stated that Sauls had "premptorily rejected Mr. Gore's reasonable request to review ballots that have yet to be counted . . . Judge Sauls' cramped interpretation of the case was mistaken" (Dec. 5, 2000). The *Washington Post*, however, titled its December 5 editorial "Running Out of Chances," noting that the Bush forces were doing "a good job of running down the clock."

4. See the story in the *Herald-Tribune Coast News*, "Author Links Bush Family to Nazis" (Dec. 4, 2000), which reports that Prescott Bush (George's father and W.'s grandfather) was a principle figure in the Union Banking Corporation in the late 1930s and 1940s, which was a front for German fascism.

5. The story was broken by Gregory Palast and Julian Borger in *The Guardian* (Dec. 4) and was developed further by Palast and Anthony York in *Salon* (Dec. 4 and 8). The reporters provided a detailed analysis of "the systematic and unconstitutional denial of voting rights to thousands of black Floridians." These reports were rich in examples and statistical analysis, but the story was not pursued by the mainstream media or Gore campaign officials, who were focused on recounting enough votes to put them over the top. The broader issues of corruption and illegality are ones that a Bushian Justice Department will probably ignore. For further developments of this story by John Lantigua—that was never taken up by the mainstream media—see chapter 10, note 11.

6. Major newspaper editorials were split on the Florida Supreme Court decision. On December 8, the *New York Times* editorialists cited the Florida ruling as "a victory for Mr. Gore" and concluded that "in acting boldly, the court also acted wisely," highlighting democratic principles of "the right to vote and the right to have all votes counted as accurately as possible." Anthony Lewis declared the Florida ruling "fair and square" and opined that after the U.S. Supreme Court's "bumbling intervention in the earlier Florida case, it is questionable whether it will review this decision." The *Boston Globe* demanded, "Let the recount begin," and praised the Florida court for "courageously ordering manual recounts of the undervote statewide," rejecting "the feverish legal maneuvering by lawyers for Bush to leave out thousands of ballots that had never been counted manually." The *Washington Post*, by contrast, saw the decision as "a jolt to the system" and expressed "grave reservations," while agreeing with the Florida court's major legal positions in a masterpiece of tortured equivocation, holding out hope that the "enormous authority" of the U.S. Supreme Court would save the day and the republic (As If!).

7. When asked if he still supported the highly controversial and discredited efforts of the Florida legislature to name its own slate of electors, the wily Baker claimed, "I haven't talked to anybody in the Florida legislature that I know is in the Florida legislature," adding that he'd never even met House Speaker Tom Feeney, thus signaling that Brother Jeb's gang was behind the Florida legislature coup that Baker had earlier threatened.

8. In the furor over the U.S. Supreme Court hearings and decisions, the media often overlooked that a U.S. circuit court had ruled eleven to four to continue the recounts, highlighting the arbitrariness of the U.S. Supreme Court ruling that eventually killed the vote-counting process, leaving thousands of votes uncounted and the true results of the Florida voting in obscurity.

6

DEMOCRACY AT STAKE

To Count or Not to Count, that is the Question.

—Pete Williams, NBC

Votes Count, Count Votes.

—Sign in demonstration at U.S. Supreme Court

The remarkable twenty-four hours from the Florida Supreme Court decision to the spectacle of Floridians of every walk of life doing the hard work of democracy ending with the U.S. Supreme Court decision to halt the counts clearly put on display two competing conceptions of democracy that had been in contestation throughout the history of the United States. The opposed conceptions pose strong democracy, a participatory democracy rooted in the sovereignty of the people, against a conception of representative democracy marked by separation of powers and the sovereignty of representative institutions and elites.[1]

The past two hundred years of U.S. history reveal a series of compromises between the two conceptions, attempting to merge the notion of representative democracy articulated by Montesquieu with a more robust participatory democracy advocated by Jean-Jacques Rousseau (and later Karl Marx and John Dewey). While the original U.S. Constitution tended to ground sovereignty in a separation of powers between the executive, legislature, and judiciary, it also granted the rights of freedom of speech, assembly, and participation in public affairs, and it rooted sovereignty, in Jefferson's phrase, in "the consent of the governed." The Founding Fathers, however, were white, property-owning men who distrusted an "excess of democracy" (more crudely, "the mob") and attempted to make sure that there was no direct democracy, that the ultimate sovereignty would be with the executive, legislature, and federal judiciary, and that there be a balance as well between state, national, and local institutions (see Beard 1916 and Zinn 1995).

However, a more populist tradition of democracy emerged in the nineteenth century. Nascent movements of the working class, women, immigrant groups, socialists, anarchists, and other popular political movements struggled for self-determination, expanded rights, social justice, and popular sovereignty, rooting democracy in the power of the people. Abraham Lincoln also articulated the tradition of popular sovereignty and democracy in his dictum that U.S. democratic government was "of the people, by the people, and for the people." The reform and extension of voting before and after the Civil War exemplified the current of popular democracy, as did state legislatures that guaranteed the right to vote and protected voting rights (for examples of these forms of popular democracy, see Zinn 1995).

Popular sovereignty and democracy were thus encoded in both social movements and expanding voting rights in which citizens chose their representatives, who were responsible to the people as a whole. After intense struggle, men of the working classes, women, and people of color received voting rights. Of course, it took decades of political contestation to achieve the right to vote for all citizens, despite race, class, gender, or national origin. But by the middle of the twentieth century, the right to vote and affirmation of voting rights and sovereignty of the people were principles shared by major political parties and participants, if not actually adhered to in practice. Yet one of the most remarkable discoveries of the rulings and arguments by the conservative majority in the U.S. Supreme Court was that the Constitution did not provide the right to vote! Instead, the conservative majority noted that it was state legislatures that had kindly bestowed upon their citizens voting rights, in which, as it says in Article II, Section I, of the Constitution: "Each state shall appoint, in such manner as the Legislature thereof may direct, a number of electors. . . ."

This clause would be fatal for Gore, since the Florida Supreme Court had rooted its decision in Florida state statutes that guaranteed the right to vote and to have one's vote counted, while the U.S. Supreme Court would ultimately use the U.S. Constitution—which did *not* guarantee the right to vote—to trump the Florida court and checkmate Gore. Hence, those in the conservative majority on the U.S. Supreme Court who blocked the actual tallying of uncounted votes in Florida uncovered and brought to attention a remarkable fissure in the American system of democracy. For, on the one hand, political power derived, in Thomas Jefferson's phrase, from "the consent of the governed." Yet there was no real grounding in the Constitution for the right to vote. Commentators noted that the Founding Fathers did not trust the sovereignty of the people and so did not put the right to vote in the federal constitution, but they set up the Electoral College so that electors, certified by the states, would be the actual body selecting the president. Constitutional scholars noted that the conservative majority in the U.S. Supreme Court was rooting its decision in part in the Fourteenth Amendment, Section 2 of the Constitution, which states:

> Representatives shall be apportioned among the several states according to their respective numbers, counting the whole number of persons in each state, excluding Indians not taxed. But when the right to vote at any election for the choice of electors for President and Vice President of the United States, Representatives in Congress, the executive and judicial officers of a state, or the members of the legislature thereof, is denied to any of the male inhabitants of such state, being twenty-one years of age, and citizens of the United States, or in any way abridged, except for participation in rebellion, or other crime, the basis of representation therein shall be reduced in the proportion which the number of such male citizens shall bear to the whole number of male citizens twenty-one years of age in such state.

Of course, later amendments changed age, gender, and ultimately race requirements for voting, but strict constitutional constructionists such as Antonin Scalia argued that the U.S. Constitution did *not* root sovereignty in the people and that the electoral system was designed to choose electors for the Electoral College, in which state legislatures would make laws and courts would adjudicate. Conservatives were also appealing to similar clauses and principles in the U.S. Constitution to defend the right of the Florida state legislature to choose its own electors, independent of what the actual votes in the state of Florida might have been. In an article in the *L.A. Weekly* (December 15–21), Harold Meyerson notes:

> Boalt Hall law professor John Yoo, a former clerk for Clarence Thomas, argued that the legislators would be remiss if they didn't prepare themselves to appoint a slate. Writing this week in the friendly confines of the *Wall Street Journal* editorial page, Yoo elaborated his argument that the very notion of popular sovereignty is a partisan plot. "Contrary to Democratic rhetoric," he asserted, "the people have no right to vote for president or even the Electoral College; that power is only delegated to them by the grace of the legislature. In appointing the electors itself, the legislature would be directly taking up its constitutional functions again."

To be sure, this conservative position is contradicted by Florida state law, political practice in the United States over the past two centuries, and the widespread belief that sovereignty actually rests with the people and that the purpose of an election is to count the votes. In any case, the adventurism of the Florida state legislature went untested, and one imagines that the outcry would have been ferocious had its attempts to present its own slate to the Electoral College been advanced. No doubt there would have been serious challenges and probably a constitutional crisis that would have to be settled by Congress, or, once again, the Supreme Court.[2]

SUPREME COURT ACTIVISM

Previously, U.S. Supreme Court decisions and other major legal decisions involving voting rights had not taken such extreme positions in denying the fundamentality of the right to vote and popular sovereignty. But the conservative Supreme Court majority aggressively advanced arguments that the right to vote and to have one's vote counted were trumped by the absence of these rights in the U.S. Constitution and other constitutional legal principles that vested sovereignty over elections with legislatures and courts. Scalia had long championed an "originalist" interpretation of federal law, grounding decisions in the "original intentions" of the Framers of the Constitution. Now, he was able to do so in a way that both provided an assault upon popular sovereignty and a road to the White House for the candidate who had deemed him and Clarence Thomas his favorite Supreme Court justices.

The U.S. Supreme Court stay that halted the vote counting and the ultimate court ruling would trigger a firestorm of legal and political commentary and debate. Analyzing the principles behind the controversy in the halt to vote counting revealed that two conceptions of democracy were being played out against each other, as well as the partisan interests of two campaigns, which were in stark contrast and with high stakes. The short spectacle of democracy in Florida put on display people determining their own sovereignty, engaging in the civic duty of counting the votes, and resolving disputations through discussion and consensus. This process displayed self-government and self-organization of the people, who attempted to solve a complex problem and come up with a reasonable solution. It involved debate and consensus, as representatives of the two parties, the local canvassing boards, and in some cases Florida judges attempted to work out a fair process of tallying the never-counted votes according to Florida law then in place.

The halting of the undervote counting by the U.S. Supreme Court, by contrast, displayed an abstract and elitist representative democracy at its worst, putting formal and legalistic democracy over substantive democracy—institutions above people—thus imposing an arbitrary solution from above rather than a negotiated one from below. Indeed, from the beginning of the Election 2000 struggle there had been combat in the courts, media, and public spaces between these competing conceptions of democracy, with partisans of one side appealing to the most abstract and arcane legalistic formal principles to defend their candidate, while the other side often used more substantive principles based on basic precepts of democracy, justice, and fairness.

This is *not*, certainly, to equate Gore and the Democrats with strong and substantive democracy and the Republicans with formal, abstract, and representative democracy. Had the situation been reversed, the Republicans no doubt would have screamed themselves hoarse to count every vote and let the people decide, while the Democrats would probably have been content if the Supreme Court had handed them the election.[3] Curiously, it was the Republican candidate who throughout the election campaign maintained that he "trusted the people" and wanted to give the people more power and resources taken from the government, thus supporting people against government. W. claimed that his party represented the people against Big Government and represented local solutions to problems rather than federal ones. Of course, this argument in the mouth of George W. Bush was merely soundbite hype concocted by his handlers for a puppet ventriloquized by representatives of the most powerful corporate interests.

One could see the hypocrisy of the Republican discourse when the Bush camp argued to trust machines, not people (in counting the ballots), and then appealed to the federal courts to halt the manual counting and give Bush the election (after insisting that the courts should be left out of the process). The Bushites also argued that one could not trust manual recounts, or the people who do the recounting, to determine the actual votes, even though Governor Bush had personally signed a Texas law mandating manual recounts in close elections, and this practice was regularly applied in Texas and most other states.

On the other hand, although the Bush campaign had used a pseudo-populism to curry favor with the voters, there was a rightwing antidemocracy position that had been circulating through global channels of discourse and that was popular with hardright legal and political scholars over the past two decades. Grounded in the political philosophy of Carl Schmitt and aristocratic elitist Leo Strauss, conservatives had throughout the twentieth century fashioned arguments against popular sovereignty and for more elitist conceptions of democracy. Strauss had celebrated Athenian democracy as a political model, in which the elite deliberated and determined the direction and policies of the Greek polis in a hierarchical society that excluded women, serfs, and slaves. This conservative tradition attacked "mass democracy" with its "leveling," its "mobs," and potential for "disorder" and "chaos" in favor of an aristocratic elitism, despotic if necessary. Such antidemocratic philosophy was popular since the Reagan–Bush era with conservatives such as William Bennett, Robert Bork, Alan Keyes, Lynne Cheney, and others. There were echoes of this aristocratic conservatism in Scalia's warning that continuing the counting might undermine the need for "democratic stability."

Such a philosophy is profoundly elitist and antidemocratic, and it is part of the philosophic basis of the Supreme Court decision to halt the counting and to give the presidency to Bush (hardly, however, the paragon of the "wise man" that a good Straussian would favor!). In any case, the U.S. Supreme Court mobilized a conservative and partisan majority to stop the vote counting and in effect to disenfranchise Florida voters. This process blocked substantive democracy and substituted elite and conservative decision making for the will of the people.

In the initial December 4 Supreme Court ruling that remanded the Florida Supreme Court call for manual recounts, Scalia and his conservative majority advanced the argument that Florida legislatures have the ultimate right to determine election rules. Their brief at that time suggested that the Florida court had overreached by basing its initial decision for manual recounts on federal and Florida constitutional principles that grounded sovereignty in individual voting and the right to vote and have one's vote counted, rather than the appropriate statutes and rules of the Florida legislature. Accordingly, in a carefully constructed retort to the U.S. Supreme Court, the Florida Supreme Court had grounded its December 7 ruling and call for counting of the undervotes in the rules for elections formulated by the Florida state legislature, as requested by the previous Supreme Court brief.

Many legal commentators thus predicted that the U.S. Supreme Court would have an extremely hard time ruling against the Florida Supreme Court decision and halting the counting, since the Florida Supreme Court judgment was now rooted in Florida state legislature rules, and the legislature seemed to have addressed the U.S. Supreme Court concerns in its ruling for the manual recounts. Moreover, commentators suggested that since the defining principles of the current U.S. Supreme Court had been federalism, providing jurisdiction to local as opposed to federal bodies, not interfering unduly in local decisions, and avoiding activist interventions in state or local disputes, it would be difficult to sacrifice its principles for political expediency and partisanship for Bush.

But, in fact, U.S. Supreme Court partisan bias and animus against popular sovereignty trumped its legal philosophy and principles. Hence, December 9, 2000, presented an instructive spectacle of a clash of the principles of substantive participatory democracy and popular sovereignty against formal, legalistic, and representative democracy. On the one hand, the current U.S. Supreme Court's major legal principles were undercut with its decision to halt the undervote counting, and, ultimately, the conservative majority of the Court was able to mobilize a five-to-four majority in a decision that went against the Court's guiding judicial principles of the last decade, with partisanship clearly trumping legal philosophy. On the other hand, while the U.S. Supreme Court decision seemed to undercut its localist principles and renunciation of "judicial activism," it also embodied Scalia's "originalist" philosophy and contempt for popular democracy and sovereignty. In a February 14, 2001, talk at Southern Methodist University, Scalia laid his philosophical cards out on his reactionary table, stating, "If something is really good, we think it must be required by the Constitution." Scalia added his observation that the federal courts are failing in one of their most important functions: "to sometimes tell the people to take a walk. The Constitution is to protect us against the will of the people."[4]

Hence, the Supreme Court conservative majority was able to provide, first, a stay of execution against Bush (i.e., stopping the votes from being counted that would show that Gore actually won) and, then, to put in play an execution of Gore, setting up Scalia, who many believed had engineered this legalistic coup d'état for big rewards from a future and continuing Bush dynasty.[5] But the justices were publicly divided as never before, and the Republican-appointed moderate Justice John Paul Stevens penned a forceful dissenting opinion to the halting of the vote counting in which he wrote, "Preventing the recount from being completed will inevitably cast a cloud on the legitimacy of the election." He noted that the "Florida court's ruling reflects the basic principle, inherent in our Constitution and our democracy, that every legal vote should be counted." Moreover, Stevens warned that the majority ruling "departs from three venerable rules of judicial restraint that have guided the Court throughout its history," suggesting that the majority opinion undercuts the very principles upon which the Court had been operating, that it would undermine the legitimacy of the election, and that it "may cause irreparable harm to the respondents" (i.e., the Gore side).

Responding to Justice Stevens's dissent, Scalia wrote, "The counting of votes that are of questionable legality does, in my view, threaten irreparable harm to petitioner [George W. Bush] and to the country, by casting a cloud upon what he claims to be the legitimacy of his election." Scalia is admitting here, it seems, that counting all the votes would indeed lead to the illegitimacy of Bush's potential election and harm the Bush candidacy, but he does not consider the "irreparable harm" that not counting the votes would do to Gore, to the voters who voted for him and whose ballots were not counted, and to the very future of democracy. Moreover, Scalia worried that "one of the principal issues in the appeal we have accepted is precisely whether the votes that have been ordered to be counted are, under a reasonable interpretation of Florida law, 'legally cast votes.' " While this concern raises important philosophical and legal questions as to what is a vote, it also sophistically appeals to legalisms and technicalities that replace substantive issues of determining the intent of the voter and counting the vote cast so that the voter could participate in the actual process of voting in the choice of a president.

In his brief, Scalia had written that "a majority of the court . . . believes that the petitioner [i.e., Bush] has a substantial probability of success," thus signifying a done deal and the cooking of Gore's electoral goose. Criticism of Scalia and the Partisan Supremes, however, was particularly intense, and, as always in Supreme Court splits, liberals were hoping against hope for the defection of the allegedly "centrist" and "moderate" Sandra Day O'Connor from the conservative male Supreme Court cabal. Henceforth, it would be difficult to perceive O'Connor as fair and reasonable, and it would be many moons before the Supreme Court would be held in such solemn respect as before its intervention in Election 2000.

The halting of the undervote counting in Florida by the Supreme Court generated a firestorm of controversy. The usually mild-mannered *New York Times* news analyst R. W. Apple wrote that in the "surreal election of 2000," for "the second time in less than 24 hours, a judicial earthquake remade the nation's political terrain" (December 9). Apple continued, "Democrats reacted with extraordinary bitterness to today's decision. Some, speaking off the record, denounced the justices as incompetents and worse, using language not often heard in the capital since the days when Southern lawmakers regularly denounced the court for its rulings on racial questions and called repeatedly for the impeachment of Chief Justice Earl Warren."[6] *Washington Post* analyst Charles Lane noted "High Court Fractures, and Exposes the Seams." Lane cited Akhil Amar of Yale Law School, who indicated that the justices have "come down off Mount Olympus," and a Washington attorney who opined, "There's really a war there."

Even more pointedly, E. J. Dionne wrote in the December 10 *Washington Post* that "the court's decision to stop all counting until it hears the case tomorrow will forever be seen as blatant political interference on the side of George W. Bush—and, yes, the heavy-handed use of federal power against a state court that was trying to ensure an honest election." Dionne argued that "the Florida Supreme Court majority wisely and bravely decided that the way to make sure neither side steals this election is to say: Let's look at all these unexamined ballots with our own eyes so we can know—really know—who won." Concluding his passionate brief for democracy, Dionne argued, "Unless one of the five justices who stopped the recounts yesterday has the prudence to switch sides in the final decision, we will face the spectacle of a narrow conservative majority on the Supreme Court allying itself with a political campaign to stop the people from knowing how the voters of Florida really cast their ballots. That cannot be good for the court, or for our country."

Salon (December 10) reported that in the twenty-four hours since the Supreme Court moved to shut down the hand recount of the uncounted ballots, the manual recount procedure had been moving relatively fast. Judges in Tallahassee had counted about half of the controversial Miami–Dade ballots, and some counties had concluded their counting. Others were well under way and believed that they could easily make the 2:00 P.M. Sunday deadline; some counties maintained, however, that they would need an extension. Television news over the weekend confirmed the complexity of the process, showing images of relatively fast and orderly counting, as well as pictures of confusion over standards and processes. Ultimately, it was not clear how many votes each candidate had picked up, with competing unofficial figures circulating.

It thus seemed that the manual recounting of the undervotes was doable, and in retrospect it appears that this should have been done immediately after the initial near dead heat on election night to determine the winner. What was not yet clear was whether the ballots would ever be counted; whether they would be available for a recount under the Florida "sunshine" Freedom of Information Act, making ballots accessible to responsible groups or individuals who petitioned for access; or whether they would be locked-up. The Republican governor of New Jersey, Christine Todd Whitman, considered one of the "moderate" Republicans, made the immoderate suggestion to seal the ballots for ten years, highlighting once again the Bush camp fear that if the ballots were actually inspected, something horrible would be revealed—such as who the voters actually chose. Some counties did allow news organizations to do recounts after the election, and the first such count of untabulated ballots in Lake County after the election by the *Orlando Sentinel* (December 19) found 376 discarded ballots that "were clearly intended as votes for Gore," with another 246 such ballots showing votes for Bush, which would have yielded Gore a gain of 130 votes (see "Aftermath"—chapter 11—below for further discussion of vote recounts by media organizations and political groups).

And so as the nation waited for the Monday morning Supreme Court hearing, two competing sets of images and spectacles embodying two different conceptions of democracy were set against each other. On the one hand, the televisual spectacle briefly exhibited heartening images of ordinary citizens taking matters into their own hands, working hard to fairly and in consensual debate determine the will of the voters through interpretation of ballots, and publicly participating in the fate of their country. These Heroes of Democracy represented democratic America, with its can-do pragmatism, its hands-on solving of problems and resolving disputes, and its good-natured "let's go out and do the job." On the other hand, there emerged the intervention of a small group of conservative judicial activists set to decide the election (i.e., in the U.S. Supreme Court) with the Florida state legislature pledged to choose Bush if the U.S. Supreme Court justices failed to carry out their partisan task).

The spectacle of raw, brute conservative power embodied in the white conservative faces of James Baker, Dick Cheney, and Antonin Scalia reveals that these Oligarchs of the Institutions are afraid of popular sovereignty, afraid of people actually administering their own lives, and obsessed with maintaining power and wealth for themselves in the dominant corporate and political institutions, which they can then deploy for their own private interests. The fact that the U.S. Supreme Court consisted largely of Nixon–Reagan–Bush appointees, whereas the Florida state legislature was dominated by the governor of the state, Jeb Bush, attested to the enormous power of the Bush dynasty and the rule of white and upper-class conservative men, determined to seize the reigns of power and to use all major institutions to advance their partisan economic and political interests. The spectacle of conservative white men seizing power in what comes down to a coup d'état provided instructive images of the dangers of oligarchy, conservatism, and restoration in the fierce struggle of Republicans to reinstate the Bush dynasty. The fate of democracy in the United States was at stake, and for the short term the prospects of substantive participatory democracy and the sovereignty of the people in the voting process did not look promising.

BUSH V. GORE

The media announced, on Sunday, December 10, that the tireless David Boies would present the Gore camp argument in the U.S. Supreme Court on

Monday. Thus, the stage was set for a titanic clash of giants between Boies, who had been leading the Gore legal campaign in Florida, versus ultra-rightwing activist Ted Olson, who had argued the Bush position in the first Supreme Court battle with the fate of democracy in the balance. The media reported (falsely) that the thousands of disputed ballots at the center of the legal struggle were to be shipped to Washington as evidence for the Supreme Court because they were part of the official court record. But the ballots never made it to the nation's capital, remaining mute witnesses to what might have been a legitimate election.

The day of the Supreme Court hearing, the *Los Angeles Times* headlined a story, "A 'Modern' Democracy That Can't Count Votes," reporting "What happened in Florida is the rule and not the exception. A coast-to-coast study by *The Times* finds a shoddy system that can only be trusted when the election isn't close" (December 11). Clearly, the entire Florida debacle dramatized the highly flawed character of the U.S. system of voting, the scandalous number of uncounted votes, the tremendous differences between more modern and older voting machines, and the embarrassing technological obsolescence of much of the country's voting apparatus. The scandal was multiplied by the fact that the older equipment was largely in place in poor and minority, largely African American, districts, but such concerns did not bother the Partisan Supremes, who were more interested in putting their conservative ally George W. Bush in the White House than addressing the injustices of the American way of voting and crisis of democracy evident in Florida—a crisis that the conservative majority Supreme Court decision immensely intensified.

Editorial commentary was quick and harsh, attacking Scalia and the other reactionary Partisan Supremes for halting the voting. Blistering legal criticisms of the five-to-four conservative majority stay brief circulated, along with analyses of the destruction of democracy and the Constitution in the process.[7] The media reported that Scalia's son worked for one of Bush's legal firms, and there were (futile) demands for him to recuse himself. Later in the day, it was also reported that a *second* Scalia son had been offered a position in the Florida law firm that included the highly visible Bush lawyer Barry Richards, Bush's point man in the Florida cases. On December 12, the *New York Times* reported that rightwing Justice Clarence Thomas's wife was working for the Heritage Foundation, a conservative Republican think tank, in assembling a list of candidates for the Bush transition team! Hence, both Scalia and Thomas, the two most partisan and rightwing justices, had clear conflicts of interest but refused to recuse themselves.[8]

Liberals, as usual, speculated on whether the Gore position arguments might turn around Justice O'Connor (and perhaps Justice Kennedy) to vote with the Court moderates and for the vote recount. Speculation circulated that since O'Connor was a former state judge she would be dedicated to preserving the integrity of state courts (another futile hope, as it would turn out). Such wishful thinking overlooked that O'Connor also had a long history as a Republican Party activist and committed partisan.

At 11:00 A.M., the Supreme Court session opened once again with a weighty Washington celebrity crowd attending and large crowds demonstrating outside. Once again, television was forbidden, though audiotapes would be released after the proceeding. (Evidently, the Supreme Court justices did not want their faces on television, and this time the reasons were clear: they were setting themselves up as the Thieves of Democracy, and members of the public would not forget this.) Once again, each side was allowed forty-five minutes for its brief, and once more there was intense speculation as to the arguments and results, with CNN commentators leaving the courtroom to provide breathless first reports of the jousting and speculation on the significance of the proceedings.

The images of citizens demonstrating outside the courtroom; the media pundits and spinners debating the relative merits of the case; and the active Internet posting of bulletins, discussions in chatrooms, and flurry of e-mail presented the spectacle of democracy in action, in all its turbulence and messiness, a stark contrast to the deliberations inside the Supreme Court. Outside the courtroom, the spectacle of popular democracy showed demonstrators with clever signs, thrust behind the CNN and other network commentators, reading "The Supreme Court Does Not Have the Right to Choose the President of the United States: Only the People Do" and "Votes Count, Count Votes." Other signs proclaimed "King George, His Fraudulency" and "The Supreme Court Coronation: Dubya George II," while a competing sign declared "5 to 4, No More Gore." Several dozen "Bush–Cheney" signs were altered to read "Bush–Cheated" and one read "W. stands for Weasel." Democrats chanted, "Oh, no, Gore's ahead; better call my brother Jeb," while Republicans yelled back, "President Bush! President Bush!" A leader of the National Black Farmers Association brought an old mule named Forty Acres from his Virginia tobacco farm to symbolize the disenfranchisement of black voters in Florida, while Susan Clark, a regular on the pro-Bush demo circuit, taunted the crowd with repeated chants of "Sore Loserman" from her bullhorn and called out, "Help a good capitalist businessman. Get a Sore-Loserman T-shirt for just $10!"

This good-natured spectacle contrasted with the formalistic and legalistic sophistry of the arguments inside the courtroom. Supposed "swing" Justice

Sandra Day O'Connor harangued Bush lawyer David Boies about the lack of "standards" in judging the ballots, not grasping the point that Florida law left the standards to local canvassing boards, a necessary consequence of having many different kinds of ballots over the state of Florida and even different situations in different canvassing boards that required varying standards in discerning the intent of the voter (i.e., when old machines were overloaded with ballots and chad, it was impossible to punch through the infamous chad, requiring vote counters to look closely at the dimple or pregnancy of the chad). O'Connor demanded that the standard be the process of the voting (i.e., the ability to correctly register one's vote on the ballot); she was seemingly not aware of the malfunctioning of machines, part of the official record of evidence, and herself displayed an elitism contemptuous of voters, their rights to have their votes counted, and the necessary complexity of the voting process. The conservatives were demanding "standards" that were impossible in the situation at hand, characterized by an overwhelming diversity of voting machines and procedures, as well as conditions, throughout Florida. Establishing such "standards" would, in fact, require illicitly rewriting the law, precisely the sin of which Republican spinners and the U.S. Supreme Court were criticizing the Florida Supreme Court.

Both O'Connor and Scalia pushed the issue of "voter responsibility," in effect blaming voters for confusing ballots, misfunctioning machines, and highly problematical conditions at balloting sites, as if voters whose votes were not counted by machines were too stupid to vote properly and deserved to have their votes ignored. This was precisely the argument that Republicans had been making from the beginning, blaming voters for their mistakes (tough noogie!), and the Partisan Supremes were just echoing these and other Republican arguments, couched in legalese. In one episode disclosing his partisanship, Scalia even jumped in and helped Bush lawyer Ted Olson with his arguments when he was faltering.

In the one moment of humor, Katherine Harris's extremely nervous attorney, Joe Kroch, mangled the names of the justices he was addressing and mumbled incoherent sentences anticipatory of the linguistically challenged president-to-be. Otherwise, the proceedings were grim and dispiriting. The brazen Republicans arguing for Bush used "the equal protection clause," initially formulated to help minority groups guarantee their participation and rights, in order to question whether the hand-counted ballots violated the rights of Florida voters whose ballots did not have this privilege—a gross misuse of an important principle attacked by Jesse Jackson and John J. Sweeney in the December 12 *Washington Post*.[9] Indeed, using the equal protection clause as a bludgeon to prevent the counting of votes overlooked the plight of those who faced butterfly ballots or the other confusing ballots circulating throughout Florida; those whose votes were eliminated because they had allegedly overvoted; those, mostly African American or poor white, who were purged from the voting lists because they had allegedly committed a felony, whereas in thousands of cases they had not or had been legitimately restored to the voting lists.

The Bush camp and their Supreme Partisan supporters shamelessly exploited the equal protection clause, committing a supreme injustice to those—mostly African Americans—who were allegedly harassed by police as they approached polling stations, or faced long lines and hostility at the polling sites and were not able to vote. And those whose votes were never counted because of improperly functioning voting machines also were harmed by the Supreme Court intervention. As noted, published analyses indicate that votes in poorer districts with the older machines were likely by odds of from 3–1 to 5–1 to fail to count votes in these districts, surely a *legitimate* problem for "equal protection" that clearly demanded actually counting these votes for redress; the conservative majority, however, *limited* their application of the clause in the Fourteenth Amendment, Section 1, that provides "equal protection of the laws" in a highly specious and later much-criticized fashion.

Thus, the conservative majority on the Supreme Court was highly selective in its application of legal principles, seemingly tailored to serve the Republican cause. Moreover, listening to the Partisan Supremes questioning the lawyers on narrow issues of legal technicality, observing their misunderstanding of the facts at issue, and noting their blatantly biased and sophisticated interpretations put on display the Supreme Court at its worst. This was the spectacle of a highly myopic legalistic and abstract (anti)democracy that was in effect attempting to settle the presidential election with extremely questionable use of legal principles, arrogating for itself the right to determine the presidency.

On December 12 as the nation awaited the Supreme Court decision, the Florida House of Representatives indulged in another spectacular display of antidemocracy. The rightwing führer of the Florida house, Tom Feeney, an activist for the Christian right, was ready to press forward with using the Florida legislature to appoint its own electors. Feeney admitted that this move would be a "radioactive hot potato," a phrase that intimated that Feeney and his storm troopers would indeed have a lethal weapon to unleash against Gore to assure Bush the presidency—assuming that there would not be a fierce backlash, as many predicted there would be. Hence, members of the Florida legislature moved ahead with their project of choosing their own electors for Bush while the U.S. Supreme Court deliberated.

Although Feeney and his Republican colleagues argued that the alternative slate of electors needed to be ready in case the outcome of the popular vote was still tied up in the courts by the time of the legal deadline, in fact, a state legislature had never chosen electors different from those elected by their citizens' actual votes. Moreover, there was no legal basis for the move in Florida law, which never envisaged such a process and stipulated that electors had to be chosen according to laws in place on election day. Thus, by beginning to choose their own slate of electors, the Florida Republicans put on a blatant display of extralegal partisanship, going far beyond the law, precedent, and the consensus in the country of what was fair in determining the Florida electors and hence the election. (No one except James Baker and extreme rightwingers thought it a good idea for the Florida legislature to disregard the Florida voting and choose its own electors, and in fact once the Supreme Court decision in effect certified the earlier Bush electors, the Florida legislature dropped its extremist measure as the radioactive hot potato that in fact it was.)

The Republican Florida House thus showed that the Bush camp was not prepared to lose and would do anything necessary to get Bush elected. It made clear that Jeb Bush's Republican cronies in Florida were partisan and undemocratic to the core, preparing to substitute their will for the will of the people, putting their own legislative sovereignty over popular sovereignty. Brute conservative hypocrisy, aggression, and ruthlessness were displayed to the world, revealing these Republicans as the Enemies of Democracy.

Although the media reported that the U.S. Supreme Court ruling would come any minute, the hours of the afternoon passed by and the suspense mounted. At 3:30 P.M., EST, it was announced that the Florida House had passed a resolution to choose its own electors, a historical first that required ratification from the Florida Senate the following day. Shortly thereafter, the Florida Supreme Court ruled that the absentee ballots in Seminole and Martin Counties should count, thus providing a victory for Bush and appearing to make a positive U.S. Supreme Court ruling the only fading hope for Gore.

The tension accelerated as the day went on. By midafternoon, the cable networks flashed "Supreme Court Ruling Expected Any Minute," but by evening CNN's banners were admitting, "No word on when U.S. Supreme Court will rule on Fla. Recount." At around 10:00 P.M., EST, however, bulletins started to flash on the screens indicating that "U.S. Supreme Court Reaches Decision on Bush and Gore."

NOTES

1. There are, of course, many competing conceptions of democracy, and the term is highly contested. I am using an ideal-type Weberian construction here to illustrate the two competing concepts circulating in the legal decisions and the public debates over the Florida voting. I do not want, as I note in the text below, to associate Gore and the Democrats with popular democracy and the Republicans with more legalistic constitutional and representative democracy, although in the actual legal briefs and political debates this was the side that they ultimately came down upon. I primarily want to disclose tensions in the U.S. theory and practice of democracy to promote reflection on what democracy is and should be. I am also concerned to promote a stronger concept of participatory democracy over representational democracy, realizing that in the U.S. constitutional system these competing concepts have been in tension with each other from the beginning. I maintain, however, that in the resolution of Election 2000 a legalistic and representative democracy trumped voting rights and popular sovereignty in an arguably illicit and scandalous fashion.

2. As a thought experiment, it would be interesting to try to imagine how far the Supreme Court would have gone to promote the Bush presidency, having already in its partisan decision evoked unprecedented public outcry and rage, and having already undermined the philosophical basis of its judicial conservatism over the past decades that had privileged state and local government over federal intrusion and judicial activism in what is one of the most activist and controversial Supreme Court decisions in U.S. history.

3. Indeed, the Republicans were eloquent in defending the right to vote, the sanctity of every ballot, and the need to avoid "technicalities" to tally every vote when insisting on the need to count military ballots even when missing postmarks and other requirements. Likewise, they reached high eloquence in defending the vote when arguing against lawsuits launched by local Democrat Party activists against Republican illegal manipulation of absentee ballot applications in Seminole and Martin counties, crying out that throwing out these votes would be an assault on democracy.

4. Scalia is quoted here in the *Dallas Morning News* (Feb. 15, 2001).

5. It was widely assumed that Scalia wanted the role of chief justice for himself and that the aging and ailing Rehnquist would retire as soon as a Republican president was elected to choose a new chief justice. Scalia had reportedly said that he would resign if a Democrat was elected president, which would block his ascent up the Court ladder, hence his entire maneuvering and power play could be read as brute self-interest. This criticism was indeed leveled at Scalia after the final decision, which many predicted had created so much ill will against the Supreme Partisans that the controversy might block his ambitions after all. It was later revealed that Sandra Day O'Connor had herself expressed a will to retire and wanted to be replaced by a conservative justice, so she too had partisan self-interest involved in her decision as did Clarence Thomas; see chapter 10 and Bugliosi 2001: 87.

6. The *New York Times* editorial regretted "the decision by five of the nine justices of the United States Supreme Court. . . . The federal courts should not have halted the counting in Florida. . . . We urge it to reject the appeal and to permit the recount to resume" (Dec. 10, 2000). CNN Washington Bureau Chief Frank Sesno also attested on December 10 that senior Democrats "have expressed their extraordinary bitterness toward the U.S. Supreme Court," that the nation is "perilously divided," and that this "is a genuine constitutional morass." Sesno also noted the intense "resentment and suspicion in much of the African-American community" and their anger about "significant voter disenfranchisement" resulting from stories circulating about the denial of ballots, uncounted ballots, and obstruction of voting rights in the election in Florida.

7. See, for example, Phil Agre's analysis in the "Red Rock Eater News Service" and Paul Rosenberg's "In Order to Preserve Democracy, It Was Necessary to Destroy It." And www.alternet.org published a dossier of articles on "A Broken Electoral System" worth consulting. An article in the *Palm Beach Post* noted that black voters were "angered by hurdles" in investigating a growing list of charges documenting systematic exclusion, intimidation, frustration with obsolete voting machines and confusing ballots, and the failure to count a disproportionate amount of the black votes cast due to the Supreme Court decisions (Dec. 10). A wide range of editorials attacked the Supreme Court in major newspapers; see the summary in Howard Kurtz, "For the First Time in a While, High Court Gets Media Drubbing" (*Washington Post*, Dec. 11, 2000). The attack on the court continued the next day as the Court deliberated; see, for example, Jack M. Balkin, "Supreme Court Compromises Its Legitimacy" (*Boston Globe*, Dec. 12, 2000), which noted, "Like some dreadful pestilence, the presidential election of 2000 seems to eat away at the legitimacy of every institution it touches. The U.S. Supreme Court has become its latest victim."

8. The conflicts of interest of the conservative majority that I have noted were downplayed in television discussions, although CNN brought it up and posted a Web report on December 12 headlined "Ethics Experts Say Scalia, Thomas Connections Not Conflicts of Interests." Other legal experts interviewed in the report, however, said that there were financial stakes for the families involved and that the justices should recuse themselves. Few mainstream commentators mentioned that the decision positioned Scalia to replace the aging and ailing Chief Justice Rehnquist and thus was vitally in Scalia's own self-interest. In any case, the Supreme Court's legitimacy was besmirched, and henceforth the Court would ooze the stench of partisanship and self-interest.

9. A postelection article in the *Washington Post* shows that the Bush legal team had early on in their court interventions pushed the equal protection clause. Their argument did not make headway with judges in Florida, or the 11th Federal Circuit Court of Atlanta, but it did catch the attention of Scalia and his allies in the U.S. Supreme Court. See James V. Grimaldi and Roberto Suro, "Risky Bush Legal Strategy Paid Off" (Dec. 17, 2000). Hence, at bottom, the Bush lawyers massaged the conservative

majority of the U.S. Supreme Court into buying an argument that no other court would accept and that has been fiercely criticized by the legal community, assuring that the conservative majority decision would be one of the most thoroughly analyzed and criticized decisions of all time. Also noteworthy is that early on in the postelection battle the Bush team turned to the courts, thus James Baker's constant mantra that the Democrats were tying up the election in the courts, or that they were the first party to ever contest an election in courts, is disingenuous and a symptom of blatant Republican lying and hypocrisy.

7

DAY OF INFAMY

Tuesday, Dec. 12, is a day that will live in American infamy long after the tainted election of George W. Bush has faded from memory. With their rash, divisive decision to dispense with the risky and inconvenient workings of democracy and simply award the presidency to their fellow Republican, five rightwing justices dragged the Supreme Court down to perhaps its most ignominious point since the Dred Scott Decision.

—Gary Kamiya, *Salon*

The 2000 election has finally ended, but in the worst possible way—not with a national affirmation of democratic principle but by the fiat of the five conservative Supreme Court justices. . . . The conservatives stopped the democratic process in its tracks, with thousands of votes yet uncounted, first by ordering an unjustified stay of the statewide recount of the Florida vote that was already in progress, and then declaring, in one of the least persuasive Supreme Court opinions that I have ever read, that there was no time left for the recount to continue. . . . The five conservatives have made this Supreme Court the most activist Court in history. They aim to transform constitutional law not, as the Warren Count did, to strengthen civil liberties and individual rights, but rather to expand the power of states against Congress, shrink the rights of accused criminals, and enlarge their own powers of judicial intervention.

—Ronald Dworkin, legal philosopher

Confusion reigned in television land as it was announced that the Supreme Court decision was about to be released. Network correspondents rushed to get on camera holding the highly opaque and complex text that would reveal the Fate of the Presidency (maybe). Shivering in the cold D.C. night, their breath visible, correspondents rapidly thumbed through the long and conflicted ruling on camera, attempting to discern its thrust, reading passages out of context, trying to get a fix on the whole. Tension crackled as they frantically speed-read the confusing document and tried to make sense of the Court's decision (this would have been seen as a moment of high-comedy media spectacle if the stakes had not been so high).

THE SUPREME COURT CHOOSES ITS PRESIDENT

On NBC, legal correspondents Pete Williams, former Pentagon press secretary during the Gulf War, and Dan Abrams, son of the legendary constitutional lawyer Floyd Abrams, poured over the document live on camera trying to decipher the ruling. There was no summary statement at the top of the ruling as is usual, there were no press releases or clarification of the ruling issued by the Court, which condemned the public to the excruciating agony of watching shivering reporters trying to make sense of the document.[1] The initial sentences read on NBC seemed to be a death sentence for the Gore presidency, with Pete Williams concluding, "There's just no way the court thinks a recount is possible."

Shortly thereafter, Democratic Committee Chairman Ed Rendell blurted out in an MSNBC interview that he thought Gore should concede, but other major Democratic Party officials firmly replied that this was "unauthorized and outrageous," that Rendell was speaking for himself, and that no concession had been announced. Indeed, NBC was using the decision to crown Bush with the presidency as one by one its anchors, correspondents, and guests proclaimed that by midnight George W. Bush would be president-elect. Not surprisingly, the Fox network also declared Bush the winner, trumpeting a Reuters report as a banner: "DNC Chairman calls on VP Gore to concede." The other networks were more circumspect, isolating NBC and Fox, who could not wait to elevate the Pretender-Select to the throne, as blatant apologists for Bush ("Pretender," since it was clear that Cheney and others in his father's inner circle were pulling the strings, and "Select," rather than "Elect," since W. had been selected by the Supreme Court and the Republican establishment and not the majority of the people).

CNN's initial deciphering registered immediately on its Web site, headlined "U.S. Supreme Court Sends Recount Case Back to Florida Court"—seeming to imply that there could still be a review and perhaps a recount. Shortly, thereafter, however, the CNN Web site headline read at 11:31 P.M., EST, "U.S. Supreme Court Reverses Recount Ruling: Democratic Party Chairman Calls on Gore to Concede." The network was careful, however, to not declare Bush president, and thereby to not repeat the mistake of election night.

Dan Rather and his legal analysts on CBS studied the convoluted text carefully, stressing the complexity of the document and calling it "stupefying," and CBS chose inconclusive banner headlines such as "Reverses and Remands Case to Florida Supreme Court." Bob Schieffer noted that the case was being sent back to the Florida Supreme Court for final ruling, but confessed to Rather, "What's not clear to me at this point, Dan, is what is the remedy when they remand it back to the Florida Supreme Court." When it became clear to CBS that the Supreme Partisans had sent the order of execution to Florida to carry out the assassination of Gore's presidency itself, Rather acidly remarked that the Supreme Court had "punted," sending the decision once more to the Florida Courts who, in effect, were asked to carry out the execution that they had ordered.

On ABC, former Clinton White House adviser and ABC commentator George Stephanopoulos declared in the first moments after the ruling's release that "effectively, George Bush wins, 271 to 267." But as the legal experts saw the complexities of the ruling, anchor Peter Jennings said that this conclusion "might be a stretch," and legal analyst Jackie Judd said that the justices had "left open the door a little bit" by sending the case back to the Florida Supreme Court, a point confirmed by their legal commentator, Jack Ford. Highlighting the confusion in the desperate network attempts to make sense of the document, the *New York Times* reported the next day that Al Gore himself "was flipping the dials, trying to find a clear explanation," and "only after listening to a report by Terry Moran of ABC News did the Gore political team understand the implications of the ruling."

Roger Simon (2001: 207) tells the story of George W. Bush, in bed watching TV, calling his political adviser, Karl Rove, also in bed watching television:

"I'm watching NBC, and it's good news," Rove says.

"I'm watching CNN, and it's bad news," Bush says.

"Well," Rove replies, "then watch NBC."

"I'll tell you what," Bush says, "I'm calling a lawyer."

Eventually, it was clear that the decision had given the presidency to Bush by allowing for no remedy to complete the tallying of the uncounted votes.

As the commentators tried to make sense of the document, noting the fierce dissents and large number of briefs and votes, James Baker came on and in an astonishingly brief statement indicated that the Bush camp was gratified that by a seven-to-two vote the U.S. Supreme Court had found constitutional problems with the recount. Baker then turned and quickly walked away, nervous eyes darting from one side to another, an election thief disappearing into the night. Following Baker's lead as always, the Republican spinners would tout the seven-to-two clause of the ruling, whereas in fact it was a five-to-four decision with Justice John Paul Stevens penning one of the most blistering assaults on a Supreme Court ruling in history, writing that the court's action "can only lend credence to the most cynical appraisal of the work of judges throughout the land." His dissenting opinion, also signed by Justices Stephen G. Breyer and Ruth Bader Ginsburg, added:

> It is confidence in the men and women who administer the judicial system that is the true backbone of the rule of law. Time will one day heal the wound to that confidence that will be inflicted by today's decision. One thing, however, is certain. Although we may never know with complete certainty the identity of the winner of this year's Presidential election, the identity of the loser is perfectly clear. It is the nation's confidence in the judge as an impartial guardian of the rule of law.

In his own dissenting opinion, Justice Breyer referred to the case as "a self-inflicted wound—a wound that may harm not just the Court, but the Nation. . . . In this highly politicized matter, the appearance of a split decision runs the risk of undermining the public's confidence in the Court itself. That confidence is a public treasure." Justice David H. Souter also dissented, strongly arguing that the Supreme Court should simply have stayed out of the case in the first place and allowed the recount, with Florida's courts left to adjudicate any legal issues: "I see no warrant for this court to assume that Florida could not possibly comply," he wrote. "There is no justification for denying the state the opportunity to try to count all disputed ballots now."

The Supreme Court conclusions were blatantly partisan and split across the usual ideological lines. The majority opinion was stunning in its hypocrisy, using the civil rights equal protection provision to justify not counting votes, many of them among African American and other minority groups that the clause was intended to protect! The conservative majority complained that there was no statewide standard to count the votes and that it was too late to set a clear standard on what constitutes a legal vote—despite Florida law indicating that the "intent of the voter" was the principle that was to guide inspection of the ballots (as it was in thirty-three other states). The Supreme Partisans also overlooked that in light of the large number of voting systems and ballots, it was up to local canvassing boards to establish standards, which would necessarily vary from place to place.

Decisively, the majority Supreme Court conservatives claimed that the Florida legislature had mandated all votes to be in by the December 12 safe harbor date. Ironically, and exposing the stench of hypocrisy and partisanship that permeated the proceedings, the Florida legislature itself was planning to choose its own electors the next day, after the safe harbor date that had supposedly been deemed sacrosanct! Opponents of the ruling bitterly complained that it was precisely the U.S. Supreme Court halting the recount that made it impossible to certify the count of the uncounted ballots before December 12 and that the court had sprung a Catch-22 trap that made it impossible to do what it claimed had to be done (i.e., finish the counting by December 12). Moreover, constitutional scholars were now insisting that December 12 imposed no absolute deadline, with some arguing that electors did not have to be chosen until December 18, while others claimed that January 6, the day that Congress certifies electors and counts the Electoral College votes, is the key date for conclusion of all vote certification and counting.[2]

Hence, the Supreme Court Gang of Five arguably misapplied key legal principles, misstated the final date for certification of Florida ballots, unduly interfered in ballot counting that was the task of the state of Florida, and indulged in a brazen act of judicial activism to select its preferred president of the United States. December 12 would be remembered henceforth as a Day of Infamy in which a divided Supreme Court picked the president while subverting its own previously held legal philosophy. During the past decade, the Rehnquist Supreme Court had trumpeted state rights and the sovereignty of state governments to determine voting laws and procedures, and had at least verbally eschewed judicial activism. But in the heat of combat, the Supreme Court had jumped in and invalidated the Florida election procedures and Florida Supreme Court rulings in the midst of the most contested election in modern U.S. history, imposing its will on the presidential election.

Several of the justices on the minority side concluded that the Supreme Court should have never halted the ballot counting, that it should not have heeded the "flimsy" Bush appeal to halt the counting, and that both the stay and final ruling (i.e., execution) had disgraced the Supreme Court, as the above passages from the dissenting opinions make clear. The ruling was hypocritical to the extreme, claiming that although the manual recount was legal under Florida law, there was no time to properly execute it within the December 12 safe harbor deadline allegedly established by the Florida legislature—no time, in fact, because the U.S. Supreme Court had itself halted the manual count of the uncounted ballots.

The Gore team announced that it was studying the document—almost immediately available on the Internet for scholars and citizens to pour over in detail—and that Gore and Lieberman would make statements the next morning. After being quoted in the media early after the ruling as indicating that Gore should concede, Harvard Law Professor Lawrence Tribe called CNN, clarifying his earlier statement. Tribe, who argued Gore's first unsuccessful Supreme Court case and was replaced by David Boies at the last minute in the second case, stated that he believed that the Gore camp should study the complex ruling more "carefully," that he was not recommending that Gore concede, and, as a fascinating late-night conversation on CNN evolved, he thoroughly took apart and criticized the decision that validated the theft of the election.

CNN spoke with Jesse Jackson, who was "outraged" with the Supreme Court ruling and said that he was planning to go to Memphis where Martin Luther King Jr. was assassinated to denounce the partisans' intervention, which he deemed equivalent to the *Dred Scott* decision in 1857 (this decision declared blacks less than human and helped create the U.S. Civil War—the comparison had already been made earlier in regard to the Supreme Court five-to-four ruling to stop the recounting). CNN correspondents cited other fierce denunciations of the ruling coming in, and in one of the understatements of the night, the mild-mannered Judy Woodruff exclaimed that the decision seemed to be provoking a "severe backlash."

NBC and its cable networks continued to prepare for Bush's coronation and the restoration of the Pretender-Select's dynasty throughout the night. MSNBC's Chris Matthews spitefully blamed Gore for running a "terrible campaign" and "blowing the election," which he said should have been Gore's in view of the booming economy and international peace and stability. Matthews attacked the "fierce anger" of the Gore campaign that was evident in the Gore camp after the decision, called upon Gore to concede, and clucked on about the dangers of Gore's "anger" spreading. The characteristically out-of-control Matthews called Gore's election officials "mad dogs" and begged Gore to call off their "bitter and partisan" attack—as if Matthews himself was a controlled and fair commentator and the Bush team members were sweet and reasonable souls. Brian Williams chimed in that "irresponsible hyperbole" was beginning to circulate, claiming that the nadir was reached when Jesse Jackson, in a phone interview with the network, compared the Supreme

Court decision to the *Dred Scott* decision—a fair comparison that would be used by many in days to come to highlight that the ruling was one of the most disgraceful and potentially disastrous Supreme Court rulings in U.S. history.[3]

The chatting continued, and the morning newspapers began preparing their headlines and analyses, posting them on their Web sites. The *New York Times* double-banner headline read "BUSH PREVAILS IN SUPREME COURT; JUSTICE RULES 5–4 TO END RECOUNT." In giant banner headlines, the *Los Angeles Times* indicated, "BUSH WINS IN SUPREME COURT: GORE IS PRESSURED TO CONCEDE." The *Washington Post* declared in its first Web site headline story, "Supreme Court Overturns Florida Recount Order," modifying it the next morning to read "In Blow to Gore, Court Overturns Recounts."

On the morning of Wednesday, December 13, the AP headlines read "Bush Team Waiting for Gore Reaction," "Gore Mulls Concession," and "Democrats Advising Gore on Decision." Neither camp was talking to the media, although Republican spinners were making conciliatory sounds on the talk shows, blathering on about "healing," and "uniting a divided nation," and signaling the tenor of the Bush camp's remarks, if indeed Gore conceded, as was now expected.

Around 10:15 A.M., EST, the media announced that "Gore would address the nation tonight, suspending the recount effort," in effect making it clear that he was to concede; the pundits went into overtime mouthing platitudes about "healing," "coming together," and overcoming divisions, once more becoming mouthpieces for the Republican line. Continuing his partisanship, Chris Matthews on MSNBC attacked Gore, predicting that Gore would make some plea for Bush not to forget the poor and would echo the "bitter populist theme" that posed "poor against the rich" and "the angry against the satisfied."

In fact, Gore had run a moderate middle-of-the-road campaign, and there would be many who would claim that he lost votes to Ralph Nader, or to apathy, precisely because he did not run an adequately rousing populist campaign. Others would blame the defeat on Nader, on strategic mistakes of the Gore campaign, such as not bringing in Clinton, or would stress the bizarre nexus of indeterminacy in the Florida election. Many others, however, including this author, would continue to believe that Gore had won the presidency with the popular vote and majority of the votes in Florida, which were not adequately counted due to the Supreme Court's Gang-of-Five decision and the Machiavellian machinations of the Bush machine.

BUSH'S COUP

If that ain't a coup d'état, what is? —Studs Terkel

George W. Bush had repeatedly announced to Florida (and national television) audiences that his brother was going to deliver the state for him in the election, and Jeb Bush had indeed done everything in his power to do so. His interventions on his brother's behalf involved questionable and perhaps illegal maneuverings with his ally, Katherine Harris, Florida secretary of state, and other cronies. These included irregular and perhaps illegal machinations by the Florida Republican Party apparatus before the election to cleanse the voting lists of as many African American and Democratic votes as possible in order to block or discard Democratic Party votes; Republican Party support for illegally inserting voter registration numbers on absentee ballots for Republican voters and then including tallying votes from arguably illegal (absentee) ballots that were missing addresses or other requirements; creating an uproar concerning allegedly Democratic Party efforts to block the counting of military absentee ballots and successful efforts to count absentee ballots missing requirements such as dates or postmarks, thus including potentially illegal ballots. Illicit Republican actions included harrassing African American voters on election day and providing inadequate facilities in Democratic Party majority precincts to register votes.

Jeb Bush and his allies did everything possible to block legally mandated recounts after the election, and Katherine Harris did all she could to certify the Florida electors for George W. Bush. During the entire thirty-six days, the Bush camp created a poisonous atmosphere that made it difficult to rationally and fairly sort out a highly charged and complex situation in Florida. Jeb Bush's virulently partisan Florida state legislature was prepared to choose its own electors, creating a certain constitutional crisis, if the votes were counted and Gore surged ahead.

One wonders what the Bush machine was able to pull off elsewhere in the country. Much was made of Gore losing his home state of Tennessee, but a Web site continues to gather evidence of voter fraud in Tennessee that illicitly swung the election to Bush.[4] Scrutiny applied to the electoral situation in Florida was greater than any previous examination of electoral processes in U.S. history and, as I argue later, suggests serious flaws in the U.S. system of democracy that require commensurate remedies.

The day after the court ruling, astute *Boston Globe* columnist David Nyhan wrote in a partly ironic and satirical December 13 piece that "Lady Luck is following George W." Nyhan described the string of lucky breaks for Bush throughout the primaries, convention, and campaign, cascading in the post-election night string of coincidences in which Bush's cousin John Ellis, working for Fox, prodded the Murdoch network to "call" the election for Bush, generating the headline "Bush Wins" and leading Gore to call Bush and concede. The "luck" continued with Bush being able to outspend Gore in Florida by a three-to-two margin, $14.5 to $10.1 million in the full campaign, with supplemental spending on behalf of gun, anti-abortion, and fundamentalist church groups, as well as help from Gulf War heroes Norman Schwarzkopf and Colin Powell to woo Florida's large community of military personnel and retirees. And Bush was fortunate that his brother's secretary of state, Katherine Harris, had promoted a "below-the-radar-screen effort to purge the voting rolls of black voters who'd had run-ins with the law." Mr. Lucky also had, Nyhan noted, an absentee vote ballot scheme whereby the GOP was able to augment its rolls with the help of various state and county officials and was lucky enough to win sensitive court cases that challenged its legality. Bush was lucky that black and poor voters in largely pro-Gore precincts had to wait in longer lines and face more complex ballots than in conservative rural areas and the panhandle "where Bush won some counties by better than 3–1 margins."

Further luck included election officials giving pro-Bush precincts laptop computers and cell phones to make it easier to confirm voter identification numbers and allow Bush-leaning precincts to vote. And after the election, in the thirty-six days of the battle for the White House, Bush was lucky to have enough lawyers to block attempts to count the uncounted votes and get a fair and accurate vote. He was lucky to get major Democratic Party lawyers such as Barry Richards on his payroll, so they could not work for Democrats. He was lucky to have his Florida recount case linger and die in the court of a conservative Florida judge, the infamous Sander Sauls, who made an absolutely flimsy legal argument against the Gore side that was overturned by the Florida Supreme Court and defended by no one, but the Sauls decision managed to derail the revote and cost Gore his best chances to get fairly elected.

The silver-spooned Bush was also lucky enough to have the Florida legislature in the background, in a state controlled by his brother, ready to choose an alternative slate of Bush electors in case the votes were counted and he came up short. But above all, he was lucky to have the Supreme Court to push through his case. He was lucky that he had mentioned that Antonin Scalia and Clarence Thomas were his favorite Supreme Court justices, that two of Scalia's sons worked for key law firms representing Bush in his titanic and successful struggle to make sure that ballots wouldn't be counted, and that Clarence

Thomas's wife was employed by a foundation gathering resumes for people seeking jobs with a new Bush administration. Bush was fortunate that Sandra Day O'Connor was looking to retire, but wanted a Republican president to choose a conservative successor, and that William Rehnquist was also ready for the easy life of Republican retirement after a partisan reign as a Chief Injustice who had fought long and hard to push through a conservative legal agenda and promote conservative interests. Bush was especially blessed that Antonin Scalia was itching to succeed Rehnquist as chief justice, and that all three of the most conservative justices fervently wanted to make sure above all that a conservative majority dominated and controlled the Supreme Court, making it a powerful arm of conservative hegemony.[5]

Lucky, indeed.[6] A less ironic analysis would attribute Bush's luck to raw and brute Republican power and money, backed by the force of the Bush dynasty and conservative groups thirsting for the White House and prepared to do anything necessary to secure its benefits for conservative causes and clients. The protracted struggle for the White House revealed the force, resoluteness, and strategic skill of members of the conservative power structure who ruthlessly used their institutions and networks to guarantee the presidency for George W. Bush. Their spokespeople and networking were able to create the image that Gore was "stealing the election" and "all votes have been counted many times and Bush won," that Gore was "ruthless" and would "do anything to win," that he was denying legitimate military ballots in an attempt to steal votes, that Gore just would not concede defeat, and that the Democrats were "using the courts" to seize power illegitimately.

Of course, all these Republican claims saturating the media every day were Big Lies, and the Republicans were in fact projecting onto their opponents their own sins. It was clearly the Republican operatives who stole the election by blocking the vote of many thousands of votes *never counted* because of flaws in voting machines or other irregularities. The Bush camp was ruthless in pursuing its aims and would obviously do anything to win. Indeed, the Bush camp was constructing a no-lose situation in which the Florida legislature would choose a set of electors for Bush in case the courts mandated the vote counting and Bush lost in the actual counting of votes. Of course, since he had a powerful phalanx of high-powered lawyers working for him and a partisan majority in the U.S. Supreme Court, Bush was able to use the courts to guarantee *his* election.

Republican propaganda team members were well organized and well financed and able to push their line into the public consciousness by using e-mail, fax, and telephone pools to organize their supporters who repeated the line of the day, who made signs and T-shirts to illustrate their points ("Sore Loserman"), who organized demonstrations and screamed loudly about the Democrats stealing the election, and who got their media spokespeople into every medium from print to radio to television and the Internet to circulate the message of the day so that all the Bush spokespeople would be "on message," mouthing the same line. Media commentators such as Chris Matthews of MSNBC repeated these lines as their own "analysis," agreed with Bush spokespeople as they pushed their message, and attacked those who would question the Republican offensive.

Bush was able to steal the election, thanks to a well-organized network of Republican activists, support in the Supreme Court, and a media all too ready to overlook his shortcomings and to reproduce his organization's media spin. In the following chapters, I dissect the ways that the Bush machine was able to seize the presidency and carry off Grand Theft 2000, but first let us look at the transition period between the Supreme Court decision, Gore's concession, and Bush's victory speech, leading to the inauguration in January 2001.

TRANSITION

We have a new president. In this democracy of 200 million citizens, the people have spoken—all five of them. —Mark Russell, humorist

Wednesday evening, December 13, was a time for the rituals of reconciliation after the acrimonious and intense struggle of the previous thirty-six days. The concluding speeches by Gore and then Bush were anticlimatic and platitudinous, but signaled that the war was over; Gore had to concede, and Bush could assume the halo of victory. Al Gore went to the Old Executive Office Building for his talk, surrounded by his wife and family, the Lieberman family, and his core set of supporters. Gore conceded, exhibited good humor and grace, said that he would continue "fighting" for the American people, but wasn't sure what he would do next. While the speech was moving, it was remarkably similar to previous concession speeches made by Jimmy Carter after his defeat to Reagan, to Michael Dukakis's concession to Bush senior, and to Bush senior's concession to Clinton—itself a deep wound that many believed fueled his son's candidacy to provide a hoped-for revenge (see Mitchell 2000). The media commentators gushed that this was the best speech of Gore's life, that he had risen to the occasion and was magnanimous in defeat. The ubiquitous Chris Matthews was uncharacteristically speechless, fighting back tears, as if he was aware that his own vicious and snide attacks on Gore had helped bring about the vice president's defeat. Matthews had clearly lost it, praising Gore's "immaculate conception," before correcting it to "concession," and then waxed poetically about Gore's "sublime masculinity," a topic that he did not expand upon.

The hard-bitten network television correspondents were almost in tears as they reported on the preparation and aftermath of Gore's concession speech, and network commentators were uncharacteristically solemn and subdued as they witnessed the defeat of the man who had deserved to win. Within moments, the scene turned to Austin, Texas, where President-Elect George W. Bush was going to address the Texas state legislature and the nation via live television. All day long, Republican spinners were saying that Bush's tone would be one of "humility," of "reconciliation," and of "uniting a divided nation." The Bush camp was now in the mode of image management, attempting to produce a positive and attractive image of its candidate to boost his popularity so that he could effectively promote the conservative agenda and get financial and other favors for his supporters.

Bush confidently strode into the history-laden halls of the Texas House of Representatives and was introduced by the Democratic Party House Speaker Pete Laney, who stressed how well Bush worked with Democrats. Bush walked up to the podium to read his speech. He controlled his smirk, tried to sound "humble," as his handlers demanded, indicated that he felt Gore's pain and asked for prayers for his family *and* for Gore and his family, and then turned to thank his wife, Laura, "who will be a wonderful first lady for America." He was proud to have Dick Cheney by his side, he was happy to be speaking in the Texas House where a "spirit of cooperation" had prevailed, and he was "optimistic" that the nation could rise above its divisions and achieve "reconciliation and unity"—the themes that his handlers had devised.

Bush likened his situation to that of Thomas Jefferson, whose first election was the outcome of a nasty partisan fight, and cited Jefferson's letter, "Reconciliation and Reform," pledging to "begin the work of healing the nation."[7] He used the term "bipartisanship" more than fourteen times, although precisely this concept, now serving as an ideological halo, would be ignored by Republicans who wanted a bigger share of the pie and it was unclear as to whether Bush would actually pursue a bipartisan agenda.[8] If Bush's speech was merely a set of platitudes with no specifics, it could be that he simply had no idea what he was going to do, though no doubt Dick Cheney and his partisan conservative colleagues had some very specific ideas and agendas that would not, however, go over well on national television. Behind the façade of the spectacle of reconciliation, the conservative operatives were sharpening their knives to cut up federal programs and regulatory programs that they opposed, to replace liberals with hardright conservative government, and to slice up the rewards and bounties of the presidency to be delivered to appropriate funders and constituents.

Bush's eyes darted nervously during his speech, which Dan Rather of CBS explained resulted from having his speech on two different teleprompters on two sides of the podium so that he would appear to be speaking to all sides of the House. Bush licked his lips and his tongue flurried about, but he appeared well sedated and made it through the speech without his usual flubs or gaffes. His furrowed brow, which he deployed to try to convey gravitas, signified, however, confusion and that he was trying very hard to say what he had been scripted to perform, but wasn't quite sure what it meant.

The Republican image management kept up its façade through the evening and into the next day when Bush attended a photo-opportunity prayer breakfast, sending a reassuring message to his conservative supporters. Dick Cheney visited Congress and tried to send out a bipartisan message that the Bush administration would work with Democrats, while quietly assuring conservatives that their concerns would be met—a tricky tightrope that would be a major challenge for a Bush administration. The rituals of reconciliation continued through the day as Bush allegedly "reached out" to Democrats (calling one). It was announced that Bush would come to Washington the following week to meet with both Clinton and Gore, and Bush "graciously" took a call from Jesse Jackson, his harshest critic. But it was reported that his brother Jeb could not get through to the President-Select, raising eyebrows and speculation.

In the United States, winning is all and it's a winner-take-all system, and so the spectacle of transition was celebratory, especially the television images and discourse.[9] Many Democrats interviewed on television, however, were surprisingly aggressive in demanding that Bush put Democrats and moderates into his administration, and they made it clear that no rightwing Supreme justices would be confirmed, that attempts to make Scalia chief justice would be harshly opposed, and that Bush could expect fierce opposition if he did not take a centrist and moderate approach. Indeed, the media were filled with centrist and moderate rhetoric, indicating that both parties had better rein in their extremes and that Bush had better assemble a moderate center—as if he wasn't funded, owned, and handled by the hardright.

Indeed, the Cheney–Bush team was bold and partisan at once, choosing not only expected centrists such as Colin Powell for its cabinet, but hardright conservatives such as John Ashcroft for attorney general, oil-industry shill Gale Norton for secretary of the interior, and conservative activist Linda Chavez for secretary of labor. Ashcroft was probably the most anti-abortion, antigay, anti-labor, anti–gun control, and blatantly bigoted hard-core member of the Christian right within the mainstream political establishment. Bush's verbal style was vintage the day that the great unifier appointed the highly divisive Ashcroft. Screwing his vacant-looking face into a serious pose while squinting his eyes, pausing for effect, Bush blurted out his soundbited message that "John Ashcroft is a man of integrity." When finished with his scripted phrase, Bush would assume a look of triumph, pleased that he had finished a sentence without mangling it, apparently not realizing that he was draining words such as "integrity" of meaning as surely as Cheney and his friends would drain the federal treasury of capital.[10]

Dick Cheney's centrality in what was appearing to be the Cheney–Bush administration came out clearly in the choice of his friend, Paul O'Neill, for secretary of treasury and his Ford administration buddy, Donald Rumsfeld, for secretary of defense—a veteran Cold Warrior who was the most enthusiastic supporter of a missile defense system, ensuring return to Reagan-era conflict over Star Wars. Although Bush had promised to choose a bipartisan cabinet that would include Democrats, he said with a smirk that while he was "not having trouble getting Democrats to return my phone calls," those he has consulted "want to stay in place." The triumphant Cheney slyly smiled, pleased that he would be the power behind the Great Pretender's throne, able to advance his hardright conservative agenda.

With the transition to the Bushian presidency, continuation of Orwellian language proceeded apace. Son of Bush's designate for secretary of defense Donald Rumsfeld's repeated affirmative responses to Richard Nixon's derogatory comments about Africans and African Americans, caught on audiotape at the National Archive, meant that he was disapproving of Nixon's racism. When the media revealed that Bush's militantly antilabor appointment for secretary of labor, Linda Chavez, had an undocumented immigrant living at her house who worked for her, but to whom she did not pay wages, and therefore social security taxes, Team Bush used it as an example of Chavez's "compassion"—leading to jokes that the "compassionate conservatism" urged as Bush's motto meant that it's "compassionate" to take in illegal immigrants and let them work in your house; it's "conservative" not to pay them. Chavez was forced to withdraw her nomination, denying her of opportunities to screw labor big time.

The partisan bickering was predictable, a return to the politics of normalcy after the dramatic spectacle of the fierce struggle for the presidency. To be sure, scandal could flare up at any time, serious Republican wrongdoings in Florida or elsewhere during the election and its aftermath could surface à la Watergate, clashes in the severely partisan capital could erupt, and perhaps the news media—whose ratings and readers were sure to dramatically decline—would be ready to promote the next big media spectacle and political confrontation. As the New Year passed, it appeared that U.S. politics had returned to business as usual with its concessions and compromises, wheeling and dealing, payoffs and paybacks, and petty bickering and infighting. The intense spectacle was over, or appeared to be, although no one could say for certain what surprises might surface in this unpredictable political episode. And so, dear reader, as the year 2001 emerges and banal transition spin and gossip once again take over the mediascape of U.S. politics, I close off this narrative of remarkable events and draw some conclusions from our story before returning in an "aftermath" with a discussion of the first one hundred days of the Bush presidency.

NOTES

1. Linda Greenhouse in the *New York Times* (Dec. 13) penned an incisive analysis of the oddity of the conditions of release, construction, and nature of the document that would probably turn out to be one of the most closely scrutinized and condemned texts in U.S. history:

> The way the court structured and then released its opinion, just before 10 o'clock at night, added to the sense of unease. The justices gave no hint of a reason for the unprecedented late-night release—whether to avoid pushing Florida over the midnight "safe harbor" deadline for immunizing its electors from Congressional challenge, or perhaps out of fear that the explosive and highly divisive decision might leak overnight if the court waited until morning to announce it. No matter. It resulted in an hour or more of frantic confusion that the court did nothing to prevent or alleviate.
>
> While the sight of network correspondents fumbling in the dark on the court plaza to make sense of the decision was deeply unsettling to viewers who urgently wanted to know whether the 2000 election was over, the fault this time was much more the court's than television's. The 65-page document omitted the usual headnote, the synopsis that accompanies opinions and identifies which justices voted on which side.
>
> Furthermore, the opinion was labeled "per curiam," meaning "by the court," a label used by courts almost exclusively for unanimous opinions so uncontrover-

sial as to not be worth the trouble of a formal opinion-writing process. There was no indication of what the vote actually was. The names of Justices Sandra Day O'Connor and Anthony M. Kennedy, one or both of whom was likely the author, did not appear anywhere on the document.

I would add that failure to provide the summary and to hide under the "per curiam" format is a sign of the cowardice and intellectual poverty of the Supreme Court Gang of Five conservative majority.

Greenhouse published a behind-the-scenes analysis of the Supreme Court deliberations in the *New York Times* (Feb. 20, 2001). She reported that Chief Justice Rehnquist played a major role in shaping the Court's response to events in Florida, pursuing the same conservative agenda that he had helped construct during his fifteen years as chief justice. He, Antonin Scalia, and Clarence Thomas wished to push the claims that the Florida Supreme Court had unconstitutionally displaced the role reversed for the Florida state legislature and had ignored their desire to get the votes certified before the December 12 "safe harbor" date (Green noted that twenty states had missed this supposed sacrosanct deadline). Instead, Kennedy and O'Connor took the lead in drafting an opinion that the lack of standards in the recount violated the guarantee of equal protection, and this argument received a majority in a five-to-four "per curiam" ruling (i.e., none of the rats owned up to authorship).

2. On December 13, the day after the safe harbor, it was revealed that barely half of the fifty states had managed to actually get their electoral slates in by the supposedly sacred December 12 deadline. One of the first to arrive safely was the earlier slate sent in by Katherine Harris (see the *New York Times,* Dec. 13). It was often pointed out that the December 12 deadline had been illicitly fetishized (by both sides as it turns out) and had no basis in significant law; see *Salon* (Dec. 11) and http://washingtonpost.com/wp-dyn/articles/A63607-2000Nov27.html.

3. In an article entitled "Bandits in Black Robes," Jamin Raskin makes a convincing case that the Gang of Five's *"Bush v. Gore"* "is actually the worst Supreme Court decision in our history" (*Washington Monthly,* Mar. 2001). The famed prosecutor Vincent Bugliosi published an article in *The Nation* titled "None Dare Call It Treason" (February 5, 2001), which drew the largest outpouring of letters and e-mail in the journal's 136-year history; Bugliosi expanded his polemic against the U.S. Supreme Court decision in a book, *The Betrayal of America: How the Supreme Court Undermined the Constitution and Chose Our President* (2001).

4. The site is found at http://www.nashvilleinsanity.com/NPbreakingnews.html.

5. In a less ironic article after the postelection battle, John Balzar, in "Some Guys Get All the Breaks," *Los Angeles Times* (Dec. 17, 2000), suggests that precisely Bush's luck may help him get through the rough times ahead and that maybe Lucky Bush is exactly the guy we need. On a more elevated plane, one could argue that Lucky Bush's election puts on display the plausibility of the chaos and complexity theory, which argues that small disturbances in initial conditions can have momentous effects. With-

out the butterfly ballot in Palm Beach County, the confusing two-page presidential ballot in Duval County, the harassment of African American voters, the Republican mob that helped prevent the recount in Miami–Dade County, the Nader candidacy, and many, many other miniscule and major events listed above, Al Gore would have won the presidency.

6. Of course, the flip side of Bush's good luck was Gore's bad luck. As Harold Meyerson put it in an election postmortem in the December 22–28 *L.A. Weekly:*

> There were times during the five weeks that followed Election Day when Al Gore seemed like one of those beleaguered archetypes in Jewish folklore, the arch-schlemiel to whom everything imaginable and unimaginable would happen as a matter of the utmost routine. Gore's losing, we should recall, required a sen-ior-friendly ballot in Palm Beach County that was all but undeciperable; creaking punch-card machines in Duval County that were no longer capable of registering votes for president; a network that entrusted its victory call to W.'s cousin; a chief statewide election officer who was a Bush partisan; a Palm Beach election board that delayed its recount, finally got it going, and finished it 90 minutes after the deadline; a Dade County election board that was dissuaded from recounting its ballots by rampaging Republican congressional subalterns; a circuit judge who refused to inspect the evidence of undervoted ballots and then ruled that no recount was permissible because he'd seen no evidence of undervoted ballots; and a Supreme Court that stayed the recount on the grounds that it might hurt Bush and then stopped it by decreeing that it would run past a deadline the court itself had set. In some weird and fatal way, Gore had wandered into the political equivalent of the Book of Job, facing a deity bent solely on his electoral demise. (http://www.laweekly.com/printme.php3?&eid=20939)

7. A Jefferson scholar noted that the Bush crew had miscited the context and text of Jefferson's letter, which did not, as Bush claimed, urge bipartisanship, but in fact was an attack on his Federalist opponents. Disregarding Bush's ridiculous comparison of himself to Jefferson, the letter in fact signaled exactly what Bush was planning to do; that is, pursue a conservative agenda and "reform" of government before any "recon-ciliation" could take place (see tompaine.com/print.php3?id=1962).

8. Jake Tapper noted in a *Salon* story the next day (Dec. 13; http://www.salon.-com/politics/feature/2000/12/14/ethics/print.html) that Bush had only invited Texas Democrats who had worked with him; Democratic legislators not invited said that Bush's "bipartisanship" in Texas was limited to allowing Democrats to do what he wanted. In days to come, centrists and Democrats wanting a piece of the action would use "bipartisanhip" as a mantra, and the Bush team would use it as an ideological wand, while the hardright that had won Bush's victory was pushing Bush to undertake a highly partisan agenda; this issue, of course, would be played out in the months to come, as Bush initially paid lip service to "bipartisanship" while pursuing a hardcore conservative agenda (see chapter 11 below).

9. Lingering resentment over the Supreme Court decision surfaced in some of the talk shows, but the central focus was on the transition and rituals of reconciliation. Major newspaper columnists and political and legal commentators continued to publish blistering attacks on the Supreme Court decision and the legitimacy of the Bush presidency, and newspapers published stories that indicated that the public was far from happy with the results. For example, on December 14, *USA Today* cited Representative Charles Rangel (D-N.Y.), calling the Court's decision "the greatest mass disenfranchisement of African Americans since passage of the Votings Act of 1965." The same day, Mary McGrory attacked in the *Washington Post* the "Supreme Travesty of Injustice"; the *Los Angeles Times* opinion page declared, "Never again will we view the judiciary as nonpolitical," with a Bush cartoon on the same page including the caption "The Grinch who stole the presidency"; and Gary Kamiya published a blistering critique in *Salon* titled "Supreme Court to Democracy: Drop Dead."

10. As noted in a previous chapter, Ashcroft had lost to his recently deceased opponent in the November election because of his extremist positions. Receiving a 100 percent rating from the Christian Coalition, Ashcroft was ranked by the *National Journal* as the most conservative member of Congress. He had received an honorary degree from rightwing Bob Jones University and had praised the ultrasegregationist pro-Confederacy journal *Southern Partisan*. Most scandalously, he had blocked the appointment of an African American to a federal judgeship by blatantly lying, claiming that the designee was soft on criminals and would not use the death penalty, when in fact neither was the case. Integrity, indeed.

8

THE MEDIA AND THE CRISIS OF DEMOCRACY

We mortals hear only the news, and know nothing at all.

—Homer

*In our time, political speech and writing are largely the
defense of the indefensible. Thus political language has to con-
sist largely of euphemism, question begging and sheer cloudy
vagueness. . . . When one watches some tired hack on the plat-
form mechanically repeating the familiar phrases . . . one often
has a curious feeling that one is not watching a living human
being but some kind of dummy: a feeling which suddenly
becomes stronger at moments when the light catches the speaker's spectacles and turns them into blank discs which seem to
have no eyes behind them. . . . The great enemy of clear language is insincerity. . . . Politics itself is a mass of lies, evasions, folly, hatred, and schizophrenia.*

—George Orwell

As the quotes from Homer and Orwell suggest, it's an old story: Power
elites lie and dissemble, their minions repeat the prevarications and evasions, and no one really knows the true story of what ruling classes are up to
and the events and actions that produce the results. We do know, however,
that Election 2000 was truly Orwellian, that falsehoods and hypocrisy masqueraded as truth, that immorality paraded itself as right, and illegality and
injustice were presented as law and order.[1] The result is a crisis of democracy
that depends on respect for truth, law, justice, morality, and rational argumen-

tation to work properly and successfully, and on the media to adequately inform the public while criticizing the spin of the party manipulators.

DEMOCRACY AND MEDIA

In a democracy, citizens require accurate news and information to make intelligent judgments and participate in the democratic process.[2] It is the democratic responsibility of the media to provide citizens with accurate information concerning issues of public importance and to present competing sides of arguments and debates so that intelligent public discussion and deliberation can proceed. For democracy to work, citizens need to obtain sufficient information to participate in the political dialogue and to help them make informed decisions. Reaching democratic consensus thus requires adequate information, rational argumentation, carefully listening to the other side of the argument, and allowing the best argument to prevail. These conditions, I argue, did not obtain in the media, in the Supreme Court, and in large sectors of the public, despite the efforts of some honorable journalists to provide accurate information, intelligent commentators to provide reasoned and informed analysis, members of the judiciary to make legally grounded and sound judgments, and members of the public who engaged in honest debate and the hard work of democracy (i.e., to count the votes in Florida).

One of the root causes of the crisis of democracy that emerged from Election 2000 and its aftermath is that the mainstream media did not provide sufficient information for the public to understand the nature, policies, and tactics of the major political forces who were struggling to win the election and subsequent battle for the White House. The mainstream media provided few sustained analyses of the differences between the two candidates before the election; few probing interrogations of their past history, policies, and limitations; and inadequate discussion of the stakes of the election and consequences of the choice being made. As documented in chapter 1, there was more emphasis on style than substance, a general trend in media coverage of political elections. Moreover, as I argue in this section, there was more stress on polling and numbers than issues. Consequently, the mainstream media failed to adequately inform the public concerning the choices that they were making in Election 2000.

In sum, the mainstream media in the United States have failed in their task of providing probing investigative journalism, intelligent analysis and critique of partisan positions, and independent analysis of the stakes of the combat in events such as the struggle for the presidency that followed Election 2000. The media was largely the terrain of partisan spin, replicating the arguments of the competing forces, rather than exhibiting independent analysis and criticism. There were all too few explications of the raw power politics in play, the lies and hypocrisy being circulated as truth, and the intensely partisan struggle to win hearts and minds in the war for the White House.

This superficial and often partisan coverage was especially true of television. The press and many Internet sources, by contrast, contained some investigative reporting, reasoned analysis, and convincing critique, which I have drawn upon in this book. But the television networks were too superficial, limited, or perhaps biased to draw upon the more illuminating and accurate analyses circulating in some of the press and on the Internet (which, of course, also contained outrageous and blatantly partisan analysis in spades).

In the early stages of the democratic revolution the media were perceived as watchdogs against lies and corruption, as the "Fourth Estate" that would contribute to a balance of power among executive, legislature, and judiciary. The U.S. Bill of Rights granted freedom of the press, in order to guarantee vigorous polemic, articulation of opposing points of view, and the ability to speak truth to power as well as to advance one's own party and interests. During the newspaper era, many papers were overtly partisan, and informed readers knew the particular biases and proclivities of the paper or journal they were reading (West 2001). Moreover, in the newspaper era, there were often hundreds of papers from which one could choose, providing a range of choice restricted in the monopoly and conglomerate eras. To be sure, during the tabloid era of the mass press and "yellow journalism," biases were often hidden, though they were recoverable by "muckrakers" and critics of the growing power of covertly politicized newspapers and press (see Schiller 1981).

With the rise of broadcasting in the twentieth century, powerful new media were emerging that created great concern for the political community. By the 1930s, broadcasting in the United States was dominated by two networks, NBC and CBS, and these networks would continue to be major forces into the television era. In the Federal Communications Act of 1934, the networks were able to defeat proposals for university, labor unions, churches, and other social groups to be given a certain percentage of the broadcast spectrum, and the networks achieved almost monopoly power. To be sure, the 1934 communications act mandated that broadcast media were to be governed by "the public interest, convenience, and necessity," insisting that the broadcast media are part of a democratic public sphere, but they rarely met this lofty obligation (see Kellner 1990 and McChesney 1995).

Officially, the broadcast media were to have important democratic obligations, which became interpreted as providing equal time to major sides in a political contest, to provide the conditions for dialogue and debate over issues of interest to the public, and to be impartial watchdogs of the stage and the political arena, rather than partisan players. Of course, there were always prejudices and preferences in the broadcast media, and deregulation during the Reagan era undercut the force of many of the "public interest" requirements. Pursuing the goals of profit in an era of intensified competition, the mainstream media became increasingly tabloid- and scandal-oriented. Politics, in turn, became focused on promoting image and spectacle and palatable sound-bites for easy consumption.

Moreover, during the past two decades, the media have been widely criticized for their bias, and there is a vast literature on their allegedly "conservative" or "liberal" leanings. These critiques intensified during the postelection struggle, creating widespread public skepticism about the fairness, accuracy, and even competency of the mainstream media. Public perceptions of the broadcast media, especially television, may have indeed been altered by the saturation coverage of the spectacle of the struggle for the presidency. Although the media produced, hyped, and benefited from the dramatic postelection events, the mainstream broadcast media, especially the television networks, ultimately could pay heavily for their short-term benefits in terms of loss of long-term legitimacy. Few will forget the painful experience of election night (for both sides), when the television networks made their series of false calls.

Henceforth, polls and network predictions should indeed be viewed with extreme suspicion, and the mainstream media—especially the television networks—should be seen as the highly flawed and limited institutions that they are. Throughout the election, the networks saturated their nightly news programs with polls focusing on who was ahead and who was gaining or falling behind, rather than on the actual issues and stakes of the election and the striking differences between the two candidates' respective experience and positions. This focus on polls was significant because the twenty-two-minute nightly newscasts were reduced to serving as news bulletins, and spending so much time on polls made it impossible to more broadly engage the key issues of the election.

Steven Hess of the Brookings Institution claims that up to election day, network news provided "the fewest minutes of campaign news in their history. . . . 2000 is 53% below 1992, and 12% below four years ago, for a new low" (see www.brookings.edu/HessReport/). NBC skipped the first presidential debate while Fox skipped all three, denoting a failure of the networks to serve the public interest in making available key political events. An Annenberg School study of the campaign primaries notes a shrinking time devoted to candidates, with a mere 36 seconds a night reporting what candidates had to say, with CBS allowing 42 seconds a night, ABC 39, and NBC 29 (in Schechter 2001: 74). And The Norman Lear Center at the University of Southern California documented that the typical local TV station in a major market aired just 45 seconds of candidate-centered discourse per night in the month before November 7 (http://entertainment.usc.edu), while the major broadcast networks performed only slightly better, airing just 64 seconds a night of candidate-centered discourse per network according to an Annenberg Public Policy Center report (both cited in "The Alliance for Better Campaigns," in Schechter, 2001: 84).

Furthermore, as noted, studies of the media presentation of Bush and Gore reveal a shocking bias for Bush and against Gore in terms of the relative number of positive and negative stories on their campaigns and persons (see chapter 1). Obviously, the television emphasis on style over substance helped Bush, who was more telegenic and more affable in his ability to connect with viewers. Likewise, the poll-driven coverage that mostly showed Bush ahead, often by 5 to 10 percentage points, aided the Bush campaign in gaining legitimacy and momentum.

Among the many lessons from the Election 2000 debacle is clear indication of the untrustworthiness of the instant polls, which are obviously biased by their sampling, the polling sources, the questions posed, and the turbulence of an often uncertain political terrain. One of the major and legitimate criticisms of the television coverage of Election 2000 was inordinate focus on the polls. Usually, the television networks start focusing on the candidates at the time of their parties' conventions and September is the month that broadcast and print journalists give more in-depth coverage of the candidates and issues, beginning in October to focus on who's ahead and who's behind and why. This year, however, focus on the polls and horse race began in the summer with little in-depth reporting. Moreover, the polls were highly unstable and fluctuating during the crucial election months from the summer up to election day; and they were especially misleading in the final days, ascribing a lead to Bush that he did not obviously possess.

Hence, in retrospect, the tremendous amount of coverage and airtime devoted to polls detracted from critical discussion of the issues and personalities involved in the election and the differences between the campaigns and the stakes for the country. By focusing obsessively on polls, the television networks signal their own superficiality, their disservice to the public, and how they are themselves a major source of the problem in the rise of increasingly vague and wishy-washy campaigns that follow the ups and downs of a highly unstable and often indiscernible public opinion, instead of focusing on crucial public issues and competing positions, with their merits and demerits, as well as the experience, qualifications, and limitations of the candidates.

While polls have a place in discerning public opinion and are of obvious interest to political campaigns and forces, they are often misleading, and their domination of airtime during important national elections and events is a major failing of the television networks and contributes to the decline of democracy, which is predicated on citizens receiving information and engaging in or following public debate, rather than pursuing the ups and downs of highly unreliable numbers. It appears that this lesson has not, however, been learned. The media continued during the transition period to Bush's inauguration and into his presidency to provide poll-driven news programming, telling citizens what they supposedly think of the President-Select, his initial appointments, and the other issues of the day.

Another oft-cited problem with television news coverage is the infotainment dimension with its collapsing of news and entertainment, and tabloidization of news. Intense competition among print, broadcast, Internet, and other modes of information and entertainment has caused journalism to become ever more entertaining, to use the frames of entertainment in news stories and debate formats, and to sensationalize news to gain public attention. The tabloidization of news and information during the era of the O. J. Simpson murder trials (1994–96) and the Clinton sex scandals and impeachment trial of 1998–99 was truly striking and can best be explained by the highly competitive nature of media in an information-entertainment society.

Interestingly, during and following the explosive thirty-six days, partisans of both sides were angered by what they saw as the biases of the major networks.[3] While for some the television networks exuded partisanship or favoritism, for others there was a disconnect between the passionate intensity of various Web sites, e-mail, talk show, and political print media (generally instantly available from the Internet) and the bland discourse and pretensions of the television networks. Some television viewers were convinced that the networks were not telling the truth about the postelection struggle and sent an unparalleled barrage of criticism of television coverage to the television networks and to sites on the Internet.

In addition, there was a disconnect between the hysteria concocted by the Republicans to bring the process to a close, with apocalyptic predictions of "constitutional crisis" and worse, in contrast to a public that was concerned to count the votes and determine, as best one could, the winner of the contest. The "constitutional crisis" was, in retrospect, a Republican spin that the media played into with their own hyping of drama and spectacle, and desire to pull viewing audiences into the process. In fact, as noted, the December 12 deadline was artificial, and had the Republicans not systematically blocked every attempt to count the votes, it would have been relatively straightforward to complete a fair, accurate, and timely vote count.

Many viewers who had not previously reflected on television news bias were shocked by what they saw as the favoritism and partisanship of the television networks as they observed the supposedly neutral commentators attack their candidates and hopes. For those who did not already know this, it must have been disconcerting to observe the Fox network in its extreme partisanship for the Republicans. In case there was any question, there should now be no doubts that the Fox network, owned by conservative mogul and ideologue Rupert Murdoch, was a propaganda machine for the right, a highly partisan instrument of conservative Republicans. For years, it had bashed the Clintons without mercy, winning a loyal conservative audience and misinforming and misleading anyone who was not aware that this was a propaganda machine and not a legitimate news and information source. The Fox network continued its partisanship in its fierce and relentless criticism of Gore and the Democrats throughout Election 2000 and avidly pro-Bush interventions throughout the campaign and the aftermath.[4]

Although CNN was nicknamed the "Clinton News Network" by conservatives during the Clinton years, on the whole CNN strove for balance during the election and battle for the White House. Traditionally, however, CNN discussion shows such as *Crossfire* are skewed to the right and often feature more ideologically pointed and effective partisans of the right than the left. Indeed, the "left" on CNN usually comprises moderate centrists while the "right" are often hard-core conservatives. A Web site, www.projectcnn.com, has been documenting what it sees as conservative bias on CNN, although I have not seen documentation of systematic bias toward Bush on CNN during the election and Florida ballot wars.

Partisanship on the various NBC networks, including CNBC and MSNBC, by contrast, was glaring.[5] The NBC networks frequently provided large segments of coverage to the opinions of the odious Rush Limbaugh, without balancing positions or refutation of his extremist blathering. Over and over, the NBC networks played the *Saturday Night Live* caricatures of Bush and Gore, which I suggested earlier were much more harmful to Gore and generally inaccurate by symmetrizing the two as dolts and buffoons. Day after day, during his three-hour talk radio program broadcast live on MSNBC, the demagogic Don Imus vigorously attacked Gore, calling him "evil," claiming that he would "do anything to win the presidency," and assaulting the Democratic Party candidate in the most venomous manner. Night after night, Chris Matthews, CNBC's hypercaffeinated and opinionated commentator, aggressively attacked Gore, repeatedly regurgitating Republican propaganda lines of the day as his own profound thought and rudely treating guests who were trying to bring up issues or positions that would put the Republicans in a bad light. The host of *Hardball* seemed to take his hardest shots at Gore, while lobbing softballs to the Republicans. His shrill voice and loud off-the-cuff opinions, however, were winning him acclaim as poster-boy media motormouth, and during the spectacle I saw several references to him on PBS and other outlets accompanied by loud guffaws and grimaces of disgust; at the same time, Matthews was amassing critics in the press including James Fallows and Howard Kurtz, and he made the "A-list" of mediawhoresonline.com.

Matthews, who served an apprenticeship with former Democratic Speaker of the House of Representatives Tip O'Neill, calls himself a "centrist" and moderate, but he was virulently anti-Gore, throwing hardball volleys of charges of "lies," "crimes," "depravity," and "evil" at Gore and the Democrats. Matthews has an annoying high-pitched voice that he projects at over-the-top decibel levels that have earned him the epithet of "Chris the Screamer." He also has annoying verbal tics like interrupting speakers with a loud "Ah huh," or "right," and then an "alright," frequently cutting off guests in mid-sentence. While he claims that he is playing "hardball," during the election and battle for the White House, as documented in earlier chapters, he frequently repeated the Bush camp's line of the day as his own position and obsessively attacked Gore.

The only commentator on television ruder than Matthews is Fox's Bill O'Reilly, one of the most vulgar and insufferable bores in the history of television. The ignorant O'Reilly hectors, lectures, and berates his guests if they are slightly left of center or represent positions he opposes. The popularity of this mediocre and obnoxious "personality" is a sign of the failure of education and culture in the United States and of frightening social regression. Only an ill-informed and resentful audience could tolerate this boorish bore, and it is perhaps his abuse of his obviously intellectually superior guests that give pleasure to a mass audience also suffering from inferiority complexes, jealousy of more educated and cultured classes, and the burden of excessive societal rage and aggression. O'Reilly is the mouthpiece of this resentment and rage, and an emblematic figure of Nietzsche's "last man," blinking vacuously into the camera while pontificating pompous platitudes.

Every time that it appeared that Bush was about to ascend to the presidency, it was Fox and the NBC networks that were the first to call it for their favorite, leading to several embarrassments. The NBC cable channel's anchor, Brian Williams, seemed especially eager to declare Bush the winner and to present a negative spin on Gore. On the whole, NBC's nightly anchor, Tom Brokaw, in turn had been at once the most indistinguished and bland and ideologically conservative anchor on television during the past two decades. Emerging into the coveted anchor spot after many years as cohost on the morning show *Today*, Brokaw is arguably the most lightweight of the net anchors. He has been visibly pro Reagan and Bush and anti Clinton and Gore during his mediocre reign as NBC anchor and was an emotional defender of Bush-era U.S. military interventions in Panama and the Persian Gulf, revealing in sensitive moments an embarrassing promilitary bias.[6]

In the months preceding the election, the NBC cable affiliates played repeatedly an incredibly propagandistic Gulf War documentary *Schwarzkopf's War* that featured Bush senior, Cheney, Powell, and others heavily involved in the Bush campaign that constituted straight-up political advertising for George W. Bush. In the aftermath of Grand Theft 2000, the NBC affiliates played repeatedly a documentary on the Bush family that was straight-up propaganda, presenting the shady Bushes as a great American dynasty. A June 2001 report of the NBC coverage of the Bush administration's first sixty days noted a massive shift in favorable reporting toward Bush in comparison to its initial reporting on Clinton: "Only 9% of its stories were negative in tone in Bush's first two months, compared with 42% of its stories on Clinton eight years earlier" (www.journalism.org/ccj/resources/index.html).

Thus, the spectacle of the battle for the White House delegitimated some of television's talking heads and revealed the grotesque prejudices of certain television commentators and, as suggested above, even networks.[7] Some media institutions are straightout conservative propaganda organizations like the Murdoch-owned Fox network and Unification Church–owned *Washington Times* and wire-service United Press International (UPI). Fox News asserts, "We report, you decide," as if they were providing facts and a range of opinion, but in fact it's a hardright spin that constantly attacks Clinton, Gore, and the Democrats, while propagandizing for conservative Republicans. Hence, while Fox commentator Bill O'Reilly opens his show with the warning, "Caution: you are about to enter a no spin zone," in fact this is Orwellian doublespeak since O'Reilly's spin is to the right.

Most bizarre, the Korean-owned Unification Church, popularly known as "the Moonies," own both a major Washington newspaper, the *Washington Times*, and a national wire-service, UPI. These institutions are highly useful to the Republicans that can use them to spin nasty rumors into the national media mix. Curiously, the Moonies are closely involved with the Bush family, with the Reverend Moon paying Bush senior over six figures for a speech after his presidency, donating over one million dollars to Bush senior's presidential library, contributing heavily to Republican causes, and holding a prayer breakfast for the President-Select after his theft of the election (which, amusingly, disturbed Baptists invited to the event who were uncomfortable with being associated with the Moonies who advocate extremist theological beliefs, as well as hardright political beliefs).[8]

In addition, the right has its mainstream media journalists and spokespeople, its organized movements, and impassioned intervention in talk radio, the Internet, and other forums of public debate.[9] The right is disciplined with its line-of-the-day, its scripted soundbites and positions, and thus is usually "on message," creating rightwing pundits who were a familiar part of the mediascape and thus have a certain credibility and clout. These familiar pundits include the sophistical and unvirtuous Bill Bennett, the supercilious light-brow George Will, the buffoonish Rush Limbaugh, and a stream of barely distinguishable mediocrities usefully exposed by Eric Alterman (2000).

Corporate-controlled media generally hire people who will not rock the boat, who can be depended on to provide the spin of the day. The corporate culture acts as a filter through which media corporations hire trustworthy personnel who in turn know that they cannot go beyond the boundaries of accepted opinion and corporate interests. Further, the organized right is able to intimidate the media, which suffer intense competitive pressures, to make sure that rightwing opinion circulates and to try to block more liberal views.

One of the scandals of Election 2000 and its aftermath was the failure of the mainstream media to investigate the Bush family history, political and economic scandals, and in particular the highly peculiar career and history of George W. Bush. Part of the reason is that significant exposé would have created a major uproar by the right and the Bush machine. Members of the Bush family themselves have been reported to have intimidated and threatened members of the media and during passionate events like the Gulf War or the battle for the White House, the Bush machine is able to mobilize significant campaigns to pressure major media institutions not to criticize their policies or action.

Moreover, in the corporate culture of safe news and information, there is little investigative journalism. To be sure, sex and scandal sell and seem to be on-limit for media exposés, but more complex economic and political activities, such as the Bush dynasty history, seem immune from media scrutiny. And so while the media have been coarsened by the merger of entertainment and information in an era of tabloid journalism fuelled by corporate mergers, they do not pursue more difficult and complex stories. In a 24/7 news cycle with a proliferation of print publications, cable television news channels, and the ubiquitous Internet, the competition for audiences has intensified, and sensational stories involving sex and scandal overshadow more mundane issues of politics and public policy and complicated stories such as the Bush dynasty history. The media in turn have been infected with the twin viruses of pack journalism and punditocracy, following en masse the latest story of the moment, with journalists chasing down the same sources and spinning up similar soundbites instead of cultivating more probing and informed commentary. The result is the decline of investigative and independent journalism, thus intensifying the crisis of democracy under way for the past decades.

On the other hand, there is a blatant difference between the critical and investigative coverage of the White House during the Clinton years and the "on bended knee" coverage during the 1980–92 Reagan/Bush I era. Never before the Clinton years had the media been so critical of a sitting president, dug so deeply into every aspect of a presidential family's personal, economic, and political life, and circulated so many scandalous rumors as "news." Yet for a variety of reasons, the Bush family was immune from similar scrutiny, perhaps because the Bushes were part of the U.S. establishment with scion Prescott Bush on the first Board of Directors of CBS, a friend of the editor of the *Washington Post*, and a U.S. Senator, while his son George H. W. Bush headed the Republican Party, was CIA director, and vice president and then president of the United States.

Yet precisely because of the lack of critical coverage of the Bush dynasty, in contrast to the Clintons, Kennedys, and other major figures in the Democratic Party, the media are suffering a crisis of legitimacy where they clearly have favored one side in an intense political struggle and have been prejudiced against the Democratic side, while letting the Bush dynasty off the hook. Since the majority of the people by a several million plurality voted either Democratic or Green Party, since it is clear that the Bush administration has taken on a hardright direction (see chapter 11), and since many people will be hurt and angered by its policies, the media may undergo pressures to do what they should have done long ago, which is to tell the people the sordid truth about the Bush family history of economic and political scandal.

Many damning stories concerning generations of Bush scandals are collected on the Internet so the material is there for Watergate-style revelations and uncovering of the most shocking political history in the history of the country. I will suggest similarities between Nixon and George W. Bush in chapters that follow, and since it was Nixon who brought the Bushes into the mainstream of U.S. politics, it would be fitting if they underwent their patron's fate and went down as hard as Nixon, with Bushgate following Watergate as a triumph of U.S. investigative journalism, a purging of the political system, and a gain in legitimacy for the American media, political system, and democracy.

THE INTERNET AND THE COMING BUSHGATE

I would submit that the material is there already for a Bushgate that will make Watergate look like a third-rate burglary and second-rate nexus of political scandal and corruption. The coming Bushgate will be the inexorable and possibly cascading torrent of revelations that will uncover the slimy political and economic history of the Bush dynasty, the particular scandals that George W. Bush has been involved in, the correlation between the contributors to the Bush campaign and his actual policies, and the hopeful uncovering and dissemination of the manipulations, machinations, and possible criminality involved in his theft of Election 2000. It might emerge slowly and undramatically with revelations of corruption in Grand Theft 2000, or in the Bush administration, and like Watergate the revelations could achieve a critical mass that could lead to the Bush family exit from American politics. It is arguable that the Bushes' trump poor Nixon in spades in financial corruption and scandal and make his dirty tricks and abuses of government pale in comparison (for material that could produce Bushgate, see the sources in Introduction, note 3, and chapter 11).

While the television networks revealed themselves to be a highly limited, unreliable, and flawed source of information and opinion during Election 2000, the Internet appears, to those of us who made sustained use of it, to be a much richer and more diverse source of information and opinion. More accurate analyses, more intelligent and reasoned commentary (on both sides), and many stories and dimensions of Election 2000 and the battle for the White House that never made it onto the television screens were accessible in print sources and from the Internet. Indeed, the Internet is now the repository of around-the-clock publication of almost every major news organization, newspaper, journal, and print publication, as well as a library of its own Webzines, Web sites, discussion rooms, listserves, e-mail, and other sources of news and information, often for free, depending on what one pays for one's Internet connections. Of course, as always and especially in this political passion play, one also observed excess, stupidity, disinformation, and grotesque flame wars on the Internet.

Interestingly, and perhaps for the first time, in the thirty-six days of the fight for the presidency, the excesses of the Internet were also observable daily on television, in the rawness and immediacy of the drama with uncontrolled commentators and guests blustering and often expressing offensive, or just ill-conceived, opinions. As the Internet absorbs ever more media like radio, television, and film, the net itself will become increasingly like the commercial and mainstream media, with all of their flaws and limitations, and television will become more like the Internet. This process of the mass mediazation, commercialization, and banalization of the Internet is driven both by technological development and the mergers between corporate conglomerates, which produces a standardization and homogenization of news and information as well as increasingly superficial and tabloidized news (see Schiller 1999 and McChesney 2000).

And yet the contradiction exists between the most astonishing information society in history with the widest range of information, opinion, and media accessible in contrast to a mainstream of news and information that is constantly shrinking, becoming more partisan and biased, and more superficial and unreliable. The news and information is there if honorable and literate people seek it, but all too many turn to television, or inflammatory and biased sources such as talk radio, instead of the wide range of Internet materials available on almost every topic imaginable. Of course, some Internet sites are among the most offensive and unreliable sources imaginable, but the wide range, diversity, and accessibility of a broad spectrum of material compensates for its limitations, although it requires information literacy and knowledge to adequately use and interpret.

In retrospect, the relatively high quality of some newspaper, journal, and Internet sources in the thirty-six days of the battle for the White House was impressive in comparison to the often mediocre and covertly biased coverage by the television networks. On the other hand, the drama was played out live on television screens, and to experience history in the making was highly exciting. To watch the crucial events of the thirty-six days unfold before one's eyes (or at least the results of key political and legal decisions and maneuverings) was extremely gripping and proved again that television's forte is you-are-there presentation of current events as they actually happen. The spectacle of the thirty-six days was one of the most electrifying television passion plays in recent history, and few who immersed themselves in the drama will forget the experience (perhaps many, like myself, have made videotapes and will discover nuances of the drama not evident during the first and live viewing).

Given the intensity of the clash and the immediacy of the live drama, there were more revealing exchanges than usually take place in the controlled contexts of television news and discussion. Often partisan debate was lively, and critical views usually not seen on television were expressed. The craving for news and information occasionally led the networks to cover explosive stories on the Internet, such as the Florida Republican Party "cleansing" of the voting lists that eliminated many legitimate voters, although the more explosive stories were not pursued or elaborated.

Writers who are later able to carry out a much more detailed and in-depth analysis of postelection 2000 combat than I can do here in my efforts to make a critical analysis of Election 2000 and its aftermath available in a timely fashion will find rich archives of news, commentary, and polemic. The videotapes of the postelection struggle are also revealing, especially the live broadcasts of press conferences, judicial hearings, demonstrations, and interviews that often provide more telling information and insight than the canned nightly news and partisan discussion. Curiously, during major events such as thirty-six days' combat for the presidency or the 1991 Gulf War, the daytime television programming that is live, direct, and often unedited can be more diverse and unpredictable than the later evening broadcasts. There are often explosive or interesting revelations during the relatively unfiltered live broadcasts of "breaking news," but as the day goes on and the events are made into news summaries they become bland and less worthy of attention.

On the whole, the mainstream media failed democracy during the battle for the White House. As I argue above, preelection mainstream journalism was atrocious in its blatant bias toward Bush and failure to articulate the important differences between the campaigns, the flaws of key participants, and the stakes involved. In particular, there were few sustained investigative analyses of the Bush family history and George W. Bush's record, or Cheney's record and role in a new Bush administration, little memorable commentary on the campaign, and a dearth of illuminating analysis, interpretation, and critique. As documented in chapter 1, newspaper and broadcasting coverage tended to be heavily biased toward Bush, and by and large newspaper articles were as poll-obsessed as the broadcast media, as focused on style and minutiae, and as lacking in substance.

It is arguable that the failings of mainstream print and broadcast media in covering Election 2000 and its aftermath can be considered one of the low points of U.S. journalism. Whereas there was plenty of important information and illuminating critique available in major opinion journals and Internet sites, both during the election campaign and the thirty-six days following election night, they rarely surfaced in the mainstream media, which either remained on the surface of the issues and personalities or leaned toward Bush. My experience in following and trying to make sense of Election 2000 and the postelection melee confirmed again the need for print and Internet material to provide a necessary context and framework for interpretation of television journalism, whose glaring limitations were all too apparent during the entire episode. While television captured the drama and immediacy of the day-to-day action portrayed during the struggle for the presidency, it was woefully deficient in probing the spectacle, in supplying adequate context and interpretation, and in providing reasoned critique of the various partisan positions and strategies deployed.

My studies show that although many of the hegemonic frames and discourses of the television election spectacle were favorable to Bush in both the election and its aftermath, many critical stories, discourses, and images circulated, as I have documented. It is conceivable that critical material will continue to surface, especially in newspaper investigations and on Internet sites, that suggest scandal that may surpass the Watergate affair in magnitude and infamy. Certainly, the way that the most explosive allegations of scandal that surfaced in the battle for the White House were marginalized could lead one to embrace Frankfurt Schoolesque theories of the culture industries and one-dimensional manipulation of news and information.[10]

And yet incidents and issues that are neglected or covered over by the mainstream media could resurface and explode. It is true that the many scandalous and damning stories that suggest systematic Republican corruption in the Florida election and the scuffle over the incredibly close official vote tallies tended to be ignored or marginalized. Yet they are part of the public record and a potentially explosive archival source that can be retrieved, mobilized, and deployed with perhaps fateful results (for the Bushes and the Republican Party). In any case, it is possible to diagnostically critique the discourse and tactics of the Bush camp based on its performance in Election 2000. Accordingly, the following two interpretive chapters attempt to show what Election 2000 and the following thirty-six days reveal about the U.S. political system and what problems are disclosed, followed by a section on lessons and conclusions that proposes some solutions to what I see as a growing crisis of democracy in the United States.[11]

NOTES

1. In George Orwell's famous novel *1984*, truth and falsity are interchangeable, war is peace, slavery is freedom, and so on, in a topsy-turvy totalitarian political system. Orwell's satire, beloved by conservatives, is, of course, an attack on totalitarian communism. In the contemporary era, conservative Republicans have taken on the tactics and odor of Stalinists and systematically deploy Orwellian language for their interests and to defend the indefensible (I make this argument in the next section). For my appreciation and critique of Orwell and analysis of contemporary examples of Orwellian language, see Kellner 1984.

2. Democratic citizens also require, as John Dewey constantly argued (1917), adequate education, which in our day requires media literacy, abilities to process information, and engaging in public forums of debate from the local community to the Internet. It also requires, as I suggest below, voter literacy, a capacity lacking in the Florida election. One could argue that our educational institutions have failed to educate the public for democracy, and that is indeed an argument that I will make in a forthcoming book; for a preview, see Kellner 2000.

3. See Elizabeth Jensen's story in the *Los Angeles Times* (Dec. 15, 2000), "*Nightline* E-Mail Goof Renews Cries of Media Bias." Jensen recounts how an e-mail announcement on ABC's *Nightline* list-serv that a new president had been chosen before Gore had conceded set off a firestorm of controversy on the program's e-mail list; the story also notes how Jeff Greenfield of CNN complained on air how partisans of both sides were flaming CNN with e-mail concerning their bias when, Greenfield said, the network was merely reporting the news. Rarely had an audience been so intimately involved in a story and reacted so passionately to what they saw as partisan bias in the media.

4. For detailed critiques of Fox News, see Neil Hickey's study at http://www.cjr.org/year/98/2/fox.asp and John Moyer's analysis at http://www.tompaine.com/features/2000/10/31/6.html. After Bush's successful theft of the election, several media published articles on how Fox ratings had been constantly rising and how Fox frequently beat CNN and the NBC cable networks during the battle for the White House (a cover story planned for *Newsweek* was allegedly pulled and demoted to an inside story in a February 2001 edition). Fox's growing popularity attests to the fact that conservative and Republican viewers see it as *their* network, obviously preferring to seeing their opinions confirmed over allegedly "liberal" views.

5. NBC is owned by General Electric, one of the most conservative U.S. corporations, out of which, for instance, Ronald Reagan emerged, transforming himself from a GE corporate spokesperson to governor of California and then president of the United States (see Kellner 1990). My research into the Gulf War revealed that NBC was the most prowar and pro-Bush administration, providing regular advertisements for GE weapons systems masquerading as news about the war (see Kellner 1992). It was clear that George W. Bush, like his father, was going to push for more military

spending and that GE, NBC's owner, would strongly benefit from the policies of a Bush administration, so perhaps its bias was not accidental.

In addition, besides owning the cable network CNBC, NBC is part owner of MSNBC, which is a joint venture of NBC and Microsoft. Major commentators on NBC and its cable networks were blatantly anti-Gore during the campaign and seemed the most eager to call it for Bush during the election night, the Florida certification by Katherine Harris, and the night after the Supreme Court ruling before Gore had conceded. Since Bill Gates's nemesis during the long and painful Microsoft trial was David Boies, who emerged as Gore's chief lawyer, and since Gates faced a potentially ruinous prosecution under a Gore Justice Department, and since Gates contributed heavily to the Republicans during the election, it would be interesting to know what, if any, influence Microsoft played in pushing the MSNBC coverage toward Bush, or if this is just the natural corporate inclination of its GE owners and the news personnel and commentators it hired.

6. In an effort to provide the superficial anchorman an intellectual lift, a bestselling book was published under his name in 1999, *The Best Generation*. Brokaw celebrated the generation of World War II as the "best" American generation, and while one would want to pay homage to its defeat of Fascism, this same generation brought us McCarthyism and the Cold War, the arms race, and an insane stockpile of nuclear weapons; it assassinated major political leaders in the 1960s while pursuing a highly divisive war in Vietnam. The "best generation" also produced the scandals of Watergate and provided the problematic presidencies of Reagan and Bush. Only a blinkered conservative ideologue would promote the gross distortions of recent history found in Brokaw's book. Brokaw thus emerges from his decades of NBC service as the perfect anchorperson to promote General Electric's corporate interests and weapons division. As Chomsky and Herman point out (1988), the corporate media select people who best represent their interests, and Tom Brokaw has been a loyal corporate flack and highly mediocre journalist.

7. Appraising the role of the Fox, NBC, and other networks requires analysis of political economy of the media, which critically dissects ownership and corporate control. Such analysis also requires critique of the actual role of the corporate owners; the employees that they choose to run the operation; and the talking heads that actually appear on-screen. It is to be hoped that future studies of the media will be able to correlate analysis of ownership patterns with scrutiny of the production process and critique of the media texts produced. Thus, a critical cultural studies requires analysis of production, text, audiences, and effects, a more systematic enterprise than I was able to undertake for this study, which is obviously time-sensitive and text-based.

8. For analysis of the longtime Bush–Moon relationship and their strange connections, see Robert Parry, www.consortium.com. On the Unification Church taking over the UPI, see Eve Gerber, "Looking for a Miracle," *Brill's Content* (April 2001).

9. Conservative foundations have training schools to cultivate young rightist journalists, fund rightwing student publications and writers, and thus invest in the creation

of a rightwing punditry. See "In Virginia, Young Conservatives Learn How to Develop and Use Their Political Voices," *New York Times* (June 11, 2001). Some of the best critiques of conservative punditry and criticism of the broadcast media comes from the Internet, including the american-politics.com "Pundit Pap Team," Gloria Ladumia of buzzflash.com, and the commentators at http://www.mediawhoresonline.com/.

10. On the Frankfurt School and the contributions and limitations of its media critique, see Kellner 1989.

11. A diagnostic critique uses media texts and events to provide critical knowledge of existing political discourses, forces, and contexts. For explication and examples, see Kellner and Ryan 1988 and Kellner 1995 and forthcoming.

9

BUSHSPEAK, POSTMODERN SOPHISTRY, AND REPUBLICAN STALINISM

If you're sick and tired of the politics of cynicism and polls and principles, come and join the campaign.

—George W. Bush

Those who cast the votes decide nothing. Those who count the votes decide everything.

—Joseph Stalin

The ascent of George W. Bush to the presidency has introduced the world to a new language and mode of political communication that we can call "Bushspeak." This discourse and discursive strategy involves both Bush's personal mangling of the English language and his systematic use of hypocrisy and lies to gain political support and manage public opinion. Bush's linguistic genocide has been widely noted and has already produced a book (Weisberg 2000) and "Bushisms of the Day" collected on the www.slate.com Web site and widely distributed through the Internet, as well as a critical compendium and analysis by Mark Miller (2001). But even more striking is the Bush administration's systematic use of hypocrisy and lies to defend the indefensible and legitimate the illegitimate.

BUSHSPEAK

It's the people's money. —George W. Bush

George Orwell introduced the concept of "doublespeak" in his novel *1984*, which presented a dystopian satire of a society where language referred to its opposite (i.e., "freedom is slavery," "war is peace," and so on; see the discussion in Kellner 1984). Bushspeak involves the systematic use of pleasant-sounding terms to camouflage a nasty reality. His "compassionate conservativism" in practice turned out to be hardright extremism, his "bipartisanship" masqueraded as a façade for carrying out a conservative agenda, and his oft-repeated promise to "leave no child behind" served as a front for systematic attacks on programs that would help families and children. And while Bush said during the campaign that "our allies must be respected" and the U.S. should play a "humble" role in the world, since becoming president, he has engaged in arrogant and hostile posturing that has incurred the wrath of the world and that is isolating the U.S. from its allies while intensifying hostile relations with "enemies" (see chapter 11).

During the battle for the White House, Bush's "trust in people and not government" involved trust in machines and not in following accepted democratic procedures of vote-counting by people in close elections; his "following the rule of law" involved his side's doing everything possible to manufacture votes while accusing his opponent of "stealing the election." And his campaign officials' pleas to keep the election contest out of the courts and virulent attacks on the courts when they ruled against them were accompanied by petitions and pleadings with every court that would listen to them, knowing that only their conservative partisan cronies on the Supreme Court would be willing to egregiously disregard precedents of law and democratic procedures to give the election to Bush and his apparatus.

Hence, while Orwell's doublespeak involved changing the meaning of words ("freedom is slavery"), Bushspeak involves concocting soft-sounding phrases for hardright and nasty policies, as well as saying one thing and then doing another. Richard Nixon's Attorney General John Mitchell warned reporters and the public to "Watch what we do, not what we say," and such advice is good in the Age of Bushspeak.

While I viewed a showing of Emile de Antonio's brilliant deconstruction of Richard Nixon, *Millhouse* (1971), the astonishing parallel between Nixon and George W. Bush became apparent, revealing a remarkable continuity of Republican Party dirty tricks and hypocrisy over the generations. In the 1968

Republican primaries and subsequent election Nixon was "a uniter and not a divider" (as opposed to Nelson Rockefeller, who had criticized Barry Goldwater and the right and was thus "dividing" the party). Nixon repeatedly made the same pseudo-populist argument that Bush made again and again, claiming that the Democrats were for Big Government, while Republicans represented the people. In the 1968 election Nixon reached out to "the forgotten man" and later "the silent majority," claiming that the Republicans respect "individual initiative" and "enterprise," while the Democrats pander to welfare cheats and "special interests," suggesting that the hardworking people should vote for the Republicans to represent their interests (the film *Millhouse* made clear that, in fact, Nixon represented the corporate elite and wealthy, just like Bush).

Moreover, Nixon carried out a series of dirty tricks and slandering of opponents, beginning with his 1948 Congressional race and 1950 California Senate race, in both of which he accused his opponents of being communist supporters. Now while it is well known that George W. Bush is not a student of American politics, clearly his adviser Karl Rove has learned his Nixon well and put it into practice. In addition to "appropriating" Nixon's ideological lines for the campaign, Rove has long followed Nixon's campaign manager Murray Chotiner in systematically carrying out dirty tricks and smearing of his opponent. Just as Chotiner slandered Nixon opponents, so did Rove and company smear Gore, calling him a "serial exaggerator," questioning his character, and trying to associate him with the excesses of Clintonism (the communism for the hardright of today). Karl Rove and George W. Bush thus emerge retrospectively as Richard Nixon's revenge, the avenging angels of Nixon's humiliation and disgrace.

Richard Nixon, of course, was George H. W. Bush's patron, naming him to a succession of jobs as ambassador to China and to the United Nations, as well as choosing him to head the national Republican Party. Audiotapes from the Watergate scandals reveal that Nixon saw George Bush as someone who could always be relied on; continuing Bush's promotion in the Republican establishment, Gerald Ford named him head of the CIA in 1975, cementing his relationship to an apparatus that he would make much use of in years to come. Thus, George W. Bush is part of a nexus including Richard Nixon and his father and their most questionable associates.

As a discursive practice, Bushspeak is programmed language, soundbited to put out the message of the day. It is circulated throughout the Bush administration and the vast conservative network that is on-target to support Republican and conservative policies. Bushspeak involves enforcing a party line wherein the Bushites parrot the same "message" and "talking points." Traditionally, conservatives attacked leftists for following a party line, for being incapable of individual critical thought, and for sacrificing values of truth and virtue for expediency and pragmatism. But in an era of 24/7 media, a flip-flop has occurred wherein the Republicans pursue a very disciplined party line enforcing conformity in discourse to "stay on message," one of the distinguishing features so far of the Bush party apparatus.

Bushspeak is presented in a daily photo opportunity by George W. Bush whose handlers engage in daily prayer to hope that their puppet will not mangle his lines and bungle the message. Its successful execution is signaled by the chimp-in-chief's smirk that indicates he has gotten his message and soundbite right and transmitted his Bushspeak of the day, allowing him to go work out or take a nap. A vacant and hollow look on Boy George's face signifies that he has forgotten what he has been told to say and is in the clueless zone.

Bushspeak involves, once again, the daily use of what one of my high school teachers referred to as "weasel words," whereby once honorable concepts had their meaning sucked out of them, just like weasels would suck the pits out of fruits. Bush has a limited vocabulary of particular words that he uses for emphatic emphasis, such as "integrity," "honor," "pride," and "humility," words that are quickly drained of meaning by Bush's misapplying and misusing these words, which are reduced to soundbites in Bushspeak. After hearing these words in Bush's snarky and smirky mouth, it is impossible to hear him say "I am proud" (or "humbled," or "honored," etc.) without feeling depressed that a once venerable language is having the meaning sucked out of it and veiling the lack of substance in Bush's pronouncements and his inability to use the language to convey thought or ideas (as opposed to scripted soundbites). The winner, however, in the weasal-word linguistic genocide sweepstakes is arguably George Bush senior, who allegedly said that James Baker was doing "God's work in Florida," a statement that reflects a stunning level of blasphemy and misuse of theological concepts.

Bushspeak involves speaking in soundbites, using cliches, images, and code words, rather than complete sentences and coherent arguments. Bushspeak uses code words with certain buzzwords to the Christian right like "faith" and "humility"; some to the corporate sector like "free markets," "free trade," and "entrepreneur"; some to average folks, when he claims that his tax plan trusts people and not government; and some to Clinton-haters, as when he promises to "restore honor and dignity to the White House." Although Bush promised "straight talk" and "plain speaking" on the campaign trail, not only does he mangle syntax and pronunciation daily, but Bushspeak empties words of meanings, uses words to manipulate and mislead, and systematically deploys a political semantic of hypocrisy and lying.

Like Orwell's doublespeak, Bushspeak often involves using words with opposite meanings. During the debate over energy policy, when Bush and Cheney refer to "free markets," they are really signaling to their oligarchic friends in the energy industry that they are for allowing the robber barons to gouge consumers, to seize any property that they want for energy production and distribution, and to promote any deregulatory measures that the industry wants, no matter what the environmental consequences. When they invoke the notion of "supply and demand" concerning energy prices, they are signaling, in the words of comedian Robert Klein, "We've got all the *supply*," [mimicking an oil company executive], so we can *demand* whatever the fuck we want." When Bush says he is for "limited government," he is indicating that he wants to limit government assistance to citizens and consumers, while doling out spoils to big corporations and the rich. When he invokes "personal responsibility," he is saying "screw everyone who can't afford higher energy prices," although he is providing Democrats with strong arguments why they should have been wary of a hardright conservative who is himself part and parcel of the oil and energy industry and totally subservient to its agenda.

The social and political consequences of Bushspeak are a systematic degradation of political language and defense of the indefensible. Bushspeak mobilizes euphemism, question-begging, vagueness, hypocrisy, and lies, which the puppet and his handlers substitute for honest political language. Feigning sincerity, Bushspeak oozes insincerity and duplicity, rendering politics a field of manipulation instead of discussion, debate, and consensus. Bushspeak also involves, as I will argue in the next section, a degradation of standards of truth and virtue and replacement of these genuine conservative values with a highly aggressive policy of "might makes right," thus subverting traditional conservative principles and values.

REPUBLICAN POSTMODERN SOPHISTRY

> You don't get everything you want. A dictatorship would be a lot easier.
> —George W. Bush

One of the most striking features of the postelection combat was the aggressive fashion in which Republicans deployed Bushspeak and engaged in a systematic practice of what could be described as postmodern sophistry. The Greek

Sophists, among other things, were presented by their adversary, Plato, as using rhetoric to make the weaker argument triumph. The sophistry and doublespeak systematically deployed by the Republican forces in the struggle for the presidency are striking and ironic, because over the past two decades cultural conservatives had attacked liberal and postmodern relativism and had defended values of truth, right and wrong, and justice over doctrines of perspectivism and constructionism. Postmodern discourse frequently argues that all discourses and values are socially constructed and laden with interests and biases.[1] Against postmodern and liberal relativism, cultural conservatives have argued for values of universal truth and absolute standards of right and wrong.

The Bush camp, by contrast, exemplified in its discourse and practices the old "might is right" relativism of the Athenian Thrasymachus, Plato's old philosophical nemesis.[2] The Gore side, perhaps opportunistically, strongly argued that the public needs to know the truth about how Florida voted, embodied in counting the votes and carefully examining the evidence to determine who got the most votes in the Florida election. The Bush camp, by contrast, employed every conceivable sophistical argument and power play tactic to (successfully) stop the votes from being counted, to block inquiry and analysis of the results, and to make it impossible to discover who had the most votes. The Bush camp also bent philosophical principles and legality to its purposes, using the law as an instrument of power rather than a tool of justice.

Hence, in Republican postmodern sophistry, it was might that determined right, with the force of the Bush legal team, political apparatchiks, and operatives plotting to block recounts and construct sophistical "arguments" to persuade the public that the votes should not be counted. Republican might trumping the process of inquiry and discovery was also visible in the organization of storm-trooper shock forces and cadres of demonstrators to ensure that the votes not be counted, that the truth not be discovered, that democratic procedures not be carried out, and that court decisions not go through (this process also bordered on thuggery and illegality).

In fact, postmodern doctrines were played out and exemplified throughout the election and postelection struggle on both sides, as it was clear that the truth (i.e., who won the Florida election) would be a hermeneutical construct and not pure and unsullied "facts" waiting to be discovered. The set of key issues, however, was whether this construct (and the winner of the election!) would be produced by empirical inquiry, debate over standards, and democratic consensus as set forth in the democratic theory of American philosopher John Dewey.[3] Or would the election result be constructed through the brute power play of the most powerful interests and forces, that is, Thrasymachus and "might is right" (as it would be)?

Another bizarre twist in the battle for the White House emerged in the sudden Republican fear of numbers. Public policy had long been made and legitimacy established through counting, census, voting, and the generation of numerical outcomes. While radicals had criticized technocracy and the tyranny of numbers used for purposes of governmentality and their final authority in the building of legitimacy, conservatives and technocrats had previously had no problems with making and defending decisions on the basis of numbers.[4] Rather than depending on constructing procedures as fair and impartial as possible to determine the outcome of the election according to the numbers—as both science and democracy would dictate—members of the Bush machine used the brute power of their supporters and the institutions they controlled to construct their victory. Their power plays revealed, in effect, that numbers themselves are the constructs of complex social processes and that strings of numbers are often results, as in Election 2000, of highly partisan interests and procedures that legitimate the powerful rather than expressing truth and objectivity.

The process also revealed a remarkable turn in an intense debate over whether machines were superior to human beings, in which conservatives were ironically flipped over to the side of the posthumanist technoculture.[5] One indeed wondered how conservatives felt in repeating day after day that only machines are to be trusted in counting votes, that machines are superior to people, and that people cannot be trusted. Such faith in machines over humans would seem to fly in the face of a philosophical humanism that most conservatives espouse, but it did not seem to bother the Bush spokespeople, who repeated the posthumanist mantra again and again. The rhetoric of machines over people as arbitrators of the election not only flew in the face of Florida law. It was also subverted by a Texas law signed by Governor Bush that in a close election hand recounts were necessary, and flew as well in the face of evidence that machines often failed to provide an accurate vote. But the mantra also undermined philosophical humanism that affirmed the dignity of persons over machines.

In Election 2000, brute power and antidemocracy thus trumped inquiry and democracy, associating Republicans with cynical "might is right" power politics and ceding the higher ground to their Democratic opponents. Hence, the arguments for counting the ballots, discovering the truth, validating popular democracy, and the like, argued by the Gore camp, were overpowered by the sheer force of the power apparatus deployed by the Republicans, including cadres of well-paid lawyers; a ruthless central committee of Bush machine political operatives; control of the state executive and legislature of Florida; powerful influence in the media; and, ultimately, the trump card of the support of the Supreme Court conservative majority.

The Bush machine's deployment of raw power politics thus put on display a particular type of Republican Stalinism in which what was important was not counting the votes but determining who won the election by means of institutional power and power politics. In this conflict, truth, justice, and democracy could not win; the forces of raw and brutal political power were just too strong. One wonders, indeed, if any cultural conservatives were bothered by the fact that the political rhetoric and tactics used to bully Bush into the White House were so antithetical to traditional conservative positions on truth, right, and legality. For a good philosophical conservative, "the ends justify the means" is the height of philosophical relativism and amorality, undermining those core values and principles that conservatives supposedly cherish above all.

One wonders how conservatives felt about the barrage of sophistry and blatant lies that James Baker, Bush's media team, and Republican spokespeople would repeat over and over every day. One Republican mantra was "All the ballots have been counted, many, many times." In fact, there were thousands of ballots never counted because of malfunctioning machines or, more disturbing and never really investigated, "irregularities." Many ballots were only counted once, because the county election boards failed to perform the legally required recount.[6] Other canvassing boards shifted votes from Gore to Bush after the recount, reverting to original tallies without justification or public outcry. And in another vote-counting scandal, absentee ballots arbitrarily and illegally went into Bush's vote tallies even if they were postmarked late or were lacking in other absentee-ballot requirements (see chapter 11 for documentation).

James Baker, with his slippery rhetoric and evocation of raw power politics, was the master of doublespeak and hypocritical sophistry. For Baker, legal decisions exhibited "partisanship" and a "usurpation" of democracy (unless the court decided in his side's favor). Forked tongue darting in the air, Baker would decry events that portended a "sorry day for our democracy," exactly when he was doing his best to undermine U.S. democracy himself. Baker and his Bushspeak brigade would decry the Democrats' use of courts, even declaiming that the Democrats were the first party ever to use the courts to decide an election. In fact, it was Baker and his crew who initiated the first major legal case, asking the Atlanta Court of Appeals to block manual recounts on the grounds they were "unconstitutional"—a charge no one bought, although Don Antonin Scalia and the Gang of Five were eager to adopt the Bush team's equal protection argument to shut down the counting of votes.

A brazen Big Lie often repeated by Republican sophists was that Gore and the Democrats were "stealing the election" by demanding that votes actually be counted. Republican passion was intense around this myth, which largely consisted in projecting onto the Democrats exactly what they were doing themselves. Moreover, Republicans fell prey to a corrosive hypocrisy as they first excoriated the judiciary, when the Florida Supreme Court voted against them, and then praised the legal system when the U.S. Supreme Court ruled for them. Copius examples of hypocrisy abound, the many daily sophistries, evasions, and outright lies that were part of the Bush machine propaganda strategy. Clearly, the truth was sacrificed by these "compassionate [but lying] conservatives," for whom power is all and principle little, for the greater good of winning the election. Ironically, the Bushites had lambasted Gore for his narrative embellishments, saying that he twisted the truth, that he could not be trusted, and even that Gore was a liar guilty of "serial mendacity." But when push came to shove, when truth (i.e., who won the most votes) was at stake, the Bush force's contempt for conservative values was unveiled, and truth and democracy were the victims.

THE DEGRADATION OF CONSERVATISM

I'm very gracious and humbled. —George W. Bush

Hence, for the Bush machine, conservative values were readily sacrificed for political power in a daily display of (effective and successful) mendacity that would have made the Athenian Sophist Thrasymachus proud and broken poor old Plato's truth-loving heart. So far, however, I have yet to hear of any U.S. conservatives' hearts breaking. Nor have I read or even heard mild conservative misgivings about the beating their cherished values took in the hands of the hard-core Bush operatives. This silence would suggest to me that cultural conservative values, often heatedly and loudly displayed in academic arguments against postmodernism and relativism, are themselves largely tactical. Moreover, it appears that conservativism itself in the age of Reagan/Bush/ little Bush has turned into a mere ideology of political power and partisan interest.

Michael Kinsley provides an instructive example of Republican doublespeak and Republicans' sacrifice of honesty and integrity for partisan purposes in his account of watching conservative pundit William Bennett on CNN (*Slate*, December 22). Bennett, a former secretary of education and author of a book on virtue, had frequently extolled the virtues of honesty and principle over the past decades, but as Kinsley tells it there was no evidence of these virtues in Bennett's performance. Bennett opened by claiming that he had not been in touch with Bush campaign officials and did not "have their talking points"—and then proceeded to advance precisely the talking points that Bush campaign officials were advocating that day. Claiming that Gore "was trying to change the rules" by asking for a manual recount, and then arguing that manual recounts are a terrible idea "because of the uncertainty in counting by human hands, the subjectivity that's introduced," Bennett was covering over that manual recounts were the accepted practice to determine elections in close contests throughout the country. When confronted with the fact that Bush himself had signed a law mandating manual recounts in Texas, Bennett sneered and offered the sophistical argument, "I've heard a lot of things from lawyers in the last few weeks," but nothing so ridiculous as the idea that "the law in Texas governs what goes on in Florida" (ironically, the Bush forces were in the process of pushing through a recount in the state of New Mexico using the same arguments that the Gore side was using in Florida, but as Ronald Reagan once remarked, "facts are stupid things" and surely stupid facts were not bothering sophistical Republican ideologues).

Moreover, another dimension of the conservative mind was also on display during the bitter struggle for the presidency, and that was belief in the absolute certainty and truth of one's positions (even if they change day by day and contradict the previous day's positions). Conservative partisans were *certain* that their candidate had won the election. They were absolutely sure that they were right, and that the Democrats were thieves and knaves stealing the election. Whereas a more skeptical and open-minded response to the demand that votes be counted to ascertain the truth and see who really won appears reasonable, this was not negotiable by conservatives, who were positive that all votes were already counted—many times—and that further counting was just a Democratic Party trick to steal the election that was their entitlement and right.

Ironically, Republicans had been intensely critical of entitlement programs over the past years that would benefit minorities and the disadvantaged. Yet they seemed to believe that they had an entitlement to the White House, that they deserved to govern. Indeed, commentators noted that from the beginning Bush camp officials had presumed that they were going to win the election, that they had indeed won it on election night, and that anyone who disputed their right to ascend to power was going to get crushed. The Bush family clan always assumed that it was born to rule, that the election was theirs through family privilege, and that anything they did to advance their ends was justified. Indeed, the brute power and arrogance of the Bush machine; the mobilizing of all of its networks and constituencies; its ability to use Florida state institutions, the media, and even the U.S. Supreme Court, were put on raw display, as the Bush machine sacrificed legal and philosophical principles in order to win the election contest. The Bush machine assumed from the beginning that it had captured the presidency, and when results seemed to suggest otherwise, it deployed all of its firepower to assure victory—law, democracy, truth, and morality be damned.

For decades, conservatives have been outspoken defenders of morality and critics of alleged "immorality" by other sectors in U.S. society and politics. George W. Bush and other conservatives have also argued for the need for civility and decency in politics today. Yet consistently during the war for the White House, the Bush team acted amorally and uncivilly. In order to not repeat previous points, I want to cite three examples of Bush machine petty viciousness and incivility that display the vindictive and brutal character of rightwing amorality and practice in the current era.

One of the first mean-spirited and petty mantras emanating from the Republican camp as the war for the presidency began was that seniors and minority groups who were victims of the butterfly ballot in Palm Beach, or the confusing two-page presidential list in Duval, were stupid and deserved to lose their votes. Rush Limbaugh and others on talk radio mouthed this mean-spirited litany, and it spread through print and television as well. Insensitivity to Holocaust victims who accidentally voted for Pat Buchanan and the mocking of African American voters and others who were voting for the first time were disgusting and typical of the aggressive and brutal Republican forces. Sandra Day O'Connor in her Supreme Court comments also attacked those who had misvoted and had the audacity to claim that the "standard" for counting a vote was proper voting procedure, overlooking all the evidence that indicated that machines had systematically malfunctioned, in addition to voter errors.

A second example of typical Bushite ruthlessness occurred during the court cases over the illegal Republican strategy of filling in voter registration numbers on Republican absentee ballots in Seminole and Martin Counties. Clay Roberts, a Republican appointee and underling of Katherine Harris, admitted that although the GOP officials who altered the ballot applications and the Republican county supervisors who allowed the alterations to take place seemed to have committed a crime and should perhaps face prosecution, the voters should not be punished and have their ballots thrown out. This mantra became the line of the day on December 6 for the Bushites, showing their willingness to sacrifice their own underlings who had worked hard for The Cause in the interests of winning the election for Bush (including a seventy-something Republican woman, Sandra Goard, who was supervisor in Seminole County). I saw members of the Bush spin brigade such as Governor Marc Raciot of Montana seriously make this argument on MSNBC, as well as lawyers from the Bush side. Once they won the case, this cruel discourse was dropped, but it showed that the Bush machine was willing to scapegoat its own loyal underlings for the great good of winning Bush a few votes and the presidency. Even the Mafia is more loyal to its underlings than the Bush camp was to its fellow election thieves.

A third example of petty Republican vindictiveness occurred the fateful day that the U.S. Supreme Court stopped the Florida balloting with a stay that halted the democratic process of counting the uncounted undervotes. Ron Klain, a legal and political adviser to Gore, noted in a press conference that the Gore campaign had won a certain number of votes already in the aborted counting of the undervotes and had reason to believe that if counting continued Gore would handily win. In a vindictive Republican spin right afterward, the vicious Governor Raciot and his colleague Republican Governor George Pataki of New York accused Klain of violating an embargo on giving out the numbers until the counting was finished, suggesting that he should be subject to legal punishment for his sin. At the same time, Republican operatives were also leaking vote counts, as was the Associated Press, and so the fair-minded Judge Terry Lewis indicated that he was not interested in pursuing violations of his orders under the circumstances. But the mean-spirited attack on one of Gore's closest advisers showed the pettiness to which Republicans had sunk in their (successful) bid to win the presidency by any means necessary.

Moreover, as documented, throughout the battle for the White House, conservatives put on display what Richard Hofstadter described as "the paranoid style in American politics." Conservative Republicans believed that the Democrats were the incarnation of evil, that they were "stealing the election," and projected day after day their own sins onto Gore and the Democrats. In fact, conservative Republicans genuinely hated Bill Clinton, who had beaten them twice in presidential elections and narrowly escaped impeachment. Republicans were outraged that Clinton had escaped their jihad, which they really believed was a holy war, and projected the imagined evils of Clinton onto Gore and the Democrats in general. This rage and resentment led Republicans into an irrational frenzy during the battle for the White House where they genuinely seemed to believe that the Democrats were stealing "their" election, and in a state of irrational hate and paranoia they repeated whatever mantras the Bushites were circulating as the message of the day, came out in droves to demonstrate, and were prepared to do anything to keep the Democrats from winning the presidency.

I have already detailed the beating that cherished conservative legal principles took in the hands of the Partisan Supremes whose decision for Bush violated their cherished principles of state's rights, respect for local judiciaries, and aversion to judicial activism. Regarding the latter, the Rehnquist Supreme Court was clearly uncovered as a very activist and engaged court—for the right conservative causes. Indeed, the intense scrutiny on the court after the election revealed the sustained conservative and partisan activism of the Rehnquist conservative majority over the past decade.

Members of the Rehnquist–Scalia Gang of Five were also unveiled in terms of their deep hostility toward popular sovereignty, their loathing of voting rights, and their contempt for popular democracy, which came out front and center in the election aftermath. Yet, the successful Bush juggernaut delegitimated some of the deepest conservative philosophical and legal principles, while revealing contempt for genuine democracy and proclivity for raw and brutal power displays.

In fact, the pragmatism and instrumentalism of the Bush forces were much more extreme and less nuanced than those of the father of American pragmatism, John Dewey. Dewey, whose pragmatism and alleged relativism were often attacked by conservatives, appeared a moderate in comparison to conservative instrumentalism in the election contest. Dewey believed that truth could be approximated by the scientific method of testing hypotheses and examining evidence (in this case, looking carefully at the ballots), and he believed that democratic debate and consensus were the way to solve political problems. He had always been a critic of sophistry, raw power politics, and undemocratic procedures, and his pragmatism showed itself to provide a reasonable philosophical basis for solving problems in contrast to conservative absolutism and hypocrisy.

The Republicans, by contrast, combined postmodern sophistry with raw Stalinist instrumentalism, discrediting conservatives for years to come with their theft of the election and corruption of language and principles to justify their coup d'état. The theft of the presidency revealed the Bush machine to be ruthlessly Machiavellian. In the Bush machine's pursuit of power, the ends justified the means and, like Comrade Stalin, so too would Commissar Harris do anything to advance the end of electing W., while Jim Baker would say anything to legitimate the illegitimate. Like Stalin, the Bush machine knew that one couldn't make an omelette without breaking eggs, and that one couldn't steal a presidency without breaking the rules of democratic legality and norms of truth and sincerity.

Thus, the Bush machine Republican Stalinism usurped the presidency by any means necessary and confronted U.S. democracy with one of its most daunting challenges. It is conceivable that the hardball tactics deployed by Republican operatives and the Bush machine to snatch the election for Bush, the lies and hypocrisy that legitimated their tactics, and the pain and scandal associated with the Bush victory could delegitimate the Republican party in a serious and sustained fashion that could help mobilize publics to oppose the Republicans for the foreseeable future. Bushspeak, the degradation of conservativism, and Republican Stalinism have now associated the Republicans with the hardright and it will be very interesting to see how voters and publics respond to this very dubious and chilling politics in the days to come.

NOTES

1. For sustained presentation and critical analysis of evolving postmodern positions over the last two decades, see Best and Kellner 1991, 1997, and 2001. I should note here that there are many types of postmodernists, just as there are opposing types of conservatives. Some conservatives are partisan Republicans who simply wanted Bush to win and did not worry much about the discourses and tactics deployed. Some hardright conservatives admired and in good conscience deployed the antidemocratic and highly partisan tactics because they believed in their cause and their principles. There is another type of cultural and political conservative, however, who typically espouses traditional values of democracy and philosophical principles of truth and morality and whose positions were directly assaulted by the Bushites. In the analysis that follows, I am drawing out the contradictions between the discourse and practice of those conservatives who vaulted Bush into the White House and traditional philosophical conservatism.

2. See the reflections by Alan Wolfe that I build upon here: "Hobbled from the start. How can George W. Bush convince Americans to trust him when he has dismissed such notions as truth and justice?" (http://www.salon.com/politics/feature/2000/12/15/trust/index.html).

3. On Dewey's concept of democracy, see Dewey 1995 [1916] and the commentaries in Kloppenberg 1986, Westbrook 1991, and Ryan 1996.

4. See, for example, Hacking 1981 and Rose 1999. Thanks to Allan Luke for suggesting this argument.

5. For the intricacies of these debates, see Best and Kellner (2001). Briefly put,

posthumanists argue that machines are simply superior to humans, that humans should welcome the coming implosion with machines and technology (i.e., development of artificial intelligence and "intelligent machines," cloning of humans, and so on) and should not be afraid of the rule of machines, which is inevitable in any case. Conservatives and philosophical humanists of various sorts have reacted violently to posthumanist cheekiness, and it was ironic to see Republican conservatives supporting machines over human beings, and thus siding with posthumanist perspectives that would normally horrify them.

6. Testimony in the Sauls court documented the high failure rating of the voting machines, especially the punch-card machines used in the contested counties. On how some Florida counties never undertook the mandated recount, see the article (http://www.herald.com/content/archive/news/elect2000/decision/078314.htm).

10

THE BATTLE FOR DEMOCRACY

*[T]he election of the president of the United States by the
Supreme Court of the United States needs to be regarded not
only legally, but also morally and historically. And morally
and historically speaking, we have witnessed an outrage. . . .
This ruling was designed to bring about a political outcome,
and it is an insult to the intelligence of the American people to
suggest otherwise. . . . Constitutionally speaking, this presidency is ill-gotten. It is the prize of a judicial putsch.*

—The Editors, *New Republic*

The Republican theft of the White House reveals that in the present era, truth, law, and democracy are increasingly sacrificed for partisan inter-ests. The struggle for the presidency revealed the continued centrality of media spectacle in U.S. politics and the ways that political struggles are played out in the media. It also showed the partisanship of the U.S. legal system, espe-cially the Supreme Court, whose conservative majority had so disgraced this august institution. In this chapter, I discuss what the events of Election 2000 and its aftermath tell us about the state of U.S. politics, the crisis of democracy revealed, and some possible solutions.

A DIVIDED LAND AND THE FAILURE OF THE DEMOCRATIC PROCESS

As I suggest in earlier chapters, Election 2000 and the succeeding battle for the White House reveal a divided country around the axes of race, gender, sexuality, class, region, religion, and political ideology. Postelection break-downs of the voting patterns dramatize the major divisions in the United States today. Inspection of the electoral map shows a split into two countries, one Democratic, liberal, and progressive, and the other conservative and Republi-can. The more progressive sector of the country includes the northeastern states, encompassing the Boston–Washington corridor; it sweeps across the northern midwestern states that are more industrial and urban, and then leaps to the West Coast from Washington to California. This America is urban, multicultural, well educated, and liberal. It includes Florida with its ethnic mix and large community of retirees, although, obviously, this state is highly contested.[1]

The Republican and conservative sector encompasses most of the rest of the states and especially the South, Southwest, Midwest (with the exception of the more industrial states), and far West (with the exception of the West Coast). This America is primarily white, heavily religious, rural, and conserva-tive. As noted, gender and race divides are significant, with men going heavily for Bush and women for Gore, while people of color were solidly Democratic. Democratic Party America also has a firm class and union base, with Gore getting 54 percent of voters within the $15,000 to $20,000 range, 6 percent higher than his overall total and a differential slightly higher than that for any Democratic presidential nominee in the last quarter-century. Twenty-six per-cent of the voters came from union households, and they gave 59 percent to Gore, following intense mobilization of labor by the AFL-CIO and other labor unions. Well-educated voters also chose Gore, with males with college degrees choosing the Democrat by 8 percent and women with college degrees by 22 percent.

These divisions have become intensified by growing differences in political ideologies between Republicans and Democrats—as well as among liberals, conservatives, and radicals of the left and right. Moreover, the intense struggles over the Clinton sex scandals and impeachment trial, and then Election 2000 and the subsequent struggle for the White House, deepened political divisions in the country and brought to a white-heat intensity the cultural wars that have been ebbing and flowing since the 1960s. One imagines that this division will continue and perhaps intensify as the media promotes ideological clash in its discussion formats and as scandals and struggles in Washington intensify with the new Bush administration encountering determined Democratic opposition and widespread lack of legitimacy within large sectors of the public.

Yet the ideal-type model of the fundamental division in the United States is complexified by three factors: there are significant radical and progressive sectors, approximately half of the country is depoliticized and could go either way, and groups of the population are fed up with both major political parties. This turbulent and volatile political situation makes it possible for independent candidates to attract large numbers of voters and makes the political future highly unstable and unpredictable.

On the whole, Election 2000 treated the world to an astonishing display of the failure of the U.S. voting system, media and polling, and its political and legal system. Almost half of the U.S. public did not vote, while many thousands made mistakes that cost the more qualified candidate the election. More worrisome, millions voted for a candidate and party that campaigned on a vacuous and hypocritical populism ("we're for people, not government") that was a front for the most reactionary rightwing interests (see chapter 11) and that fronted a candidate who was the most underqualified presidential contender of the last fifty years (watch the Dumb Son any given day, and go to the Slate.com site that collects his almost daily gaffes and stupidities). The Bush camp was so intent on winning that it did everything it could get away with, inside and outside of the law, to pull off the most audacious and stunning theft of an election in U.S. history.

Clearly, Election 2000 put on display the technological obsolescence of the voting system in the United States. The election revealed the contradiction between technological overdevelopment in many sectors of U.S. society and the technological underdevelopment of the system of voting, especially in districts that used outmoded and unreliable punch-card voting machines. The clumsy chad-infested ballots in predominantly African American precincts in Florida, the infamous butterfly ballot in Palm Beach County and two-page presidential ballot in Duval County, the difficulty in ascertaining voter intent in recounting ballots, and the strong partisan bias to the entire process obviously pointed to the need for a radical overhaul of the voting process.

U.S. democracy was supposed to be the world's most advanced, the model for the rest of the world. Whereas G. W. F. Hegel perceived the Zeitgeist riding into Germany in the form of Napoleon, who he thought would bring the French Revolution, democracy, and modernity into a provincial Europe, in Election 2000 the spirit of democracy became constipated in chad-stuffed ballots stuck in voting machines, and American democracy appeared a farce. Intelligent observers stressed the need to make voting registration easier and more efficient, using computerized voting rolls and not just printed-out registration lists; the need to standardize and rationalize voting with clear and well-designed ballots and machines, like automatic teller machines (ATMs), that would accurately register one's preference, inform the voter of her or his choice, and provide an opportunity to void the vote if one made a mistake; and the need for an electoral process not controlled by partisan groups.[2]

It remains to be seen if the political parties will undertake a reform of the voting and electoral system. Immediately after the struggle for the presidency had ended, Jeb Bush and Katherine Harris submitted proposals to form a commission to study ways to reform the Florida electoral system. Scientists at Cal-Tech and MIT announced a joint project to devise new high-tech voting systems within the next six months, and the company that produces election machines said that it is prepared to radically retool its product.[3] Jesse Jackson called for more radical reform of voting registration and guarantee of voting rights, insisting that this would be a major civil rights issue for the future (see my comments on the outcome of these efforts as of this writing in chapter 11).

The obsolete voting machines in Florida and elsewhere are one of this country's greatest technological embarrassments of recent times, and one imagines that serious efforts will be undertaken to remedy the problem. Less certain is whether the even more shocking civil rights violations of African American voters, who were illicitly removed from voter registration lists, whose efforts to vote were blocked, and whose votes were not tabulated, will be remedied. It is obviously not in the interests of the Republican Party to empower a voting bloc that will vote against it, nor is it likely that a Republican-controlled Justice Department will vigorously pursue the allegations of systematic discrimination against African Americans and other minority groups—allegations that if pursued could elicit evidence of widespread illegalities and systematic discrimination that would further delegitimate the already grossly illegitimate Bush theft of an election and lack of a mandate.

The refusal by the voting machines of more than 20,000 ballots in Palm Beach County, and perhaps more than that in Duval County, reveals striking deficits in ballot design and voting literacy, which in turn highlights striking limitations of the U.S. system of democracy. It is a scandal, first of all, that poorer counties and districts would be forced to use voting machines and procedures that are technologically obsolete and prone to dysfunctionality. Second, it is outrageous that machine malfunctioning, overvotes and undervotes, and thus disenfranchisement of large sectors of the public have been going on for years and yet no one has done anything about these issues, or even raised them as serious concerns. It is also shameful that in light of obsolete and poorly functioning machines, more effort was not exerted to design ballots that would compensate for voting-machine problems, and that voters were not better educated about how to vote, how to make sure that their vote registered, and what they should do if they were having problems in voting.

Curiously, many absentee ballots were also disqualified because voters did not read the requirements for absentee voting or made mistakes in voting. It is scandalous that while there have been heroic efforts at voter registration and turning out the vote, there have been few efforts in voter literacy. This is in part a failure of the political establishment and in part a failure of the schools. Learning how to read a ballot, how to register choices, and how to properly submit the ballot so that it is counted should be part and parcel of all education, starting at an early age. In particular, all citizens of voting age should know how to vote. Of course, it is now technologically possible to devise a voting system and ballot that are as simple to use as an ATM, that allow feedback so that people can confirm their choice, and that thus overcome many of the limitations that punch-card voting machines possess. Computerized voting, of course, brings up the problem of manipulation and corruption, problems intensified in importance after the experiences of Election 2000. An argument for the older style of paper-ballot voting is that at least ballots leave a paper trail, that there is a record to examine and sort out. The paper trail left in Florida was a catastrophic mess, as I document further in chapter 11. But there is a technological solution to worries about computerized ballots and the lack of a paper trail. Assuming that a workable high-tech computerized voting-system could be devised, it would also be useful to print out a copy of the ballot results, as one's ATM record is printed out; a voter could inspect the print-out, sign it, seal it in an envelope, and deposit it in a voting box as one now does. If there was an extremely close election or suspicion of fraud and corruption of the computerized process, the paper ballots could be examined and the election results certified—hopefully by courts and not partisan election boards.

In any case, drastic reform of the voting system is necessary in the light of Election 2000 and the crisis of democracy that it disclosed. But a functional democratic voting system requires literate voters to work, so that voter literacy should be part of any and every campaign and should also be part of civic education in the public schools and even college.

VOTING REFORM AND A NATIONAL VOTING DAY

Ballot design and voter literacy have long been problems in U.S. politics with little, however, focus on and discussion of the issue. A 1998 article by Susan King Roth found serious problems in ballot design, compromising the ability of people to make accurate and informed electoral choices. Her study points to endemic problems of usability in the U.S. electoral process, driven by the dual goals of fitting a large number of candidates and issues on the ballot and counting them mechanically as quickly as possible (see http://www.informationdesign.org/pubs/roth1998.html).

The Florida election made as clear as could be desired the problems with Votomatic punch-card ballots, truly a national embarrassment, but also revealed the limitations with optical scanning devices that yielded an often stunning number of overvotes. Here, the problem is literacy, of teaching voters how to vote, of letting voters know what they have to do to get their vote completed and counted. One of the upsides of the Florida recount wars is that there is increased consciousness concerning this issue and efforts are being undertaken to remedy the situation. The *Los Angeles Times* (April 5, 2001: B3) reported that in preparation for the April Los Angeles municipal elections, voting sites were preparing signs reading: "Got Chad? Check Your Ballot Card." Los Angeles county was also promising voters that they would receive a provisional ballot if they were not on voting lists and were providing an emergency hotline to provide ballots and poll workers in case precincts were closed down or understaffed. Officials were reassuring minority voters that they would be able to vote and have their voices counted. "This effort is to assure the people of Los Angeles that they should not fear being ripped off when they vote, as happened in Florida," said Councilman Mark Ridley-Thomas.

Hence, perhaps gains in voter literacy, fairness, and accuracy might follow immediately from the Florida fiasco that so dramatically presented the sad state of U.S. electoral processes and technology. But the most ludicrous commentary during the battle for the White House and its dispiriting aftermath was provided by those vacuous pundits who said that the entire process shows how well the system works, how vigorous U.S. democracy is, and how marvelous the U.S. Constitution is. But, in fact, the debacle shows that the system does not work, that U.S. democracy is in crisis, and that the system functioned disastrously to produce an entirely illegitimate result. Indeed, the legitimacy of every major institution was severely stressed and undermined during Election 2000 and the ensuing struggle for the presidency, from the failure of the voting process to register millions of votes nationwide, and crucial votes in Florida, to the shameful intervention of the U.S. Supreme Court, tarnished forever by its infamy.

Election 2000 and its aftermath have shown U.S. democracy at its worst and best, with emphasis on the former. The tradition of popular sovereignty, of democracy rooted in the activity and will of the people, evident in the attempts at the Florida counting of disputed votes, had been defeated by a more conservative and antidemocratic tradition grounded in the institutions of the state and judiciary. While the Florida Supreme Court stressed the primacy of the right to vote and to have one's vote counted, the U.S. Supreme Court affirmed the will of the legislature and the court, and ultimately the will of the five majority justices, over the sovereignty of the people. Hence, democracy in the United States was deeply imperiled in Coup d'État 2000, and its future remains in question. What lessons can we learn from the debacle, and what conclusions should we draw?

One of the key lessons of Election 2000 and its aftermath is the technological obsolescence and flawed character of the U.S. voting process. If the equal protection clause of the Constitution were to be applied to voter registration in the United States, the maintenance of voting lists, the organization of precincts for voting on election day, the availability and use of effective voting machines, and the presence of helpful election workers and fair-minded monitors, tremendous discrepancies would be revealed, clearly evident in the Florida election aftermath. Impartial examination of the U.S. voting system would show severe prejudice against voters in minority, poorer, rural, and often Democratic Party areas. Unions, organizations such as the National Association for the Advancement of Colored People (NAACP), the National Organization for Women (NOW) and feminist groups, and gay and lesbian organizations did a tremendous job in getting their constituencies registered and out for the vote. Yet the problems that blacks, other minority groups, the poor, and seniors had in actually voting and getting their votes counted in Florida disclose tremendous shortcomings in the U.S. electoral process that are a national scandal and need to be addressed.

No doubt U.S. scientists, technicians, and corporations will be able to produce better voting machines that have more intelligent design, are user-friendly, and provide feedback as do ATMs. It is clear that the punch-card machines used by more than one-third of U.S. voters in Election 2000 are obsolete and need to be replaced, and there are no technical reasons why a voting machine could not be devised that would be relatively easy to use, reliable, and fair that could provide accurate tallying of votes protected from manipulation and corruption.[4] Devising an accessible and secure voting system might postpone Internet voting at home, and there are arguments besides security for having voters assemble in public spaces, interact with other voters, and be able to appeal to election officials if they are having problems, and for having a system in place that allows monitoring of voting to make sure that mischief is not being done.

But reforming the U.S. electoral process will require more than creating better machines and more effective voting procedures. It will require improving the voter registration process and creating "equal protection" to poorer communities, making sure that their machines are as proficient as in wealthier districts. This will also require reform of the social system of voting, so that voters know where their polling places are and are treated respectfully and equitably at their voting precincts independent of race, class, or other factors. Moreover, citizens require education in voter literacy so that they are aware of how the electoral system works and how to vote. Further, there should be fair and equal support systems to help voters with problems on election day.

Obviously, the reformed voting system will also have to be devised to minimize corruption and manipulation of the balloting process, which might require an independent electoral commission to run the whole process, as in Canada and many other countries, rather than local officials, often political appointees and even party militants. Election workers are undertrained and underpaid, and the debacle of Election 2000 shows the need for reform of multiple facets of the process. Since the Supreme Court made equal protection a fundamental aspect of election law, it will now be possible to apply this to every part of the election process to propel and legitimate necessary reforms, whose absence have denied substantial numbers of people their basic voting rights.

Hence, the equal protection clause could again be a progressive instrument of electoral reform, reversing its shameful abuse by the Supreme Court Gang of Five in the theft of Election 2000. Every citizen should have equal access to voting, encompassing clear and straightforward voter registration; access to functional and fair voting machines; the right to accurate and reliable tallying of voting; access to county officials who could help with problems; and the guarantee that the entire voting process is being professionally and justly administered, free from partisanship and partisan corruption (which so sullied every aspect of the Florida election and the battle for the White House).

One simple reform that would advance equal protection of all voters would be to make presidential election day a national holiday to facilitate voting for everyone. Voting could take place the first Monday in November, which could be declared a national holiday. This would create a three day weekend with intense focus on the election where citizens could take it as civic duty to become informed, intelligently weigh the choices, engage in debate, and make a more informed vote. In the Age of the Internet a tremendous amount of information is available and an educated and involved citizenry could choose their candidates more judiciously. Moreover, given the intense media competition to broadcast results and the span of four time zones across the United

States, it would be necessary to organize voting times so that the entire country voted at once, with polls opening and closing at the same real time across the country. This could help assure that election results were released at the same time *and* only after every polling place had closed. A national election day with a uniform voting time could involve expanding the voting day to twelve to fifteen hours so that polls would be open a sufficient span of time to allow all voters to vote and have their votes registered before the media begin their frenzied rush to predict winners. It would not be excessive censorship of freedom of speech to mandate that no election results could be released via exit polls and interviews before the polls close. It is even conceivable that the media would readily agree to a fair stipulation such as this to atone for their embarrassment in the series of miscalls in Election 2000, when they made several (questionable) predictions before polling places had even closed in Florida and while West Coast voting still had hours to go.

Moreover, new residents or voters should be allowed to register on national election day, and there should be adequate computers and staff to make registration easy, to eliminate the danger of multiple registration and voting, and to ensure that only eligible voters can indeed vote. On this latter issue, there should also be a national debate on whether felons should be excluded from voting, as is now the case in many states, and whether rehabilitated citizens should have fair voting rights—as seems preferable in a democracy. Providing voting rights to individuals who have gotten into trouble with the criminal justice system and are trying to reform and reintegrate into society might help to rehabilitate them. It is already scandalous enough that it is largely the poor and people of color who constitute the majority of the population of the prison-industrial complex, and to further deny individuals their voting rights intensifies their societal alienation and makes it more likely that they will continue to operate outside the law and the system.

ELECTORAL COLLEGE REFORM

The abuses evident in Election 2000—and their potentially catastrophic consequences—also reveal the obsolescence and dangers of the highly outmoded and dangerously undemocratic Electoral College system. This highly complicated issue requires careful examination of past official dissections of the Electoral College, up-to-date study of its inequities, intelligent and fair recommendations for reform, and sustained public debate and discussion before any revisions of the electoral process go up to vote—which would require amendment of the Constitution and thus ratification of any changes in the electoral system by two-thirds of the two houses of Congress and votes in two-thirds of the states, a process that will clearly take years.[5]

In any case, Election 2000 made clear that the constitutional system of the U.S. electoral process is historically obsolete and dangerous. There is no legitimate reason in the twenty-first century to allow state legislatures to have primary responsibility for choosing electors, as in the infamous Article II, Section 1 of the Constitution, which holds that state legislatures appoint electors, not the people—a fateful clause that the conservative members of the Gang of Five in the U.S. Supreme Court relied upon in their outrageous ruling. Allowing state legislatures to choose electors for the president is clearly unsuited for a genuinely democratic polity in which sovereignty should ultimately be rooted in the people and not with the legislature and judiciary. Citizens should directly elect their president, with legislatures and courts having the authority to set rules and to determine legitimate outcomes. But there should be no constitutional basis for allowing legislatures to actually choose a slate of electors, as the Florida legislature was prepared to do. Rather, there should be a direct election for the president, without the mediation of electors, as is the case with the House and the Senate. Direct election of senators, in fact, required a constitutional amendment in 1913 because election of the U.S. Senate also originally operated with the mediation of electors who choose senators, rather than through direct voting by the people, which is now the case and should also be so for presidential elections.

The current Electoral College system, as many have commented, is based on eighteenth-century concerns and is arguably obsolete and in need of systematic reconstruction in the twenty-first century. Initially, the Electoral College was part of a compromise between state and local government. Allowing electors to choose the president provided guarantees to more conservative politicians who wanted the Electoral College to serve as a buffer between what they perceived as an unruly and potentially dangerous mob and the more educated and civic-minded legislators who could, if they wished, overturn actual votes by the people. Moreover, as Yale Law Professor Akhil Reed Amar argued in a November 9 *New York Times* op-ed piece, "the Electoral College is a hopelessly outdated system and . . . we must abolish it." Amar went on to argue:

In 1787, as the Constitution was being drafted in Philadelphia, James Wilson of Pennsylvania proposed direct election of the president. But James Madison of Virginia worried that such a system would hurt the South, which would have been outnumbered by the North in a direct election system. The creation of the Electoral College got around that: it was part of the deal that Southern states, in computing their share of electoral votes, could count slaves (albeit with a two-fifths discount), who of course were given none of the privileges of citizenship. . . . The Constitution's pro-Southern bias quickly became obvious. For 32 of the first 36 years a white slaveholding Virginian occupied the presidency.

The Electoral College also exhibited a gender bias, fixing the number of electors in each state with no incentive to expand suffrage, as well as bias against popular sovereignty, designating electors to choose the president rather than following the cumulative will of the voters. In practice, state legislatures began binding electors to popular vote, although as was abundantly clear in Election 2000, "faithless electors," electors who vote for whomever they please, were theoretically possible (half of the states attempt to legally bind electors to the choice of voters in their state, but it would still be possible to shift one's vote, an intolerable outcome for a genuinely democratic society and a possibility much discussed in Election 2000).

Moreover, the proportional representation system in the Electoral College has serious problems that have come out in the heated debates over Election 2000. Smaller states are disproportionately awarded with Electoral College votes, so that voters in less populated states such as Idaho or Wyoming have more proportionate influence in choosing the president than in states such as California or New York. As Duke University's Alex Keyssar argued in a November 20 *New York Times* op-ed piece, disproportionate weighting of the votes of smaller states

> violates the principle of one person, one vote that most of us believe in and that, according to a series of Supreme Court decisions in the 1960s, lies at the heart of our democracy. "To say that a vote is worth more in one district than in another would . . . run counter of our fundamental ideas of democratic government," the court announced in 1964. "Legislators," wrote Chief Justice Earl Warren, "represent people, not trees or acres." Yet 18 million people in New York now get 33 electoral votes for the presidency while fewer than 14 million people in a collection of small states also get 33.

Thus, the current system of proportionate state votes where all states get two votes and then the rest are divided according to population is unfair; for example, as Jim Hightower notes, Wyoming's electors and proportionate vote represent 71,000 voters each, while Florida's electors each represent 238,000. A more reasonable system would simply allot states proportionate votes according to their populations, so that each vote throughout the nation would be equal in choosing a president.[6] Hightower and others also propose an instant runoff voting system to encourage third and fourth parties and to help get more individuals involved in the election process and voting. In this way, instead of only having to choose one presidential candidate, one could vote for one's first choice, say Nader, and one's second choice, say Gore. If no candidate received a majority, second choices would be alloted proportionately, so one could vote for one's candidate of choice without worrying about boosting a candidate that one strongly opposed.

Proposals to eliminate the Electoral College as a shield between voters and election of the president, as has now been done for decades with the Senate, seems reasonable, and I can conceive of no reason to oppose such a measure. In addition, the winner-take-all rule operative in most states means that 100 percent representation could go to a 50.1 percent majority in state presidential elections. Maine and Nebraska are exceptions, and it would be possible to follow their example and to split presidential state votes proportionately according to the actual percentage of votes candidates get in each separate state, rather than following the winner-take-all rule, where a handful of votes in a state such as Florida gives the entire state, and even the election, to one candidate.

Hence, the Electoral College must be seriously debated and reforms must be undertaken if U.S. democracy is to revitalize itself in the new millennium after its most scandalous debacle. As just argued, there are strong reasons for proportionate representation in something like an Electoral College, but it must be without electors and with the public directly electing the president in a more proportionately fair and just electoral system, as opposed to a winner-take-all state vote and subsequent ratification by electors. "Electors" are rather mysteriously chosen in any case and could potentially be "faithless" and vote for a candidate not chosen by their state. Other options would be a winner-take-all national popular vote, but this would seem to contradict the desire to have a balance of power among the states and to ascribe the states a significant political role, as was envisaged in the original U.S. Constitution. On the other hand, any number of reforms to the current system could be proposed and should be seriously discussed.

CAMPAIGN FINANCE, THE MEDIA, AND OTHER REFORMS

A popular government without popular information, or the means of acquiring it, is but a prologue to a farce or a tragedy, or perhaps both. —James Madison

For U.S. democracy to work in the new millennium, it needs to immediately adopt crucial reforms and appoint high-level commissions to study how to modernize and update the system of electing the president. Since the political establishment cannot be counted upon to undertake these reforms under the most intellectually challenged president in recent history, it will be necessary for publics—academic, local, and national—to devise reforms for the hopelessly obsolete system of "democracy" in the United States, a system that hardly deserves the name of this illustrious concept.

Furthermore, it is clear that money has corrupted the current electoral system and that finance reform is necessary to avoid continued corruption by lobbies, corporations, and the influence purchasing and peddling that a campaign system fueled by megabucks produces. The current election system financing scheme and millions of dollars needed for a federal election ensure that only candidates from the two major parties have a chance of winning, that only candidates who are able to raise millions of dollars can run, and that those who do run and win are beholden to those who have financed their campaigns—guaranteeing control of the political system by corporations and the wealthy.

In Election 2000, the excessive amount of money pumped into the $3 billion–plus electoral campaigns guaranteed that neither candidate would say anything to offend the moneyed interests funding the election, assuring that both parties would pitch their campaigns to the middle, avoid controversy, and thus avoid key issues of importance and concern. The ways that expensive campaigns indebt the two major parties to their contributors were obvious in the initial appointments made by the Cheney–Bush transition team, which rewarded precisely those sectors and personnel who most heartily supported the Bush dynasty presidency. Republicans are not subtle about this form of blatant corruption, and the Clinton administration competed fiercely with Republicans to raise money and to give favors to its friends. The only way to curtail this blatant and growing corruption is to have dramatic election campaign reform.

In the last months, the McCain-Feingold finance reform bill that has been circulating in the U.S. Senate has been widely discussed, but there is a strong case to go further and argue for public financing of elections. Four states currently allow full public financing for candidates who agree to campaign fundraising and spending limits (Arizona, Maine, Massachusetts, and Vermont), and this would be a splendid model for the entire nation. Public financing for elections at local, state, and national levels would only be viable in a media era with free national television, free access to local media, and Internet sites offered to the candidates. Indeed, the television networks should also be required to provide free airtime to presidential candidates to make their pitches, and television paid political advertising should be eliminated (see the elaboration of this argument in Kellner 1990). The broadcasting networks were given a tremendous bonanza when the Federal Communications Commission provided a wealth of spectrum to use for digital broadcasting, doubling the amount of spectrum space it licensed to television broadcasters with estimates of the value of the space ranging up to $70 billion. Congress failed to establish public service requirements that used to be in place before the Reagan-Bush-Clinton deregulation of telecommunications and as a fair payback for the broadcast spectrum give-away, broadcasting institutions should provide free time for political discourse that strengthens democracy.

To be sure, efforts were made and defeated to get the television networks to provide resources that would enable the public to get messages from the candidates, clearly presenting their positions. President Clinton appointed an advisory panel to assess how to update public service requirements of television broadcasts in the wake of the spectrum giveaway. The panel recommended that television broadcasters voluntarily offer five minutes of candidate-centered airtime in the thirty days before the election. Clinton proposed this recommendation in his 1998 State of the Union address, but broadcasters fiercely rejected the proposal, and in the Senate, John McCain and Conrad Burns announced that they would legislatively block the FCC's free airtime initiative. In fact, political advertising is a major cash cow for the television networks who regularly charge political candidates excessively high rates, although they are supposed to allow "lowest unit charge" (LUC) for political advertising; such LUC rates, however, mean that the ads could be preempted, and desperate campaigns want to make sure that they get their advertising message out at a crucial time and thus are forced to payer higher rates.[7]

Obviously, campaign finance reform is going to require taking a hard look at the role of television advertising and serious consideration of the providing of free television time to major political candidates. A fair election requires that candidates be able to present their ideas to the public and to have a chance to respond to their opponent's criticisms, whether via television ads, interviews, or televised speeches. The current situation of the necessity of high-priced ads in a presidential campaign requires record levels of fund-raising and ensures that money will corrupt the political process.

In light of major television networks refusing even to televise key presidential debates in Election 2000, perhaps specific requirements to broadcast conventions and debates should also be put in place. Having heard and made copious proposals for reforming network television over the years (see Kellner 1990), I am skeptical, however, as to whether the commercial television networks in an era of growing competition are going to reform themselves, and I fear that they are hopelessly corrupt and will never undertake their democratic responsibilities. Moreover, with their scandalous performance in Election 2000 and its aftermath, I predict that, if anything, the mainstream media will continue to pursue scandals, tabloid journalism, and infotainment, exhibiting a decline in terms of traditional journalistic standards and ethics in the foreseeable future. I thus propose the need for expanded media criticism, the cultivation of critical media literacy in the schools to create a media-literate public, and the creation of alternative media to help overcome the limitations of the mainstream media in an accelerating crisis of democracy (see Kellner 1998, 1999, and 2000 for some interventions along these lines).

As the James Madison quote used to open this section indicates, without popular information a democracy cannot function. In an era of corporate media, this means that democratic alternatives must be created and supported by the public that produces and circulates the essential information needed so that democracy can function. The age of the Internet makes the creation of democratic media possible and offers the potential to provide a diverse range of opinion and information, to allow the public to participate in public dialogue and debate, and to create an informed public that could make democracy work (see Kellner 1998 and 1999).

There is also an issue raised by the catastrophe of Election 2000 concerning the responsibilities of citizenship and the need to rethink citizenship in a high-tech era. For democracy to work, citizens must be informed and able to access information on candidates, make judgments for themselves, and use voting technology to register their informed judgment. Democracy also requires participation in dialogue, debate, and political processes for the sovereignty of the people to be exercised. The tragedy and scandal of democracy in the United States in the Third Millennium is that large sectors of the voters are not adequately politically informed, do not participate, and allow political elites to manipulate elections. The broadcast media, as I have argued in this book and elsewhere (Kellner 1990, 1992), have not undertaken their democratic responsibilities, have not adequately informed the public on political candidates and issues, and have contributed to the crisis of democracy that we are now experiencing.

On the other hand, and this is a major contradiction of the contemporary era, we are currently living in an age that makes accessible via the Internet more information resources available to more people than any period in history. Moreover, the Internet allows participation in political dialogue and debate, the amassing and disseminating of political information via list-servs and Web sites, and the possibility of circulating political discourse outside of the limitations of the party system and mainstream media (see Kellner 1999 and 2000). Participating in the new public spheres, however, requires access to new technologies, a certain degree of technological literacy, and willingness to get informed, to participate in political debate, and thus to engage in what is called "deliberative" or "strong" participatory democracy.

Thus, the responsibilities of citizenship require that the public has to take responsibility for not being informed, for living in a world of mythology, for falling for the spin and soundbites of the Bush campaign, and particularly for allowing the hardright of the Republican Party to become a major political force. Although the mainstream media were biased toward Bush and did little solid investigative reporting into his character, record, and agenda—to the lasting disgrace of American journalism—plenty of information on Bush was easily available through books, Internet sites, and publications (see Introduction, note 3, chapter 11, and the sources cited throughout this book). The events of Election 2000 and its Grand Theft reveal that large segments of the U.S. public live in a world of mythology and phantasmagoria, lost in images, lies, and entertainment, easily seduced, mislead, and manipulated by the powers that be. Many of those supporting Bush hated Clinton and the Democrats so much that they projected their hatred onto Gore, whereas others lived in self-contained and complacent worlds of myth, fantasy, and entertainment, oblivious to the issues and the stakes of the election. Conservatives got their opinions and ideas from Fox news or other rightwing media sources, participated in wingnut chatrooms or Internet sites, and read rightist publications. These people were True Believers who genuinely hated Clinton and Gore and were happy to vote for Bush and the Republicans. A large segment of the moderate public and independent voters, however, were arguably fooled into thinking that Bush was a "compassionate conservative," "a uniter and not a divider," a man who would bring Democrats and Republicans together to get things done in a bipartisan fashion, and who would "bring dignity and a more civilized tone to Washington." In the first 100 days of Bush's presidency, these Bushian mythologies were self-deconstructed and the public was confronted with the fact that the Bush agenda was hardright and that Bush was a front for reactionary social interests and corporations (see chapter 11).

There is little doubt that U.S. democracy is in serious crisis, and unless there are serious reforms, its decline will accelerate. Although electoral participation increased from an all-time low in 1996 of 49 percent of the eligible electorate to 51 percent in Election 2000, this percentage is still extremely low, putting the United States near the bottom of democratic participation in presidential elections. Obviously, about half of the country is turned off by politics, and the centrist campaigns of both sides in Election 2000, geared toward a mythical center and suburban swing voters and governed by polls and focus groups, were not likely to inspire voters and bring them into the political process (although partisans of both sides became deeply involved in the election aftermath, as I have documented in this book).

LESSONS FOR THE POLITICAL CLASS

Yet all of the intense focus on the spectacle of Election 2000 and the battle for the White House, which dramatized in its perverse way the importance of every single vote, provides an opportunity for repoliticization of a polis that had been marked by steadily declining participation in the political process (see Boggs 2000). Moreover, a message for the Democratic Party is that the majority of the people (if one counts the three million–plus Nader votes) could be mobilized if an adequate appeal is made to traditional Democratic groups (barely evident in the Gore campaign of 2000) and if the Democrats can reach out to independent voters and bring those outside of the political process, including many cynical and alienated younger voters, into the electoral process. If they do not, they will either lose to the Republicans, who have more money, corporate power, and a fanatic, disciplined, and well-organized base at their disposal, or we will see the political spectrum fragment into a proliferation of political groups, in which third- or fourth-party movements could be decisive, throwing the election to one side or the other in a highly unpredictable and turbulent process (as indeed arguably happened in 1992 and 2000).[8]

Further, while one might be sympathetic toward Gore for having the election stolen from him, one can draw conclusions about the limitations of the Democratic Party and the centrist liberalism that the Democrats have pursued during the Clinton era and the Gore 2000 campaign. Clinton, Gore, and the "New Democrats" pursued centrist policies that undermined traditional Democratic New Deal liberalism, cutting back on the public sector and social programs, while promoting the private sector, in ways that provided Ralph Nader and other critics of the centrist Democrats with ammunition for critique. During Election 2000, Gore was even more timid than Clinton in pursuing a narrow agenda of reform that no one except the superrich and Republican ideologues could dispute, but that failed to inspire the electorate. (Polls showed that moderate, independent, and undecided voters overwhelmingly sided with Gore on key issues such as tax cuts, Social Security and Medicare reform, and the other centrist positions he was advancing, but simply liked Bush better than Gore, and thus voted for a candidate who had fuzzier positions than Gore and was in fact a puppet for hard-core rightwing interests who was also dangerously inexperienced.)

Predictably, a spiraling cascade of Gore campaign criticisms was unleashed after Gore's concession and through the present. The Monday morning quarterbacking and rethinking campaign strategy in retrospect is a longtime and venerable spectator sport in politics, and no doubt Gore could and should have won with better strategy (ironically, the same could be said for the Bush camp). Yet there are two major mistakes that had the Gore camp avoided in the postelection combat for the presidency (this is my Monday morning retrospective) it could have won Gore Florida's votes and given him and the Democratic Party the high ground in the struggle for democracy that was a subtext of the election agon.[9] First, the Gore campaign should have demanded an immediate systematic manual recount of undervotes and overvotes in all counties in Florida (chapter 11, "Aftermath," suggests that this would have won the presidency for Gore, as well as been the right thing for democracy). Second, the Gore campaign and Clinton administration should have pursued a more sustained strategy of pursuing Republican irregularities in Florida involving systematically blocking, harassing, and not counting votes from African Americans and other minority communities. This dual failure, I believe, points to the limitations of Democratic Party centrism and the pursuing of narrow strategic interests instead of broader goals that would strengthen democracy.

Although Gore twice made a halfhearted pitch to the Bush camp in a televised speech to pursue manual recounts of all of Florida, and although his lawyers and campaign managers frequently expressed their willingness to negotiate with Bush a statewide manual recount, the Gore team never really pursued this avenue. Yet mentioning the possibility revealed that the Democrats were aware that another strategy was open to them. They were rightly criticized by Republicans and others for pursuing recounts only in heavily Democratic counties that were sure to yield them votes, and they could have overcome this criticism had they pursued a broader strategy. There is reason to believe that the Florida Supreme Court would have supported the call for a statewide manual recount if the Gore forces had requested it. As the statewide manual recount of the undervotes begun on December 9 and killed by the U.S. Supreme Court the same day made evident, it would have certainly been doable. Moreover, it would have been harder for the Republicans to criticize this strategy and more difficult for the U.S. Supreme Court to rule against it. Yet, in retrospect, there was probably not much that the Gore campaign could have done to prevent the theft of the presidency. Had they been able to persuade the Florida Supreme Court to carry out a statewide recount earlier, no doubt the highly partisan Rhenquist/Republican Supreme Court majority would have stepped in to block the results. And no matter what happened in the courts and the voting contest, the Florida legislature was prepared to name its own electors and force through the election for Bush. Hence, given the closeness of the election, the ruthlessness of the Republican Party, with its control of the Florida legislature and a highly partisan Supreme Court in Washington to step in, there was probably no way that Gore could have prevented Bush from seizing the presidency.

Thus, it is debatable whether a statewide recount was or was not possible under the conditions in which the Bush machine controlled the legislative apparatus of Florida and had high executors on the partisan U.S. Supreme Court, as is whether or not it would have yielded Gore enough votes. Nonetheless, I argue that this was the right course of action to pursue for the cause of democracy. For a statewide manual recount would have seriously validated the importance of counting *every* uncounted vote and carefully examining the overvotes to see if voter intent was discernible on ballots that contained two votes, as well as the undervotes. Observers of the aborted recount and other election officials who engaged in recounts indicated that on many of the double-voted ballots, such as the infamous Palm Beach County butterfly ballot, voters wrote in "Al Gore" to dramatize their intent, but these ballots were not counted by the machine because of the double punch or writing on the ballot, which nullified the vote. Moreover, in one Republican county (Lake; see chapter 11) in which a newspaper carried out a recount after the election, hundreds of never counted ballots were found that yielded a plurality of 128 votes for Gore. Therefore, a full manual recount might have won Gore a decisive plurality and thus victory.

The Gore campaign also made a serious strategic mistake in accepting the December 12 deadline for certifying state electors for the U.S. Electoral College meeting on December 18,[10] when there was no state law that mandated this and when many states sent in their slates after the date. Of course, in a situation of unprecedented complexity it is perhaps uncharitable to demand that forces in the heat of battle clearly see the terrain and act with Solomonic wisdom, but it is clear that the Democrats made important mistakes during the struggle for the presidency that result, I argue, from inadequate commitment to democracy and failure to take the high road.

The limitations of Democratic Party centrism were also evident in the refusal of the Clinton administration and the Gore camp to more actively pursue the many irregularities and perhaps illegalities in Florida that had come to light during the thirty-six days. On November 9, just after the election, Democratic Party stalwarts William Daley and Warren Christopher dramatically exclaimed in a press conference that there was evidence of "serious and substantial irregularities" that demanded investigation. This is a grave statement, and stories were rapidly circulating of the butterfly ballot that many claimed was illegal; of tens of thousands of ballots that manifested double voting in Palm Beach and Duval Counties, suggesting irregularities; of a heavy undercount in Miami–Dade County; and in systematic harassment of African Americans throughout Florida, including police blockades where voters were stopped and intimidated, long voting lines without adequate staffing, the disappearance of many African American and other minority voters from voter registration lists, even though they were registered; and many, many other stories of irregularities.

Perhaps the most dramatic and undercovered story of irregularities in Election 2000 involves a scandal uncovered by investigative reporter Gregory Palast published first in England. The account documents how before the election Florida Governor Jeb Bush and Secretary of State Katherine Harris ordered local election supervisors to purge more than 64,000 voters from voting registration lists on the grounds that they were felons and ineligible voters; as it turns out, many of these individuals were not felons, or had felony records in other states and were eligible to vote in Florida. This "scrub list" was funded by $4.3 million of state funds, was carried out by Database Technologies, a firm that had close ties to the Republican Party, and was highly inaccurate, never confirming whether those scrubbed from the voting lists were really ineligible and were thus illegally denied their vote. Palast published his initial findings in the British *Guardian,* there was a follow-up study published in *Salon,* and a few newspapers mentioned the scandal, but the mainstream media and Democratic Party activists ignored the story.[11]

The above examples are violations of the equal protection clause of the U.S. Constitution, which the Democrats could have used in the clash for the presidency. But the Gore Democrats never systematically and seriously pursued these issues, nor did the U.S. Justice Department (at least as of summer 2001). Ignoring a wide array of irregularities in favor of focusing on the recount of a few Democratic counties was, in retrospect, an appallingly limited strategy for the Gore campaign, and it angered African American voters who had turned out in record numbers for the Democrats in Florida and throughout the country. In fact, the Gore campaign had taken pains to distance itself from African American causes and groups throughout the election, as well as the aftermath.[12] This failure to embrace important political constituencies shows the limitations of Democratic Party centrism and the need to overcome the timid poll and focus group–oriented centrist campaigns that are aimed at white middle-class "undecided" and "swing" voters.

Of course, the media, the Justice Department, and other groups such as the NAACP may pursue the irregularities, and justice may be achieved. Nonetheless, it was a violation of the imperatives of democracy and social justice *not* to pursue the voting rights violation of minority groups under the equal protection clause during the battle for the White House. If the Democratic Party is to deserve the votes of the majority of the citizens in the next election, they must make redress of the violation of rights in Election 2000 and work hard to secure voting rights for all in future elections.

While Democratic Party centrism was not able to win the election or defeat Republicans in the battle for the White House, the Republicans appear to be headed on a far-right course that may alienate broad sectors of the public—or may produce a new conservative hegemony for years to come. Despite lip service to "compassionate conservatism" and "uniting rather than dividing," both in the battle for the White House and the first one hundred days of the new Bush administration, the Bush machine has pursued a highly aggressive rightwing agenda in which the gap between haves and have-nots is likely to dangerously escalate, as political divisions intensify. It is apparent that the Bush–Cheney machine represents the most corrupt and greedy sectors of the ruling class, that Bush and Cheney were going to pursue economic policies largely in favor of their corporate supporters and donors, that they are pledged to transfer as much wealth as possible from the government coffers to the wealthiest and most powerful Republican constituencies, and that they will undo every social program possible that works to distribute wealth and promote social justice, while at the same time pursuing as hardright a social agenda as they can get away with. Of course, the razor-thin Republican majority in the House and flip-flop in the Senate, the lack of support in broad sectors of the public for the Cheney–Bush agenda, and the widespread sense that the Republican coup was illegitimate and violated the basic precepts of democratic legitimacy could create stalemate and gridlock, making it difficult for the Bush machine to push through the hardright Republican and corporate agenda. It remains to be seen if the Republican program advanced by the VP-CEO Cheney, supported by Bush père and his friends, and hawked to the public like a new car or toy by George W., the Great Pretender, will succeed. It is thus now too soon to say whether the Republicans will or will not be able to bamboozle the public and exploit their theft of the election to maximize their robbery of the public assets and implementation of a rightwing social agenda.

If the Republicans are able to successfully implement their program of class warfare, it will certainly aggravate divisions between the have and have-nots to a dangerous degree, which could create a highly volatile political situation that might generate the conditions for fascism. Just before undertaking this project, I sent to press a collection of unpublished studies by Herbert Marcuse (2001) including an analysis of "The Dilemmas of Bourgeois Democracy." Written in a state of despair after the overwhelming electoral victory of Richard Nixon in 1972, Marcuse compared the situation in the United States to Germany in the 1930s in which the fascist party of Adolf Hitler rose to power after a tightly contested election. The dilemma of "bourgeois democracy" for Marcuse was that the people could elect someone like Hitler or Bush, or their parties could use the machinery of democracy to seize power. To prevent the misuse of democracy, Marcuse suggested, required political education of the people, the strengthening of genuinely democratic institutions, and the resolute opposition to reactionary and antidemocratic forces.

Only a militant democratic opposition from the day of the inaugural until the thieves leave the White House can prevent the worst from happening and create the conditions for a democratic revival, that is, a revival of genuine democracy and not just the interests of the Democratic Party. It is possible, of course, that if a vibrant movement for popular sovereignty and genuine democracy were to emerge, it would be hijacked for partisan purposes by the Democratic Party. Nonetheless, those who believe in and want democracy should seize the time, understand that the United States is in a clear and present danger of losing its democracy, and realize that now is the time for militant struggle and new radical democratic politics.

Crucially, those of us who experienced Election 2000 and the remarkable thirty-six days that followed must never forget the theft of an election and the Republican coup d'état. Aldous Huxley in *Brave New World* described a society satiated on consumer pleasures, multimedia escapism, and the intoxications of sex, drugs, and drink—a prescient allegory for the condition of the United States and other overdeveloped capitalist societies in the new millennium. Unfortunately, George Orwell's vision in *1984* of a society governed by doublespeak and doublethink that overpowered concern for truth, freedom, and democratic self-determination was also visible in Election 2000 and its aftermath—as I document in this study. Huxley and Orwell described societies marked by historical amnesia, lack of social conscience, and conformity to the powers that be.

While aspects of Huxley's and Orwell's warnings have come to pass, the battle for the White House also exhibited a serious struggle for democracy. Outrage over the theft of the election produced unparalleled criticism of the Republican Party, the Supreme Court, the media, and the U.S. political system that allowed such a crime, thus creating conditions for protest and social reform. Now is the time for partisans of democracy, justice, and social progress to stand up and speak out, to fight for reform of the institutions that made the Republican theft possible, and to struggle for democratization and social justice. Grand Theft 2000 should never be forgotten, and those who participated in its infamies should be held responsible and be made accountable.

ELECTION 2000 AND ITS REPERCUSSIONS

On the whole, the ultimate consequences and effects of the postelection struggle for the White House are highly contradictory and unpredictable. While the winner-take-all mentality in the United States privileges the side that gets the prize, the pungent partisanship and intensity of the struggle set up the winners to later be toppled, if incriminating information concerning the messy Florida election process surfaces. Intense focus on the election would circulate the spectacle of the scandal that could multiply and bring down the Bush dynasty and its allies, as occurred during the Watergate affair after Nixon's triumphant victory in the 1972 election.

It is possible that the aftermath of Election 2000 has produced an acrimonious division in which both sides will be prepared to go to protracted war without compromise against the other if provoked. After the closely contested battle for the White House, there was speculation that precisely the destructive partisanship could drive members of both sides to centrist reconciliation and a new era of cooperation. As is usual after any election, the competing parties underwent rituals of reconciliation, with the Bush camp promoting discourses of bipartisanship and the Democrats going along with the ride (or biding their time). The Bush machine lip service to unity and bipartisanship turned out to be a cover for hardright conservative policies and hegemony in the making, as my analysis of Bush's first 100 days suggests in chapter 11.

There is definitely a large reservoir of anger, and Election 2000 might mobilize African American and potentially oppositional groups to struggle for radical social transformation. Reforming election laws, replacing obsolete voting machines, and streamlining the entire electoral process would immensely aid minority and potentially anticonservative voters, who were so shamelessly violated by the disgraceful Florida voting system. There will be intense pressures from many sides to reform the electoral system that could have long-term progressive effects on the U.S. political system.

Moreover, the raw display of conservative Republican power may help elicit new coalitions targeted against the Bush machine, in reaction against the ruthlessness of its operatives and tactics, and it may highlight the need for unity to overturn the conservative hegemony. Of course, and such are the movements of the dialectic, the animosity may further fragment oppositional groups, increase cynicism and apathy, and produce a new era of conservative rule.[13] Or not. Shortly before Christmas, the *Washington Post* (December 22) published an article predicting that more than 750,000 people were planning to come to Washington to protest Bush's inauguration, and that scores of leading political groups and movements were planning to participate. Obviously, nowhere near that many protestors appeared, but there is growing evidence that many people are dissatisfied with politics-as-usual and would support radical political change.

Obviously, it is still too soon to say if Bush's election will produce a new conservative hegemony, or if the highly contested and divisive election denotes the end of the conservative hegemony of the two final decades of the twentieth century. As of December 22, Al Gore was declared to have beaten Bush in the popular vote count by 540,435 votes, a substantial plurality that dramatizes Bush's lack of a mandate and popular support. Gore and Ralph Nader to his left won the strong majority of votes, so if the voting patterns of the last two decades of the twentieth century in the United States leaned toward the right, perhaps a shift to the left was visible in the beginning of the new millennium.

No doubt, the dramatic events of the battle for the White House helped shape strong images of its major players that will continue to resonate. In such events, the resonant images are often those of personalities, and many of the public will henceforth see James Baker as the raw and brutal face of Republican power and doublespeak, Katherine Harris as the face of the corrupt party hack, and Republican politicians such as Tom DeLay or Marc Raciot as fanatic partisans, the voices of brutal hypocrisy at its worst. Those on the Republican side, however, will see these same figures as the Heroes of Victory, avatars of conservativism who fought the good fight and won.

Those who paid attention to the deliberations of the Supreme Court will not soon forget the role of Antonin Scalia, who emerged as an evil genius of Machiavellian intrigue, and the Supreme Partisans will live on in the eyes of many as major villains of the U.S. political mediascape. Sandra Day O'Connor, a previously respected centrist justice, forever disgraced herself in the face of the public with her shrill, hectoring tone and shortsighted focus during the hearings and in her siding with the conservative majority at the end. *Newsweek* (Dec. 25, 2000) reported just after the Gang of Five's partisan decision for Bush that when Supreme Court Justice Sandra Day O'Connor heard during an election-night party that Florida was first called for Vice President Al Gore, she was very upset, exclaiming, "This is terrible." The report went on to note that her husband, John O'Connor, explained to friends and acquaintances that his "wife was upset because they wanted to retire to Arizona, and a Gore win meant they'd have to wait another four years" because O'Connor "did not want a Democrat to name her successor."

Vincent Bugliosi notes how Felonius-Five Justice Sandra Day O'Connor served three terms in the Arizona State Senate, once as Republican senate majority leader, and was a co-chairperson of the Arizona state committee to elect Richard Nixon president. Bugliosi also notes that Gang of Five Justice Anthony Kennedy, often presented as a centrist or "moderate," was a Sacramento lawyer-lobbyist "who, for no pay, traveled the state on behalf of then-Governor Ronald Reagan's anti-tax initiative." While the rightwing initiative did not pass, Kennedy "won a soft spot" in Governor Reagan's heart who urged Nixon to appoint the Republican lobbyist for nomination to the U.S. Court of Appeals, where a third Republican sponsor, Gerald Ford, gave him the nod for Supreme Court Justice (2001: 26–27). Big surprise that these hardcore Republicans picked young Bush as president.

In one of the more comical episodes following the Supreme Court decision, Clarence Thomas, the silent justice who always follows the lead of Scalia, gave a talk to some high school students; "there's no politics in this court," the Rehnquist–Scalia court has "no axes to grind, we just protect this," Thomas said, holding up a copy of the Constitution (Associated Press, Dec. 13, 2000). Thomas revealed that he was either monumentally stupid or hypocritical by making such a ludicrous statement the day after one of the most political and partisan decisions that the Supreme Court had ever made, in what many were perceiving as one of the most political and partisan courts in U.S. history. Later, the usually silent Thomas rambled on at a February 13 speech to the American Enterprise Institute about attacks on him for refusing to conform to majority opinion and for being conservative and outspoken, revealing a garrulously whining and self-pitying dimension to the justice who never speaks up in court and always votes conservatively. While the five majority conservative partisan Supreme Court justices will be remembered by many as election thieves, the four justices who voted against the conservative majority will be remembered by many as Heroes of Democracy and celebrities of justice, and perhaps their impassioned polemical briefs for democracy and against the partisan majority will ironically redeem the image of the Court that the majority so dishonored and besmirched.

Likewise, the four justices on the Florida Supreme Court who ordered the recount will be remembered by some as Heroes of Democracy and by others as partisan liberal Democrats.[14] N. Sander Sauls will be remembered by many as a bumbling and provincial conservative judge who stalled efforts to recount the votes and then offered a harsh ruling against Gore that was ungrounded in law and quickly challenged, but that, in retrospect, tipped the election. In fact, the judiciary at all levels may be seen for decades as a highly partisan institution, an instrument of raw political power. The attack on the partisanship of the Florida Supreme Court by Baker, Bush, and others can be read as part of a conservative effort to delegitimate public institutions that block their will, and it is ironic that it was precisely the judiciary that came to their rescue after the Republican theft of the presidency was put in peril by the Florida Supreme Courts.

Yet, if efforts by the Republican Party and Bush machine in Florida to manipulate the vote, the counting, and the blocking of recounting and counting of the never-counted ballots are as scandalous as many believe, and if the legal system prosecutes alleged crimes and the media publicizes them, it could be that the judiciary and the media will emerge again as Heroes of Democracy, the uncoverers and undoers of political scandal and corruption. On the other hand, if major scandals materialize from Election 2000 that threaten the Bush machine coup, one can look for a conservative attack on the media and judiciary to follow.

One striking and often replayed image of George W. Bush, who lay low during much of the presidential war, is his first appearance after election night: a scared, frightened man with a bandage over an alleged boil on his face, his nose and cheeks red and splotchy. Bush looked as though he could not deal with pressure and as though he was out of his element and over his head. Throughout the battle for the White House, this political figurehead of the Republican conservatives avoided the political stage and battlefield, as James Baker, Dick Cheney, and his political operatives ran the show, calling him on the phone to report on progress or setbacks. It was reported that W. did not even have cable or satellite television at his ranch in Crawford, Texas, where he sought refuge from the pressures. And the London *Economist* suggested that Bush's ranch and escape be titled "The Lazy W" (December 15).

Bush was obviously disconnected from the whole process, appearing, in

Thomas Patterson's words, as "a callow youth allowed to serve as front man—a dauphin in a restoration monarchy," with the grown-ups running the show as the immature boy goes off to play. Patterson noted that it was disconcerting every day to hear that Bush was in a gym engaged in a three-hour workout when Jim Baker, Al Gore, and the rest of the adult political class were watching Supreme Court deliberations and engaging in the intense political combat going on in many fronts. For Patterson, "The clearest impression to have emerged of Bush these past weeks is of an exercise fanatic—a man who has replaced his much-documented earlier addiction to alcohol with a fitness compulsion" (*Boston Globe*, December 15).

For his critics, it appeared that Bush is almost completely scripted and controlled by others, that powerful conservatives run his operation, and that he is but a front man and puppet for powerful social forces including the friends of his father and Dick Cheney, James Baker, and other hardright conservatives. Indeed, Bush is arguably the most managed U.S. politician since Ronald Reagan; every move and word were scripted by his handlers, who perfected the daily routine of photo opportunities, soundbites, and media spectacles to dramatize his major policies and goals (see Hertsgaard 1988 and Kellner 1990). Yet Reagan had a core of firm beliefs and principles to which he was long committed, and there were limits to what he would say and do, thus his handlers had to manage him carefully and work with his political ideology to make him a competent actor for the conservative Republican agenda. George W. Bush, by contrast, seems to have few convictions, or principles, and it appears that he will say and do whatever his handlers tell him.[15] And while Bush, like Reagan, appears likable and able to connect with audiences, he is even more unpredictable than Reagan and emerges as a loose cannon who may shoot anyone, including himself, in the foot or worse at any time.[16]

Thus, for many, the image of George W. Bush that emerged from the spectacle of the postelection hostilities is that of a puppet of the forces who produced his soundbites and stage-managed his few public appearances. By contrast, for conservatives Bush emerges as The Winner and as the repository of Republican Party hopes. Winning is the great prize of American culture and politics, and whoever wins the big ones—the Super Bowl, the World Series, the Oscars, and the presidency—is afforded the honors and awards that a highly competitive society can bestow. Winning is the American religion, and winners are the deities and idols of spectacle culture. By winning, Bush joined Clinton (the great survivor), Michael Jordan, Bill Gates, and others as the Icons of Victory, the victors of the passion play of the great American game of competition.

Yet in the blood sport of the increasingly vicious and partisan terrain of American politics, winning sets one up for losing, and in the acrid aftermath of the battle for the White House it was far from certain that Bush would succeed and survive. To many, it appeared he was simply not qualified for the job. The postelection combat was Bush's first real political crisis, and his retreat to the ranch and from the public sphere during much of the thirty-six days raised questions about whether he had the skills, mettle, and fortitude to handle the problems and crises that were sure to arise.

Al Gore, by contrast, seemed able to deal with crisis; he was a micromanager fully engaged in the intense struggle for the presidency. He appeared mature and seasoned, while George W. Bush appeared immature and not yet ready for prime time. Of course, Bush's handlers would carefully engage in image management to repair the damage to his public perception suffered in his disengagement from the marathon postelection battle, and it remains to be seen if he will mature and grow from the traumatic process that obviously had overwhelmed him.[17]

On the other hand, Gore had emerged The Loser, and U.S. politics and culture celebrate winning and abhor losing. *Time* magazine chose George W. Bush as Man of the Year in its December 25 issue, having determined that it would present its coveted award to the candidate who won the White House. Consequently, despite his razor-thin and highly problematic victory, Bush joined Adolf Hitler and Joseph Stalin in the pantheon of *Time* Men of the Year. In the aftermath of Election 2000, Bush would assume the Mantle of Winner and Gore would be assigned the dismal category of Loser, forced to endure endless speculation concerning whether his career in U.S. politics was over.

But for some Democratic partisans, Al Gore, Joe Lieberman, and their troops will be remembered as fighters for democracy. For those on the other side, by contrast, the Democrats' politicians and lawyers will appear as heavies in a drama where the sneaky liberals tried to steal the presidency from their candidate. Likewise, Gore was a repository of major sympathy and support by many during the struggle for the presidency, but the fact that he ultimately lost the tussle means that his leadership of the Democratic Party will be contested by those who would like the plum that he was unable to pluck; hence, his symbolic and actual political fortunes are indeterminate.[18]

Other images may appear more complex. Dick Cheney, as raw and brutal a political operator as there is, escaped this harsher image because of his heart attack, which softened his image and made him sympathetic to the public. Yet the heart attack and images of a fragile Cheney emerging from the hospital also weakened him as a figure of strong and decisive political power and threatened the conservative hegemony with the loss of one of its more effective players. Cheney and his wife are longtime conservative activists, and it was clear during the postelection combat and Bush transition that Cheney was a major player, overshadowing the inexperienced and largely absent Bush. Whether Cheney's health will allow him to maintain this key power position and whether his hardright politics will make him a target of critique and conservative partisanship remain to be seen, although, as noted above, in the transition period he has emerged as what many see as the central figure in the Cheney–Bush administration.

Certain resonant representations also linger in the collective media pool of epochal images from the postelection spectacle and linger in the minds of those who watched and experienced the events. The juxtaposition of ordinary people attempting the difficult task of counting the uncounted ballots in Florida on December 9 with the televised images of the U.S. Supreme Court justices who halted the counting provides a condensed allegory of two conceptions of democracy and sovereignty, one participatory and rooted in popular sovereignty, and the other institutional, grounding sovereignty in the biased and partisan chambers of the U.S. Supreme Court, signaling to many an illegitimate presidency and theft of democracy by a powerful ruling elite.

The main questions are: What images from the battle for the White House will resonate in the media, the public mind, and within individual voters' consciousness? and Will distressing images and anger produce a backlash against the Republicans? It is possible that voters will remember the theft of Election 2000 with resentment and will eventually punish the Republicans for their infamy, or else passively accept it, forget the contentious conditions of the Republican coup, and vote them back in as winners. It is possible that Bush's coup d'état has wrecked the Republican Party for the foreseeable future, or positioned the Republicans to control the presidency and Congress into the new millennium, enabling them to push through a militantly conservative agenda. While there is no evidence yet of Republicans facing major guilt or defections, or the public turning against the Republicans in serious numbers, the U.S. political situation is volatile and the future, as always, is uncertain. If conflicts around the Bush administration multiply, and if Bush himself stumbles and makes serious mistakes, there is bound to be a backlash that will cost the Republicans heavily in future battles for democracy.

NOTES

1. Statistics used in this discussion draw on the initial analysis of voters' preferences in the *Washington Post* (see Thomas B. Edsall, "Analysis: Bush Cut into Democratic Coalition," *Washington Post*, Nov. 8, 2000); the November 13, 2000, *Newsweek* and Simon 2001: 293f.

2. See Paul Zielbauer, "Doubt over Election Outcome Spurs Plans for Change," *New York Times* (Nov. 26, 2000). Also see the articles by former conservative, now independent Arianna Huffington (*Los Angeles Times*, Nov. 14, B9). I remember repeatedly asking political scientists at the University of Texas why the obsolete voting system in the United States was never reformed and brought up-to-date, and they explained that the mainstream establishment was never really interested in registering the will of the people and was indeed chary about the potential results. Election 2000 dramatically demonstrated the dirty little secret of the political obsolescence of the U.S. voting system, how it is bent to serve the interests of wealthier voting districts and dominant parties.

3. On the MIT and Cal-Tech project, see the *Los Angeles Times* (Dec. 16, 2000, B1), and on the rush to retool in the voting machine industry, see "Armed to Send Chads into Voting Oblivion" (http://www.nytimes.com/2000/12/17/technology/17ELEC.html). The MIT/Cal-Tech preliminary report was released February 5, 2001 and is available on-line at www.vote.caltech.edu. One imagines that scientists would want to design a better voting system in light of the U.S. technological embarrassment and that corporations would want to produce and market improved voting technology. It remains to be seen if conservative politicians will show enthusiasm for reforming the voting process when such reform could contribute to their demise.

4. In a fine *Columbia Journalism Review* study, "Voting Technology: Who Knew?" (Jan.–Feb. 2001), Stephen J. Simurda documents the scandalous history of the failures of the punch-card machines, the studies criticizing them, their susceptibility to error and manipulation, and a list of other problems with the machines. According to Simurda, there were only two major newspaper stories on the failures of the machines prior to the election, and the author urges local journalists to publicize the scandalous malfunctioning of punch-card voting technology.

5. Hillary Clinton, senator-elect from New York, was the first to propose an overhaul of the Electoral College system, the day after the dead-heat election of November 7, and other major politicians have come out to support commissions that would investigate problems with the current voting system and propose solutions. Many others have warned against tampering too quickly with the Electoral College. It will be interesting to see if reforms develop from the current debacle, or if the serious shortcomings of the current presidential voting system, difficult for foreigners and many Americans to understand, will be allowed to continue.

6. See Jim Hightower's proposals for Electoral College reform at www.alternet.org. In his December 4 online netcast, Howard Kurtz noted that Gore would have won the

Electoral College if every state received electoral votes in proportion to population: "Bush won 30 states for 271 and Gore won 21 for 267. But if you take away the two electors for each senator, and just apportion electors by number of Representatives (i.e., in proportion to population), Gore wins 225 to 211" (http://www.washington-post.com/wpsrv/liveonline/00/politics/media backtalk120400.htm).

7. On the history of efforts to reform television advertising, see Charles Lewis, "You Get What You Pay For: How Corporate Spending Blocked Political Ad Reform & Other Stories of Influence" (Schechter 2001: 62–73) and the Alliance for Better Campaigns, "Gouging Democracy: How the Television Industry Profiteered on Campaign 2000," in Schechter 2001 (77–92). In another important article in Schechter (2001: 75), Lawrence K. Grossman notes that one of broadcasting's "dirty little secrets" is its sustained and high-priced lobbying against finance reform."

8. I am writing this as a political critic and not as a partisan for the Democrats. I myself would support developing an independent thirty-party movement and am for progressive social movements as key vehicles of change. Such movements, however, should pursue a politics of alliance and solidarity and be ready to support Democratic Party candidates in certain crucial elections, and they should avoid becoming chumps for the Republicans and conservative corporate interests. Interestingly, Roger Simon notes conservative fear that Election 2000 evidenced a swing to the left with a liberal-moderate majority (2001: 295f.).

9. See Richard T. Cooper, "A Different Florida Vote, in Hindsight," *Los Angeles Times* (Dec. 24, 2000, A1, A12), which describes the behind-the-scene pressures on the Gore and Bush legal teams and some crucial mistakes that the Gore team made in not going for a statewide recount, in not accepting Katherine Harris's proposal that all of the legal issues being adjudicated in local Florida courts be sent to the Florida Supreme Court (that, according to the story, made the Bush camp "livid" and that the Gore camp turned down because it thought that this was a Harris/Bush trick), and by insisting that December 12 was the legitimate deadline to conclude the counting process.

10. That December 12 had no legal status as a deadline for state vote tallies to be included in the December 18 Electoral College vote was convincingly argued in articles in *Salon* (Dec. 11, 2000) and in the *New York Times* (Dec. 20, 2000).

11. There were hearings on the purging of the voting list in the civil rights violations of African American inquiries after the election, and Palast published a long account of his investigations in *The Nation* (Feb. 5, 2001). He also participated in a fifteen-minute BBC segment on the Bush–Harris voting list purge, the transcript of which circulated through the Internet, receiving tens of thousands of hits, according to a later story where Palast notes how CBS planned a segment on the incidents, then dropped the story; see "Silence of the Lambs: The Election Story Never Told," mediachannel. org (Feb. 28, 2001). The failure of U.S. media to thoroughly investigate the Bush/Harris DBT voter scrubbing scandal and countless other examples of irregularities in the Florida election discloses the shamelessly conformist state of mainstream media

journalism in the United States. The fact that Democrats have not pursued these and other issues in the postelection era disclosed how they let Republicans beat up on them by not pursuing important and legitimate issues. A study by Pulitzer Prize–winning journalist John Lantigua, "How the GOP Gamed the System in Florida" (*The Nation* [April 30, 2001]), investigated the Florida state program of "scrubbing" alleged felons off of the Florida voting lists, the complicity of Jeb Bush administration officials, and the wrongs committed in the project. Building on Palast's research into Florida's voter list "scrubbing" program, Lantiqua concluded that "some 200,000 Floridians were either not permitted to vote in the November 7 election on questionable or possibly illegal grounds, or saw their ballots discarded and not counted. A large and disproportionate number were black." Lantiqua argues that the DBT/Choicepoint computer program that eliminated suspected felons from voting lists was part of a systematic Republican program to target black voters and that it was Florida state Republican officials who asked DBT to "use its national databases to provide the names of felons from other states who might have moved to Florida and registered." As it turns out, other states had restored their voting rights. Lantiqua also provides further documentation of how defective voting machines in predominantly black and poor districts, ill-informed precinct workers, and confusion and harassment at polling places blocked thousands from voting. See also the U.S. Commission on Civil Rights report *Probe of Election Practices in Florida during the 2000 Presidential Election* (www.usccr.gov/vote2000/flmain.htm), which I discuss in chapter 11.

12. See the documentation in Tamala M. Edwards, "O Brother, Where Art Thou?" http://www.salon.com/politics/feature/2000/12/19/gore/index.html.

13. In particular, Ralph Nader and his supporters were remarkably quiet during the aftermath of the election and the thirty-six days of battle for the White House, and it is not clear if there will be a long-term schism between his supporters and Gore supporters, or if the groups could form a progressive alliance. It is also not clear if Nader helped to unify the progressive community or if his candidacy did not ultimately divide and marginalize the left. No doubt, there will be much discussion of these topics, but, so far, they have not entered the mainstream media spectacle that I am interrogating in this study.

14. The *New York Times* (Dec. 20, 2000) reported that already campaigns are under way to unseat the judges who voted for the recount. One of the Florida Supreme Court justices, Henry Anstead, will stand for reelection in 2002, and reportedly Florida Republicans are undertaking efforts to replace him. On the other hand, Florida Democrats are geared up to take on and take out Jeb Bush and his Republican establishment. One imagines that Florida politics will be intense partisan battleground for years to come.

15. The Reagan team also had to deal with the strong-willed and opinionated Nancy Reagan, who was highly protective of her husband, wielded considerable power, and was a force to reckon with. Insiders of the Reagan administration later confessed this in their memoirs. One insider, Don Regan, came into conflict with the imperious

Nancy and sought revenge by telling the story of how her astrology reader dictated Reagan's travel schedule. It appears that Bush's handlers have no constraints on his thought and behavior and that he will say and do whatever he is told.

16. In what might be a Freudian slip, after a meeting with congressional leaders in Washington, D.C., on December 18, 2000, Bush noted, "I am mindful of the difference between the executive branch and the legislative branch. I assured all four of these leaders that I know the difference, and that difference is they pass the laws and I execute them." The first words out of Bush's mouth after his first meeting on Capitol Hill with congressional leadership are also worth citing: "If this were a dictatorship, it'd be a whole heck of a lot easier, heh-heh heh-heh heh, just so long as *I'm* the dictator, heh-heh heh huh heh-heh!" This witticism led Tamara Baker to label Bush as the "Butt-Head" of U.S. politics, as in the MTV cartoon *Beavis and Butt-Head* (http://www.american-politics.com/20001219ButtHead.html). For an extensive archive of Bushisms that will no doubt continue to grow by leaps and bounds, see http://slate.msn.com/Features/bushisms/bushisms.asp and Miller 2001.

17. Writing the morning after Bush's February 27, 2001, budget speech to Congress, Steven Johnson warns in *Feed* of "the dangers of underestimating Dubya" and focusing critique on his perceived stupidity and obvious mangling of the English language rather than on opposing his policies and actions. See http://www.feedmag.com/templates/default.php3?a id = 1635.

18. Not surprisingly, when Lieberman was announced as Gore's running mate, there was a deluge of anti-Semitic literature and comments on the margins of U.S. political culture, and there was speculation that choosing a Jewish vice presidential candidate could harm Gore's prospects with the electorate. I have yet to read any studies of whether Lieberman helped or harmed Gore in the election, although during the postelection battle Lieberman received positive media coverage and was a forceful advocate for the Democrats. Thus, I am suggesting that Lieberman has ascended into the high echelons of political celebrity, along with the Clintons, Cheneys, Bushes, and Gore.

11

AFTERMATH

*People would submit to slavery, provided that they were
respectfully assured that they still enjoyed their ancient
freedom.*

—Edward Gibbon, *The Decline and Fall
of the Roman Empire*

They misunderestimated me.

—George W. Bush

George W. Bush was inaugurated forty-third president of the United States
on January 20, 2001, greeted with miserable weather and tens of thousands of demonstrators. Although the 700,000-plus protestors earlier forecast
in a *Washington Post* (December 22) article failed to materialize, a diverse
range of groups assembled in front of the Supreme Court, in parks near the
parade route, and along the itinerary itself, greeting Bush with jeers and boos,
a rotten egg splattering on the window of the presidential car, and signs that
read "Hail to the Thief!" and "Bush Stole It." Protest was so spirited that
Bush's motorcade was held up for five minutes at one point, and he was not
able to get out and walk until the final leg where all the spectators were paid
Republicans who had bought prime seats.

The days before the inauguration were dramatic with revelations concerning
Bush's designated secretary of labor, Linda Chavez, and her illegal employ-
ment of an undocumented worker from Central America. Chavez had allowed
a Guatemalan woman to live in her house and serve as a maid, while failing to
pay her, thus forcing Chavez to withdraw her nomination. There were also
Internet rumors that the Jeb Bush–Katherine Harris liaison would be uncovered in national tabloids just before the inauguration, but instead Tabloid

Nation was treated to banner stories of Jesse Jackson's lovechild and mistress, causing Jackson to temporarily retreat from politics and to cancel participation in a voting rights rally in Tallahassee on inauguration day.

In the days leading up to Bush's coronation by Justice Rehnquist, who had helped seize the presidency for Bush, Bill Clinton cut a deal with the special prosecutor, pleaded guilty to lying in the Lewinsky affair, and was pardoned from further judicial inquisition (at least by the "special" prosecutor). Clinton then pardoned a long list of friends, supporters, allies, and others, leading to a torrent of criticism, especially concerning his pardon of financier Marc Rich, whose ex-wife had contributed to Clinton's campaign.

In fact, the Bush propaganda machine and the full array of Clinton haters continued their daily assaults on the ex-president, attacking his pardons, gifts he'd received in the White House, his proposed New York office building, and allegations that his staff had trashed the White House after leaving office. The Bush slander patrol also alleged Clinton's people had stolen items from Air Force One on the trip to New York, which appeared for sale on the Internet shortly thereafter. These stories were headlined in the press and endlessly dissected on talk radio, television, and the Internet, overshadowing Bush's early days in the White House. Put in context, it appeared that the stories of White House vandalism were greatly exaggerated, the claim of theft on Air Force One was pure disinformation, Clinton's gifts were not significantly larger than those of Reagan and Bush senior, and, bowing to pressure, Clinton negotiated an office suite in Harlem.[1] There were, however, continued investigations of Clinton's pardons, especially Marc Rich, and Senator Arlen Specter darkly hinted that this deed could win Clinton a retrospective "impeachment," while others threatened legal consequences.

Bush's spin and smear specialist, Karl Rove, was well known in Texas politics for his whispering campaigns to tarnish opponents, and it was clear that the Bush public relations strategy was to tar Clinton and his administration to the maximum so that the Bush crew would look good by comparison. Bush's White House would leak rumors to friendly journalists, or those managing rightwing Web sites such as the Drudge Report, and the stories would quickly circulate and be taken up by the mainstream media; there would then be days of impassioned discussion, and eventually reputable newspapers such as the *New York Times* would publish stories deflating claims, for example, that the departing Clintonites trashed the White House or took mementos from Air Force One. Reporters looking into Clinton's last days in the White House did not find that he took any more gifts or objects from the White House than his predecessors, and W. himself was forced to concede that there was no truth to the rumor that the Clintons had stolen items from Air Force One on their last trip. But the damage had been done, and the Bushites were able to present themselves as a "clean" and virtuous contrast to the departing Clinton administration.

HARDRIGHT

It's clearly a budget. It's got a lot of numbers on it. —George W. Bush

It was clear from the get-go that the Cheney–Bush team was pursuing a hardright conservative agenda, spearheaded by some of the extreme policies that Bush had soft-pedaled in his election campaign, such as a national missile defense system and war on environmental regulation. His most deeply felt and key proposal, however, was to cut taxes, and in a moment of exuberance he increased his proposed cut from $1.3 trillion to $1.6 trillion. While economic czar Alan Greenspan, the Ayn Rand enthusiast who many believe runs the U.S. economy, was at first reluctant to support big tax cuts and stressed the importance of continuing to pay off the deficit, he eventually endorsed the tax cut. As the hogs gathered to feed in the federal trough, the main conflict was over how much taxes would be cut and who would get the most public wealth.[2]

The process recalled the first big Reagan tax cut when David Stockman, budget director, began devising across-the-board tax cuts for individuals, ending with a corporate greedfest that sent the national debt and interest rates soaring. Later, Stockman recalled, "The hogs were really feeding. The greed level, the level of opportunism just got out of control."[3] Indeed, in pondering Bush's brazen tax give-away-to-the-rich program, one might recall the effects of the Reagan tax cut, which helped raise unemployment and interest rates, while the stock market declined and the federal deficit soared.

The first Bush family scandal emerged on February 10, 2001, when it was announced that a Navy submarine "practicing emergency ascent" hit a Japanese fishing boat used to train students, killing nine. It was reported and confirmed by video footage that fifteen civilians were aboard the sub, and although the Navy at first refused to release their names, it was discovered that the group comprised largely Bush supporters who had contributed heavily to his campaign. Some of the civilians aboard were also members of a group headed by Bush's father that was raising money to restore the U.S. battleship *Missouri*, on which Japan surrendered at the end of World War II. It was also later reported that the civilians were at the controls of the sub when it was performing the fatal "maneuver," that the civilians had distracted the crew, and that the ascent was not really an approved military test, but a procedure to entertain the visitors. Japan was further outraged when on April 2, a U.S. nuclear submarine appeared unannounced in a Japanese port, violating an understanding between the countries. Eventually, the U.S. profusely apologized to the Japanese, and will no doubt pay millions of taxpayers' money to amend for the crime, but the crew was let off without a court-martial or harsher punishment, although senior members were disciplined.

These embarrassing stories started to circulate and replace Clinton scandal stories. Wagging the dog,[4] Bush bombed Iraq on February 16, attacking five Iraqi radar and military sites near Baghdad. Although Bush called the assault "a routine mission," Secretary of State Colin Powell admitted a few days later that the undertaking was "more aggressive" than the usual bombing retaliation and that he was surprised over the clamor against the strikes in the Arab world where he was visiting. The British press saw the bombing as a "tribal" attempt in "settling his father's old scores" and warned Britain against getting involved in Bush family adventurism (*Independent*, February 18, 2001). The Pentagon eventually admitted, however, that most of the bombs missed their mark.

By mid-March 2001, it was clear that there were fierce power struggles in Bush's White House, invariably resolved by the most conservative line that Cheney supported. Secretary of State Colin Powell declared that U.S. policy would "pick up where President Clinton left off" on talks with North Korea, while Bush stated flatly that he had no intentions of negotiations with Pyongyang. Similarly, Secretary Powell stated that he supported streamlined sanctions against Iraq that would get UN weapons inspections under way again, but Cheney expressed doubts about these policies, and conservatives talked openly about taking a hard line and getting rid of Saddam Hussein.

Consequently, a hardright foreign policy reminiscent of Cold War tension at its highest emerged in Bush's first fifty days as president. In the opening weeks, Bush bombed Iraq and heightened tensions in the Middle East, threatened China, told Russia to expect reduced aid, worried much of Europe with his insistent approach to national missile defense (NMD), and made clear that he does not intend to pursue constructive negotiations with North Korea—an alleged missile threat that if reduced would question the Bush administration's harebrained missile plan. Thus, the world has returned to the hard-line Cold War paranoid universe of the military-industrial complex warned about by a departing Dwight Eisenhower, while Dr. Strangelove is alive and well in the U.S. Defense Department, concocting Star Wars missile systems that will cost trillions of dollars and have yet to be proved functional.

Bush, Cheney, and Secretary of Defense Donald Rumsfeld had also resurrected the dangerous concept of "rogue state," a concept retired by the Clinton administration, that was sure to increase tensions and the possibility of war. The dangers of the aggressive new Bush foreign policy were soon evident. On March 24, the *Washington Post* published a report that Bush had a meeting two days before with Defense Secretary Rumsfeld who was preparing a report that China had supplanted the USSR as its Number 1 Enemy and should be the focus of U.S. military policy. Some days later, an "accident" occurred when a Chinese plane and U.S. spy plane off the Chinese coast collided, and the U.S. plane, loaded with high-tech surveillance equipment and the latest military computers, made a crash landing on a Chinese off-shore island and the crew was held hostage for eleven tense days as the crew's release was negotiated.

The resulting crisis made clear the consequences of how militarist Bush administration policy and aggression toward perceived "enemies" had created a climate of hostility that could explode at any time into crisis and war. During the initial weekend of meet-the-press offensives by the Bush administration, they put out their more moderate spokespeople like Powell and National Security Adviser Condoleeza Rice to explain the administration position to the media and public. Bush, incurring the wrath of the frothing right of his party, was forced to lose face and apologize for the death of the Chinese pilot.

The day after the crews' release, a highly agitated Secretary of Defense Rumsfeld was let out of the cage to emote against China. Rumsfeld was extremely agitated during a press conference in which he attacked the Chinese. His hand gesturing wildly, his foot tapping ferociously, the Strangelovian defense secretary put on display the conservative rage pulsating through his body, wanting to go nuclear. A couple of days later, Strangelove "ordered the suspension of military exchanges and contacts with the Chinese armed forces," and then abruptly reversed the order the next day "after the White House objected, Pentagon officials said" (*New York Times*, May 3, 2001). There are obviously deep divisions within the Bush administration over defense and foreign policy between the hardright and the harder right.[5]

Bush's top-level appointments to foreign policy positions included a who's who of rightwing zealots with a healthy dose of Iran-Contra scoundrels who were friends of his father. Richard Armitage, a close friend of Bush senior, who like the father was heavily involved in Iran-Contra, was nominated as deputy secretary of state, putting a fierce interventionist and Cold Warrior high in the State Department. Armitage has an unusually colorful history and it was quite a shock to see him return to power. During the Vietnam era he was reputed to be involved in the Phoenix assassination program, in which the U.S. systematically assassinated Vietnamese villagers believed to be associated with the Vietcong—former Senator Bob Kerrey admitted his participation in such atrocities but the media failed to make the connection with the Phoenix program and Armitage. The Phoenix program was rumored to be partially funded with drug sales and there were persistent rumors linking Armitage with drug rings and then shady arms dealers in the 1970s—his connections with drug and arms networks emerged again in the bizarre Iran-Contra operation in the 1970s and, guess what!, here we go again (on Armitage, see http://prore v.com/bush3.htm).

For UN ambassador, Bush nominated John Negroponte, a former ambassador to Honduras who was heavily involved in covert operations in the illegal war against the Sandinistas and has been accused of directing contra activities in Honduras and suppressing information about the Honduran military's civil rights violations and involvement in the drug trade. For assistant secretary of state for the Western Hemisphere, Bush nominated longtime anti-Castro Cuban American Otto Reich, who was also highly active in the contra war as head of the "Office for Public Diplomacy," a propaganda wing of the government for the contras. Reich has a long list of unsavory connections and there were predictions that his nomination would be blocked (*The Nation*, May 7, 2001; on Negroponte, see "Cold War Stalks Bush's U.N. Pick," *Los Angeles Times*, May 7, 2001).

John Bolton, a relentless critic of arms control, was named by Bush as undersecretary of state for arms control and international security. Jesse Helms endorsed the candidate as "the kind of man with whom I would want to stand at Armageddon" (*Boston Globe*, April 2, 2001), a statement not likely to calm those worried about nuclear war. Those concerned about the effects of genetically engineered foods and biotechnology were not cheered when Bush appointed a Monsanto executive, a leading developer of biotech foods, for the second-ranking job at the Environmental Protection Agency, letting in the foxes again to guard the hen-house. And to properly award his Supreme Court Godfathers, Bush responded to the Scalia–Rehnquist coup by appointing Eugene Scalia, Don Scalia's son, as solicitor of labor, the top legal position at the Department of Labor, while Janet Rehnquist, the Chief Executioner's daughter, was nominated to be inspector general of the Department of Health and Human Services. No subtlety or false decorum for the brazen Bush syndicate, ruled by the law of properly greased hands.

As for Bush administration embassy appointments, *USA Today* (May 4, 2001) reported that "Bush is rewarding Republican donors and loyalists with plum ambassadorships at an unprecedented pace. Of 27 ambassadors announced so far, 22 went to people with political or personal connections and no diplomatic experience." Thus, while appointment to an ambassadorship usually requires an advanced degree in international studies, fluency in one or more foreign languages, expertise in the history and culture of a region, years of experience in the foreign service, and proven diplomatic ability, in Bush's case it was buds and campaign contributors who got the plums. Major GOP donors who received ambassadorships include Richard Egan, who contributed $491,100 and was nominated ambassador to Ireland; Charles Heimbold Jr. contributed $367,200 and was awarded Sweden; and John Palmer got Portugal for $167,850. Howard Leach, a San Francisco investment banker who put up $282,000 for Bush and other Republicans last year, was rewarded with France (une scandale: le mec ne parle pas français!). Leach also was one of W.'s "pioneers"—the insider group of corporate fat cats who collected at least $100,000 for his campaign.

Bush was also considering awarding ambassadorships to two of his buddies who had supported his major business ventures, helping bail Bush out of failure in the oil business when his company went bust in 1984 and then helping to raise money so that Bush and associates could buy the Texas Rangers baseball team. Former business partner Mercer Reynolds was nominated as ambassador to Switzerland and while it was rumored that biz bud and baseball team owner William DeWitt would also be offered an ambassadorship, Dewitt reportedly said that "he has no intention of following his business partner into striped-pants service for his old pal George W. Bush" (*St. Louis Post-Dispatch*, March 22, 2001).

On the domestic front, Bush's chief of staff, Andrew Card, announced that Bush was phasing out offices for AIDS policy and race relations, but the resulting uproar forced the new administration to backtrack and retract. Bush then called for cutting off aid for birth control and prenatal counseling for women in developing countries, throwing red ideological meat to his salivating anti-abortion fanatics. He next overturned "ergonomic regulation reform" that Clinton had signed, to the great joy of business but to the dismay of labor, and put into jeopardy funding for Advanced Technology, a research-and-development fund for high-tech. To assure continuation of the Clinton wars, Bush's attorney general, John Ashcroft, undertook steps to harass Clinton with investigations of every one of his 177 pardons. On March 16, Bush's legal advisers told the American Bar Association that they wanted to end the group's role as a semiofficial screening panel for judicial nominees, and they geared up to pack the judiciary with hard-core conservatives recommended by the ultraconservative legal group the Federalist Society. Just as on legal issues the har-dright Federalist Society emerged as highly influential, it was clear that the conservative Independent Women's Forum was serving as the most powerful force on women's issues. Its project was to attack feminist organizations and cut back the Violence Against Women Act and efforts to help girls in schools, claiming that it is boys, not girls, who are shortchanged in education. The national advisory board of the foundation is headed by rightwing ideologue Christina Hoff Sommers and includes Labor Secretary Elaine Chao, Linda Chavez, and Lynne Cheney as member-emerita. Many members of the organi-zation have entered the Bush administration and others are under consider-ation. The Bush administration also closed the White House Women's Office of Initiatives and Outreach, signaling an intention to undo the progress made for women during the Clinton period. The office had encouraged all women, regardless of party affiliation, to participate in government and had encouraged programs that would benefit women.[6]

With divisiveness accelerating over Bush's "faith-based" aid program, key senators attacked Bush's plan to channel more government money to charities, a plan that had religious groups and secularists alike up in arms. On March 13, Bush broke a promise to cut carbon dioxide emissions standards from power plants, a pledge that would have addressed growing global warming but that Bush's supporters in the power industry and conservatives opposed. The next day, Bush called for expanded drilling rights under national monuments, providing another boon to his oil-biz contributors. Bush also declared himself against stem cell research, which would use cells from human fetuses to attempt to find cures for intractable diseases such as cancer and Alzheimer's and which his secretary of health and human services and the entire scientific community support.

On March 20, Bush stopped implementation of new rules scheduled to reduce the level of arsenic in drinking water, returning to regulations adopted in 1942 that allow what is now perceived as a dangerous level of arsenic in drinking water. In another concession to the mining industry, the Bush administration suspended tougher standards for hardrock miners digging for gold and silver on public lands and called for suspension of surface mining regulation that included forcing hardrock miners to post financial bonds guar-anteeing that they would clean up water and other environmental damage, leading one critic to claim that "The barbarians are no longer at the gates, the barbarians have taken over."

Revealing what "compassionate conservatism" and his pledge to "leave no child behind" meant in practice, Bush cut child care grants by $200 million, reduced spending on programs dealing with child abuse by $15.7 million, planned to eliminate the $20 million provided by Congress for improved child care and education for preschool children, and planned "to cut to the bone a $235 million program to train pediatricians and doctors at the nation's children's hospitals" (see http://www.salon.com/mwt/feature/2001/03/23/child cuts/index.html). On a hardright freefall, the Bush administration also dropped testing in school lunch programs for salmonella in ground beef, eliminating a program "that caught five million pounds of meat that had salmonella in it last year," and allowed schools to use irradiated beef that many believed to be dangerous (*New York Times,* April 5, 2001).

After a flurry of attacks on their war on the environment, the Bushites checked their focus-group and polling results, pulled back on environmental extremism, and just in time for Earth Day declared that they would follow some of the Clinton environmental regulations. But the message was clear that the Bush regime was paying off their big business contributors and were prepared to undo regulatory gains of the past decade. Big Oil had contributed millions, and the electric utility and coal-mining industries gave nearly $560,000 to Bush; he responded by refusing to put price caps on oil and energy prices, thus allowing these robber barons to gouge consumers with sky-high profits based on grotesque price hikes, which, if Bush's tax bill went through, would multiply their ill-gotten gain immensely. The forest-products industry contributed $300,000, and Bush responded by suspending new bans on road building and logging in national forests, and as he continued to produce policies favorable to his biggest contributors, it was clear that investment in the Bush machine would pay off.

Meanwhile, Bush continued to push his shameful $1.6 trillion giveaway where 1 percent of the country would reap around 39 percent of the benefits. Furthermore, it had become clear that Bush, traveling more than any president in history to sell his economic and military "plans," is not in charge, and when Dick Cheney had a heart attack in mid-March there was intense concern. Days later the stock market felt the panic, with the Dow falling below 10,000 for the first time in years while the NASDAQ continued to plunge, losing half of its wealth from its high of last year. Every sane economist has attacked Bush's $1.6 trillion tax-giveaway-to-the-rich, but the dumb son continued to pitch it to large audiences, who applauded lower tax bills as the U.S. economy carefully nurtured over the past decade of sane economics and political policies goes to hell.[7]

It was thus clear that Bush was putting out to the max for his corporate contributors who had funded his campaign. To the energy industry clients who had contributed so much to his election, Bush went back on his pledge to toughen CO_2 emission standards and was even brazen enough to suggest that national monuments in the U.S. National Park System be opened for energy exploration, that drilling underneath monuments is A-OK for the corporate Johns as long as they keep greasing Bush's palms. The credit card industry, which had contributed heavily to Bush's campaign, got its payback in mid-March when Congress approved stricter bankruptcy laws, making it easier for Bush's corporate buddies to seize homes and property of individuals not able to pay debts. And of course Bush's continual pushing of his tax cuts and deregulatory agenda showed that the Whore in Chief was prepared to do anything to please his high-paying clients.

In fact, Bushian politics is simple: You contribute X number of dollars and you get X dollars worth of favors; then you contribute XX dollars again so that the round of public theft of the federal coffers and government-supported extortion of consumers can begin anew to the enrichment of the Bush election team and his corporate-crook supporters. If you contribute enough money, like Kenneth Ray of Enron, you can call the head of the Federal Energy Regulatory Commission (FERC) to dictate policy so that the energy producers and middlemen can maximize their manipulation of supply and demand, extortion of markets, and continuing soaring profits at the expense of consumers and the states; if that doesn't work, you can call Dick Cheney to demand a new head of the energy agency to do your bidding. (This extortion scheme by the Cheney–Bush and Enron Robber Barons was exposed by a June 2001 PBS *Frontline*, "The California Energy Crisis.") The cycle of getting money from corporate contributors, giving them favors, and receiving more money to mobilize votes to win more elections, and then providing a new round of tax breaks for the rich, deregulation, and hardright policies could go on forever, ensuring brazen robbery of federal wealth, shameless pandering to corporate donors, and ever more whorish government in Washington.

The sluttish Bush has long been a for-sale kinda guy. As governor of Texas, he promiscuously consented to the demands of his major campaign contributors, resulting in the worst environmental record in the country, the gutting of state regulatory agencies, the depletion of the state surplus after distributing large tax breaks to the wealthiest sectors, and a bonanza of special favors to large benefactors. Bush's largesse to his corporate Johns often raised eyebrows, even in the corrupt Lone Star State, and in one case resulted in a full-scale scandal. In what has become known as Funeralgate, Bush tried to get his state regulators to lay off an investigation of Service Corporation International (SCI), whose CEO, Robert Waltrip was a longtime friend and contributor to

Bush's father who had also contributed to W.'s campaign. The head of the Texas Funeral Service Commission, Eliza May, however, undertook investigation of SCI's funeral homes, due to complaints about their shoddy service, including using unlicensed embalmers. May requested documents from the company, Waltrip went off in a rage to Austin where Bush, the CEO, and his chief of staff, Joe Allbaugh, met up and within an hour May received a message to call Allbaugh. May was asked by several of Bush's senior aides to call off the investigation; she persisted and fined SCI $450,000, but the company got a ruling in court from Bush's close ally, Attorney General John Cornyn, that dropped the fine. Shortly thereafter, May was fired; she sued, and questions are being raised about the extent of Bush's role in the case (see Dubose and Ivins 2000: 101–6).

On May 1, while the rest of the world had May Day celebrations and there was an unusual outbreak of antiglobalization protests, Congress passed the largest tax cut in over 20 years, a $1.3 trillion reduction, and Chimp smirked with satisfaction. The same day, the Resident-in-Thief announced that he was going ahead with his Star Wars missile defense program, which had already wasted $100 billion and would cost over $100 billion more over the next years. On May 2, W. triumphantly touted agreement on a budget plan, allowing federal spending to grow by 5 percent next year. Evidently, someone had forgotten to tell Boy George that Daddy had condemned the combination of a giant tax break for the rich, an increased federal budget, and mushrooming military spending as "voodoo economics," and that it just wasn't possible to do all at once. But once again the nation was engaged in debate over whether a never-tested missile defense system made sense, whether it was wise to declare the end of the ABM Treaty, and how the proliferation of new weapons could be paid for.

The common denominator, of course, is that the rich in general, and the Bush machine corporate and military-industrial complex friends in particular, would benefit hugely from the puppet's largess in federal give-aways, probably the largest and most irresponsible in history. And while Bush attacked Gore and the Clinton administration during the first presidential debate for renting out the Lincoln Bedroom in the White House to donors, Bush contributors who kick in at least $15,000 to a Republican campaign committee will be invited to the White House for a "private reception" and photo opportunity with Don Evans, secretary of commerce and Bush's previous campaign manager. Big donors also get meetings with Bush cabinet members and can buy "the exclusive opportunity to dine with diplomats and embassy officials." A donor can also buy time with influential GOP senators; for $5,000 "you can go play golf with Majority Leader Trent Lott next weekend in Hilton Head" (*Washington Post,* May 6, 2001).

There had been much Republican condemnation of the Clinton administration using the White House for fund-raising, so it was not surprising that there was a barrage of criticism in May 2001 when it was disclosed that Dick Cheney was using the vice presidential mansion for Republican fund-raising. As to why the Bush administration did not use the White House, NBC comic Jay Leno explained that Cheney "originally wanted to hold the party at the White House, but the donors that gave $100,000 . . . said, 'No, no! For the kind of money we're spending, we want to meet the top guy!' "

Thus, the Bush administration was aggressively pursuing hardright social policies to placate its conservative partisans, while providing its corporate supporters and contributors federal money, deregulation, and whatever other favors they had purchased from the Bushites. While rightwing commentators cluck-clucked about Clinton's pardons and hinted that they may have been purchased with donations or payoffs, they turned their back on the whoring carried out on an unprecedentedly brazen and shameless level by Bush, Cheney, and others for sale in the Bush brothel.

While the U.S. media went down on bended knee for Bush during his first 100 days in office, blistering attacks appeared in the global press. In the conservative *Times* of London (April 5, 2001), Anatole Kaletsky wrote a withering critique, arguing: "By simultaneously destabilising global security in China, Korea, the Middle East and Russia, by recklessly abrogating the Kyoto climate change treaty, by bullying his allies in Europe and Asia, by pursuing a tax policy that will turn America into the most unequal society in modern history, George W. Bush is fully living up to my expectation that he would become the worst U.S. President since Herbert Hoover." Polly Toynbee wrote in *The Guardian* (April 4, 2001):

> In his own inimitable words, let no one "misunderestimate" George W. Bush. He is the most rightwing president in living memory. If this is compassionate conservatism, what does the other sort look like? In less than 100 days he has turned America into a pariah, made enemies of the entire world, his only friends the dirty polluters of the oil industry who put him there. His foreign non-policy is a calamity, brilliantly uniting Russia and China with gratuitous offence and threat.

Der Spiegel in Germany presented a cover story on Bush as "the little sheriff," and referred to the Bush administration as "snarling, ugly Americans."

The French Foreign Minister said that the refusal of the Bush administration to abide by the Kyoto protocol is "not so much isolationist as unilateralist." And, showing righteous contempt for Bush administration arrogance and aggression, the UN booted the United States out of the UN Commission on Human Rights for the first time since its founding in 1947, and then took away the U.S. seat on an international drug monitoring body.

Attacking Bush's policies, misstatements, and comportment in office, Jonathan Freedland described the "Presidency of dunces" (*Guardian*, April 25, 2001), concluding that: "It is an appalling record, assembled in less than 14 weeks. What it amounts to is the wish list of the wealth wing of the Republican party, granted in full. Big business does not just have influence over this administration—it is this administration." One-upping his *Guardian* colleague, Henry Porter complained (May 6, 2001) that the reaction around the world to Bush's speech proclaiming that the Anti-Ballistic Missile Treaty of 1972 was no longer appropriate "contained a common element and that was indignation that the fragile structures and trust of the nuclear stand-off had been ended by a man with neither the intellect nor humility which this issue requires. Slim Shady and his chainsaw were now in charge of world peace."

The United States was now considered a rogue nation by much of the world. Bush's roguish State Department official Richard Armitage was bombarded by eggs in Korea and once again the "ugly American" was the image abroad of U.S. citizens, thanks to Bush administration unilateralist policy. Bush's refusal to honor the Kyoto Treaty and decades of antinuclear agreements led to criticisms that the United States was exhibiting "hostile isolationism," "great-power greed," and casting itself as an "unrepetent outlaw." A British Labour Party lawmaker called the Bush blast against nuclear arms agreements the "equivalent to launching a nuclear attack whose missiles will land across the globe over the next 30 years," and a variety of groups called for an international boycott of American products (*Los Angeles Times*, March 31, 2001).

During May 2001, the Bush administration warned U.S. citizens about the dangers of traveling abroad because of terrorism, unintentionally signaling the price paid for aggressive U.S. policy. On the home front, since Bush political adviser Karl Rove was a longtime shill for the tobacco industry, there was little likelihood that there would be tobacco protection for U.S. citizens. As energy and gas prices soared and California and other parts of the country faced energy blackouts, Cheney and Bush refused to curb prices or promote any meaningful energy policies, guaranteeing billions for their Robber Baron friends in the oil and energy industry, who would pocket billions more if the

Bush–Cheney tax cuts went through, threatening the viability of the U.S. economy.

One of the euphemisms of Bushspeak is the Resident-in-Thief's constant invocation, "I have a plan." In fact, Bush has no plans but to perform his soundbites of the day. The "plans" of the Bush administration are to rob the federal treasury and the people for rapacious robber barons—that includes their own friends, families, and corporate allies. Hence, when you hear Bush intone, "I have an energy plan," or "I have a missile defense plan," be aware that this is a plan concocted by Cheney, Rumsfeld, or others to rob billions, to enrich greedy corporations who in turn will be expected to contribute millions to Bush and the Republicans and to keep the merry cycle of robbery going until people wise up and see they are being ripped off and taken on a ride.

Cheney's "energy plan" amounted to unleashing the oil, gas, and energy industries' ability to increase production without consideration for environmental concerns, which enabled the government to take over private property to build plants and transmission, and which thus undid decades of environmental regulation, without meaningful concern for energy conservatism or alternative energy sources. The theft of federal resources, treasury, and people's wallets was in full swing by summer 2001, along with the hardright takeover of government. All of this was perfectly predictable, and had the media informed the public of the full thrust and destructiveness of the Bush–Cheney agenda it is likely that many voters would have not fallen for the "compassionate conservative," "uniter and not divider," and "new kind of Republican" Bushspeak with which the tawdry Texan sold his candidacy. But the Bush machine successfully stole the election and could now go on to rob the country.

By late May, it was clearly apparent that Bush was a divider and not a uniter, as Senator Jim Jeffords (R-Vt.) jumped parties, abandoning the hardright Republican blitzkrieg and providing ecstatic Democrats with the control of the Senate. Suddenly the Hardright Cheney–Bush Express encountered obstacles to stacking the courts with rabid conservatives, undoing environmental regulations of the past decades, creating a space-based missile system, and providing unlimited resources and favors to their corporate contributors while screwing everyone else. Most important, one of Bush's Big Lies was unraveling, in the exposure of his false claim that he had been able to work in Texas to bring Republicans and Democrats together to "get things done," and that he would do the same in a "bipartisan" fashion in Washington. In fact, in Texas Bush twisted the arms of conservative Democrats to go along with his hardright agenda and those who did not he ignored. In Washington Bush's plan was to pick up a couple of conservative Democrats for his hardright agenda, which required that all Senate Republicans stay on board the Far-right Express. When Jeffords and other moderates bulked, they were subject to ferocious attack, driving Jeffords to abandon the Republicans, with others threatening to leave.

Bush had also campaigned on "changing the tone in Washington," and after his first 100 days he repeatedly bragged about how he *had* changed the tone in Washington. In fact, Bush's administration began with blatant lies and personal attacks on departing Clinton staff members, who allegedly trashed the White House and Air Force One upon leaving office, setting up a propaganda frame that the unruly and immature Clintonites had left and that order and decorum had been returned to Washington with the arrival of the Bush administration. In fact, George W. Bush, Karl Rove, and other of Bush's political advisers are among the most vicious, vengeful, and uncivil in U.S. politics. Bush and Rove have a history in Texas of viciously going after their opponents, often with slime and lies, as in their successful campaign against Ann Richards (see Dubose and Ivins 2000). Bush/Rove were notorious in the Chotner/Atwateresque dirty lies slandering of John McCain in the South Carolina primaries where they leaked ugly stories that McCain was unbalanced as a result of his imprisonment in Vietnam, that he had betrayed Vietnam veterans, that his wife was an addict, and that they had a black child (they had indeed adopted a dark-skinned daughter whose picture was circulated in South Carolina; see Simon 2001: 109ff). When Jim Jeffords left this disgusting cabal of slimers after repeated attack and bullying, and threw the balance of power to the Democrats in the Senate, he was subjected to an unparalleled barrage of insults, vilification, and even threats on his life—behavior typical of the Bushites who had "raised the tone" and created a "more civilized" Washington.

It was also clear by May 2001 that Bushspeak was not only the rhetoric of campaigning (see chapter 9), but constituted Bush's mode of governmental discourse as well. Bushspeak involves blatant Big Lies and cooking statistics. As Princeton University economics professor and *New York Times* economic columnist Paul Krugman argues: the "fiscal predictions that enable Bush to pay for his tax cut and contingency fund are not mere errors but deliberate efforts to deceive the public. The Bush administration understands better than anyone that if its math were honest, its tax cut could never pass." Krugman argued that the Bush figures were misleading in terms of its budget projections for a surplus; the amount of money needed for meeting Social Security and

Medicare obligations; and the budgetary impact of the tax cut on the federal budget and paying off the deficit.[8]

Upon the May 26 passing of Bush's tax bill, Krugman minced no words, writing in an op-ed piece "The Big Lie" that

> Throughout the selling of this tax cut, its advocates have engaged in a disinformation campaign unprecedented in the history of U.S. economic policy—misrepresenting who would benefit from the plan (pretending that a tax cut mainly for the rich is actually aimed at the middle class) and understating its effects on revenue. Indeed, the pretense that taxes can be sharply cut without undermining the fiscal integrity of the nation has been maintained through a financial fakery that, if practiced by the executives of any publicly traded company would have landed them in jail. . . . This is white-collar crime, pure and simple. We should call in the Securities and Exchange Commission, and send the whole crew . . . to a minimum-security installation somewhere unpleasant. (May 27, *New York Times*)

Bush had derided Gore's tax cut that would most benefit low-income and middle-class families who needed tax breaks and would support energy-efficiency and other socially valuable ends as "only benefiting special people, only those they want to choose," while Bush's plan "would benefit everyone." In point of fact, Bush's tax scam pays off those upper-income people and corporations who the Bush gang chooses, although no one has yet figured out exactly who is going to benefit the most in what informed commentators have derided as the most confusing and gimmicky tax bill in memory. There is little doubt, however, that Bush's major contributors and allies have made sure that *they* are getting the breaks, that the benefits will go into their bank accounts, while the public is bamboozled and flim-flammed by Bushspeak and the Bush propaganda machine.

A study by the Citizens for Tax Justice reported that almost half of those in the bottom 60 percent of income earners will receive no tax rebates, while the top 20 percent of taxpayers will get the full promised rebate, with the top 1 percent getting the lion's share (*Washington Post*, May 31, 2001: A7). A *Business Week* commentator derided the bill's "gimmickry and false promises, describing it as "the most disappointing piece of tax legislation I've ever seen" (June 1, 2001). *USA Today* cited Robert Greenspan, director of the Center for Budget and Policy Priorities, who concluded that: "None of us can remember any major budget or tax bill in recent history that comes close to this bill in the magnitude of budget gimmicks included" (May 31, 2001). Other critics noted how the tax bill will bust the current budget and allows no allocations for promised defense programs and education (*Washington Post*, May 28, 2001: A1). Bloomberg.com cited a former IRS commissioner who described it as "the most confusing bill ever" and a *Christian Science Monitor* commentator described it as "one of the most convoluted pieces of legislation ever produced by the peculiar machinery of Washington fiscal politics" (June 7, 2001). And subverting his own plan to have faith-based charities replace welfare and social programs, the bill eliminated $90 billion in charitable tax breaks!

During the weekend of June 2–3, while all hell was breaking out in the Middle East, Bush retreated to Camp David with his parents and two teenage daughters, who had been busted for attempting to buy alcohol with a fake ID the week before, with the wild(er) twin, Jenna, facing jail due to Draconian Bushian Texas legislation that three criminal citations for drinking could land teenagers in jail thanks to a "zero tolerance" bill in Texas passed by Bush. Returning to the capital on Sunday night, Bush rushed to the event that was of utmost importance to his presidency, playing T-ball on the White House lawn with Little Leaguers and Hall of Famers. Meanwhile, violence escalated in the Middle East, energy prices soared, California faced energy blackouts, and poll support plunged with an ABC/*Washington Post* poll showing Bush's overall rating dropping 8 points over the past month, with 58 percent opposing his energy policies and 40 percent viewing the Democrats takeover of the Senate as "a good thing," while only 20 percent perceived the Republican loss as "a bad thing."

Bush's promises and rhetoric in his December 14, 2000, "victory speech" in Austin, Texas, after Gore's concession, make an instructive contrast to the reality of his administration. Bush promised to "set a new tone" in Washington and to overcome "the bitterness and partisanship of the past." Bush did set a new tone—which was to increase bitterness and partisanship as a result of his hardright agenda. Bush promised in his victory speech a bipartisan agenda that would first pursue education, and then social security and medicare reform, followed by tax cuts, since on the former issues there was more bipartisan agreement. In reality, Bush pushed hardest for his divisive tax cuts and antienvironmental and anticonsumer energy program, benefiting his wealthiest and most powerful contributors.

Bush promised in his victory speech to "work hard" for the bipartisan agenda, and while his handlers have worked very hard for his hardright agenda, Bush keeps slacking and limiting his involvement to cosmetic appearances and salesmanship, just as he did for seven years in Austin. Bush had the audacity in his victory speech to quote Thomas Jefferson and speak of commitment to a "sense of purpose," to "stand for principle," and to "do great good for freedom and harmony." So far, Bush's purpose has been to enrich the feeding-trough of his richest corporate contributors; his principles are to follow the hardright and screw the moderates; and the "freedom" he has promoted involves the untrammeled sovereignty of oil, gas, and energy producers to gouge consumers and states to the maximum, and the freedom of corporations from pesky environmental regulations that blocked their raping of the land and irresponsible exploitation of natural resources.

In the area of foreign policy, Bush evoked "American responsibilities" and the "promise of America" (a phrase used by progressive Herbert Crowley). In reality, Bush pursued a highly irresponsible politics of unilateralism that renounced global environmental treaties, rejected arms limitations treaties, recklessly pushed ahead to build a missile defense system strongly opposed by U.S. allies, and accelerated tensions with Iraq, North Korea, China, and Russia to generate "enemies" that would justify a missile defense system and increased military spending. During a June 2001 trip to Europe, Bush was savaged by the foreign, and even U.S. press, for his policies, encountered demonstrations against his administration, and has clearly emerged as the most embarrassing U.S. president in recent history, held in contempt by a growing number of world leaders and peoples.

And as for the "reasonable," "honorable," and bipartisan" politics that Bush promised in his victory speech in Austin and January inauguration speech, the Bush administration has proven itself to be the most dishonorable and mendacious in recent history. Already Bush has broken all of his promises in his December 13 Texas Legislature speech where he first defined his presidency. Bush's "political strategist," Karl Rove, joins Nixon's campaign manager, Murray Chotiner, as the sleaziest political operative in history, the master of the slime and slander—a technique that Rove honed in Texas politics, applied to John McCain in the Republican primaries and then to Al Gore during Election 2000, and aimed at the Clinton's as they left office. Rove is not only the numero uno slime maestro in U.S. politics, but is the most consistent and radical proponent of the Big Lie since Goebbels and Hitler. Lying is not just an accidental side-policy of Bushian politics, a normal business-as-usual where white lies and bending the truth are part of political normalcy (Wink! Wink!), where everyone does it and no one could expect norms of truth to govern all the time. No, Bushspeak lying is Big-Time Mendacity, the Big Lie as the politics of everyday spinning, lying as the very substance of Bushspeak.

We now see in retrospect that Bush was never a compassionate conservative, he is a hardright radical whose record in Texas, and so far as president, shows no compassion whatsoever for the poor and oppressed, for workers and working mothers, for children and the aged, for prisoners and the wayward, or for the environment or democratic polity. The Bush administration has no compassion toward anyone except the tobacco companies, the oil and energy companies, and the Republican Party and Bush crime syndicate that steal as much as they can from the federal treasury to reward their allies and contributors in the theft of an election, Grand Theft 2000.[9]

THE FLORIDA RECOUNT (Cont'd)

The great thing about America is everybody should vote. —George W. Bush

While the media and the political establishment were eager to get on with business as usual, in response to criticisms of illegitimacy and complaints about the election, the Republican mantra was "get over it." In a visit to William Daley's Chicago just after the inauguration, Bill Clinton congratulated Daley on the Gore campaign and said that Gore would have won the election if the votes were counted. In early February, the new head of the Democratic National Committee, Terry McAuliffe, attacked the Florida fiasco and promised "voter intimidation hearings all over the country" and broad electoral reform. Web site democrats.com posted Al Gore's steadily increasing margin of victory in Florida, as news organizations inspected the ballots in various regions of the state.

Many media and political organizations wanted to count the ballots after the Supreme Court halted the tallying of the never-counted undervotes and awarded the presidency to Bush by a five-to-four decision. While there were some Republican attempts to end the "inspection" of the ballots after the premature closing down of the vote counting, Florida's "sunshine laws" allowed inspection of ballots, and many media and political organizations paid local counties for the right to examine them. Hence, a wide range of groups undertook to see who would have prevailed if a fair hand count had been taken of the ballots throughout the state of Florida.

The first count of untabulated ballots in Lake County after the election by the *Orlando Sentinel* found 376 discarded ballots that "were clearly intended as votes for Gore," with another 246 such ballots showing votes for Bush, which would have yielded Gore a gain of 130 votes (December 19). Gore gained 120 more votes than Bush in a recount of Hillsborough County's disputed presidential undervotes done by the *Tampa Tribune* (December 30). The *Orlando Sentinel* undertook further recount operations, tallying overvotes as well as undervotes in some "inspections." They found that overvotes were regularly yielding more votes for Gore even in Republican-dominated counties that had optical-scan systems. Mickey Kaus concluded in an article in *Slate* that had Gore pursued a statewide recount of under- and overvotes he would have won in a walk (December 28).

While initial inspections focused on the undervotes that the Florida Supreme Court had mandated should be counted throughout the state of Florida, a consortium of eight press organizations (*New York Times, Washington Post, Wall Street Journal,* Associated Press, Tribune Company, CNN, *St. Petersburg Times,* and *Palm Beach Post*) planned a recount of the overvotes as well as the undervotes. A study by the *Washington Post* (January 27, 2001) in eight of Florida's largest counties of the overvotes had indicated that Gore's name was punched on more than 46,000 of the double-punched ballots while Bush's name was punched on 17,000 of them.

One group, democrats.com, was also counting overvotes, and in an inspection of overvotes in Gadsden County they found forty smudged ballots for Gore, eliminating the vote, and no smudged ballots for Bush, leading the group to suggest "official misconduct." Focusing on evidence of voter fraud, group members examined overvotes where punching out an extra chad or marking an optical scan would eliminate votes; they were suspicious that a large number of overvotes deprived Gore of so many votes.[10] The group was also searching for evidence of a concerted effort by unregistered and ineligible members of the Cuban community to vote for Bush in retaliation for the Clinton administration's seizure of Elian Gonzalez and his return to Cuba. A right-wing group, Judicial Watch, was also investigating voter fraud in South Florida involving felons who voted for Gore (on these surveys, see Anthony York, "The Florida Recount Continues!" *Salon,* January 17, 2001).

Surprisingly, an inspection by the *Palm Beach Post* (January 14, 2001) of the 10,600 previously uncounted ballots in Miami–Dade County revealed that Bush would have picked up six votes and that the majority of undervotes appeared to register no choice. A later inspection funded by the *Miami Herald* and *USA Today* indicated that Gore gained only 49 votes in the recounting of the 10,644 Miami–Dade undervotes. These results suggested that the Republican "bourgeois riot" that stopped the Miami–Dade manual counting of untallied ballots was not necessary and that had Bush agreed to the recount of the four counties proposed by the Democrats he might have narrowly won.[11]

However, an array of inspections throughout Florida suggests that Gore would have decisively won if the Florida Supreme Court recount had not been stopped. A study by the *Palm Beach Post* (January 27, 2001) indicated that examination of the 4,513 ballots declared "no vote" in Palm Beach County showed that closer inspection and a liberal chad standard would have yielded Gore 682 votes. A *Miami Herald* study (January 28, 2001) revealed that spoiled ballots that had been invalidated because of misalignment between card and ballot holder had cost Gore 316 votes; the report indicated that there was evidence of both machine error in the ballot alignment problems and voter error. An *Orlando Sentinel* (January 28, 2001) inquiry concluded that in a study of discarded votes in the state's fifteen counties with the highest rate of error Gore would have picked up 366 votes. A later survey by the newspaper in Orange County (February 11, 2001) disclosed that Gore would have picked up a net gain of 203 votes from inspections of 799 ballots rejected by voting machines.

Many of the votes were lost in smaller, rural areas that accounted for 8.6 percent of the state's lost ballots. The *Orlando Sentinel* inspection indicated that an optical-scanning system used in fifteen of Florida's sixty-seven counties resulted in 5.7 percent of all ballots being rejected, compared with a 3.9 percent rejection rate in counties that used punch cards, due to voters writing in the names, erasing votes, or making other errors. Thus, while the punch-card machines regularly created undervotes, the optical-scan system seemed to be generating large numbers of overvotes.

On April 4, 2001, the *Miami Herald* and *USA Today* released their recounts of the entire undervotes in Florida and their headlines, repeated in the Associated Press, *New York Times*, and most major newspapers, suggested that results indicated that Bush would have legitimately won the election if all undervotes throughout Florida had been counted. But closer inspection of the story showed that the study claimed that if the loosest interpretation was used that counted every uncounted ballot with a hanging chad, indention, or dimple, that Bush would have won by 1,665 votes. Whereas if the strictest standard that only counted clear punched-through had been used, Gore would have won by three votes, and if the more liberal standard had been applied in all counties, including Broward and Palm Beach, Gore would have won by 393 votes. Critics of the papers' recount argued that two courts in Florida had dismissed the most lenient standards and noted that if the overvotes had been counted it would have been a clear victory for Gore (a full recount of undervotes and overvotes by a consortium of major newspapers has not yet been completed).

The *Miami Herald/USA Today* inspections of the ballots suggested that assumptions of both the Bush and Gore camp were erroneous in regard to where their respective votes might be found in the uncounted ballots. The April 4 results indicated that many would-be Bush voters had made mistakes in their ballots, as had Gore voters, raising again the issue of voter literacy and the need for voter education. An April 5 *USA Today* follow-up on the recount indicated that: "Voters in Florida's majority-black precincts were nearly four times as likely to have their 2000 presidential election ballots invalidated than voters in precincts that are overwhelmingly made up of white voters." A *New York Times* report on April 5 headlined that "Counties Can't Account for All Ballots Reported in 2000," noting that "only 8 of the 67 Florida counties were able to produce for inspection the exact number of undervotes they reported on election night" and that 330 undervotes were missing in Orange County, 137 in Hillsborough, and 67 in Pinellas, disclosing once again the diciness of Florida's antiquated system of voting.

Most startling, however, were studies conducted by the *Orlando Sentinel*. On May 7, 2001, they reported that more than 10,000 mismarked or torn absentee ballots that counting machines couldn't read were duplicated to feed into voting machines and tabulate, more than 2,400 in Escambia County alone. This means that local canvassing boards took ballots that were torn, smudged, and even mangled in which they could discern "clear intent" and reproduced the "intended" votes on clean ballots so that machines could tabulate the votes and the votes could be counted. Since this operation was done primarily in Republican counties and since Bush dominated absentee ballots by a 2–1 margin, hundreds, maybe thousands, of votes were "manufactured" for Bush!

The previous day, May 6, the *Orlando Sentinel* published an article that documented how the optical-scan machines were not properly programmed to identify misvotes and provide the possibility of correction, especially in poor districts that were largely African American. They found that thousands of votes were wasted in poorer Florida counties because of misprogramming of optical scan machines, "bad pens," and other machine errors, costing Gore scores of votes.

Vote counting was extremely chaotic in Florida after the initial dead-heat election. Although all 67 counties were mandated to recount the ballots after the election night draw in Florida, Nick Baldick of the Gore campaign claimed that in 20 Florida counties the recount never took place (Simon 2001, 259), while a *Washington Post* study concluded: "18 of the state's 67 counties never recounted the ballots at all. They simply checked their original results. To this day, more than 1.58 million votes have not been counted a second time" (June

1, 2001: A1). The *Post* study also pointed out that although some counties had sophisticated technology designed to catch ballot errors, some switched off the mechanism. "Eight counties printed Spanish ballots for large blocs of Hispanic voters, but one elections supervisor chose not to do so. In 26 counties, ballots were disqualified if people voted for a candidate and wrote in the same candidate's name on their ballots" (June 1, 2001: A1).

Further, it was reported that in 8 counties, mostly Republican, there were manual recounts after the first machine recounting, gaining Bush hundreds of votes, even though the Republicans did everything they could to block the manual recounts in the four largely Democratic counties that the Gore campaign had requested. While there had been no formal requests of either side of counting overvotes, Jackson County tallied overvotes on election night, boosting Bush's total (Tapper 2001: 452). Although a ferocious battle went on in public over the tallying of absentee ballots, many of which did not contain legally required signatures, witnesses, or postmarks, some Republican counties quietly added illegal absentee ballots to the totals, leading a *Washington Post* reporter to conclude: "Without his Thanksgiving stuffing, Bush would have fallen behind. Gore would have had a lead of 22 votes—a lead that could have changed the entire public relations dynamic" (2001: 133). A later *Washington Post* inspection of the ballots found that many military absentee ballots were counted which were mailed after the required November 7 election date and that scores more were counted without postmarks. The *Post* even found a sailor who admitted mailing his ballot a week after the election hoping to help elect Bush and discovered that his ballot was found to be tallied in the Duval County results (June 1, 2001)!

Edward T. Foote II, chancellor of the University of Miami and co-chair of a task forced appointed by Florida governor Jeb Bush to study the election, concluded: "It was different systems, with different standards, different technology, different expectations and different procedures. . . . That's a prescription for nonequality of treatment." From this perspective, had the "equal protection" clause of the Constitution been applied to the Florida votes, the entire state's voting results and electors should have been thrown out as fundamentally flawed! Indeed, a report on the 2000 election by the U.S. Commission on Civil Rights concluded that Florida's conduct of the 2000 presidential election was marked by "injustice, ineptitude and inefficiency," singling out Gov. Jeb Bush and Secretary of State Katherine Harris "for allowing disparate treatment of voters" (*Washington Post*, June 5, 2001: A1*)*. Summarizing the "key findings," the *Post* noted:

- African Americans were nearly 10 times as likely as whites to have their ballots rejected. Poor counties populated by minorities were more likely to use voting systems that rejected larger percentages of ballots than more affluent counties.
- Some Hispanic and Haitian voters were not provided ballots in their native languages, and physical barriers sometimes kept disabled voters from entering polling sites.
- There were no clear guidelines to protect eligible voters from being wrongly removed as part of a statewide purge of felons, people with dual registrations, and the deceased.
- Elections supervisors in the counties with the worst problems failed to "prepare adequately" for the election or demand adequate resources.
- The Florida Division of Elections failed to educate Florida's residents on the mechanics of voting.

The U.S. Commission on Civil Rights report, *Probe of Election Practices in Florida during the 2000 Presidential Election*, was published on June 7, 2001, and contains a damning indictment of the Florida system of voting and rich detail on the problems and irregularities in the Florida voting-process, singling out Jeb Bush and Katherine Harris for criticism. Bush and Harris and the Commission's Republican members attacked the report, which the Commission made available to the Justice Department for possible criminal investigation and posted on the Internet for the public to scrutinize (see www.usccr.gov/vote2000/flmain.htm).

However one interprets the recounts, it is clear that a large number of ballots were not counted, votes were manufactured in dubious ways, and the Florida vote revealed, in the words of *Miami Herald* reporter Martin Marzer, "a world of imprecision and chaos" (April 4, 2001). Both the optical-scan method of voting and the punch-card system produced thousands of ballots in Florida where votes were not counted, revealing a system of voting in crisis and needing serious remedies.

The confusion uncovered in some of the ballot inspections and recounts points to obvious voter literacy problems, and indicates that serious efforts must be undertaken to ensure that individuals learn how to vote. Indeed, one of the scandals of Election 2000 is that Governor Jeb Bush of Florida vetoed a $100,000 state allotment for voter education, while approving a $4.3 million budget to purge felons from the voting list, a procedure that eliminated thousands of eligible voters, mostly poor and African American. The political bias involved in such decisions is obvious and was arguably part of a Bush–Harris campaign in the 2000 election to minimize potential Democratic voters and maximize Republican ones in a systematically partisan distortion of the state election process.[12]

Contrary to popular perception, the punch-card system—with the hanging and other chads—was not the worst offender in disenfranchising Florida voters. Ballot design was also crucial, with the infamous Palm Beach butterfly ballot helping to produce more than 19,000 overvotes. The two-page ballot in Duval County helped generate 20,000 overvotes. Moreover, it was accompanied by a sample ballot that wrongly advised citizens to "vote on every page" and contained on the second page the phrase "write-in candidate," which led many voters to scrawl in the candidate's name and have their vote thrown out because the machine rejected it. In fact, optical-scan machines threw out votes where citizens had used pens or markers rather than pencils, had tried to erase a vote and change it, or had smudged the ballot (there is also the possibility of systematic mischief in the producing of overvotes, as some suspected had occurred in Florida).[13]

It is thus clear that the current U.S. electoral process is highly flawed and requires new technologies, voter education, and a more professionally supervised electoral process. The Republican-dominated U.S. Congress got off to a slow and unpromising start on vote reform. Speaker Dennis Hastert (R-Ill.) proposed a bipartisan House select committee to review a range of issues from voting technology to the Electoral College, seeking new legislation to bring U.S. elections into the twenty-first century. The *Roll Call* reported, however, that Bush had been warning House Republican members against Hastert's reforms, at the very moment when he was assuring members of the Congressional Black Caucus that he favors electoral reform (February 5, 2001). Republicans said that Bush feared Democrats would use the panel to revisit the Florida recount melee and question his legitimacy. Democrats in the House and Senate have promised their own electoral reform measures, with Democrats calling for hearings, but so far there is no consensus on how to proceed or what to do.

The bottom line, however, is that the Bush team did everything possible to prevent the votes from being counted, to manufacture votes for their candidate, and even to prevent votes for Al Gore to be cast. They stole the presidency in Grand Theft 2000 through the machinations of a slim majority on the Supreme Court, thus casting in doubt the legitimacy of Bush's election and putting in crisis the U.S. system of democracy. As of summer 2001, it appears that much of the independent auditing of votes after the U.S. Supreme Court and Bush-machine theft of an election suggests that Gore won the plurality of votes in Florida, as well as the national popular vote by more than 500,000 votes. Election 2000 thus represents one of the great thefts and political crimes in U.S. history and should be investigated. Who, then, was most responsible for the Theft of an Election, and what might be the consequences of this crime?

GRAND THEFT 2000

I didn't, I swear I didn't—get into politics to feather my nest or feather my friends' nest. —George W. Bush

In concluding my tale, I recognize three sets of villains who emerged to pull off the Theft of an Election. First are the members of the Gang of Five on the U.S. Supreme Court who halted the recount in Florida mandated by the Florida Supreme Court and then ruled for Bush in a split five-to-four decision that is certain to be one of the most controversial in U.S. history. The conservative partisan five who stole the election for Bush are clearly enemies of democracy and have been condemned by Vincent Bugliosi (2001) as criminals. On January 13, 2001, 585 law professors published a statement in the *New York Times* comparing the Supreme Court justices who voted to stop the manual recount to propagandists who suppressed the facts and acted as "political proponents for candidate Bush, not as judges." The legal documents from Election 2000 were collected in a Brookings Institution publication, *Bush v. Gore* (2001), which contains legal rulings and commentary, supplemented by a Web site.[14] As Justice Stevens remarked in his dissent, confidence in judges as arbitrators of law will be indelibly harmed and the legacy of the Rehnquist Supreme Court has been deeply tarnished by the highly partisan and problematic decision to intervene in the election and select Bush president.

Second, the Florida Republican Party and in particular Governor Jeb Bush and Secretary of State Katherine Harris emerge as brazen thieves who abused their authority and did everything possible to help Bush win, engaging in highly problematic and perhaps criminal procedures before the election, and then doing everything in their power to block the manual recounting of ballots and to rush to certify Bush during the Florida ballot wars. Harris was rewarded for her labors with an appointment to the prestigious Council on Foreign Relations, but both her political future and Jeb Bush's are in question, potential victims of their abuse of their offices to get George W. Bush elected.

Reports indicated special anger of citizens of Florida over the suppression of their votes in the election. The *St. Petersburg Times* published a series of

585 LAW PROFESSORS SAY

By Stopping the Vote Count in Florida, The U.S. Supreme Court Used Its Power To Act as Political Partisans, Not Judges of a Court of Law

We are Professors of Law at 115 American law schools, from every part of our country, of different political beliefs. But we all agree that when a bare majority of the U.S. Supreme Court halted the recount of ballots under Florida law, the five justices were actings as political proponents for candidate Bush, not as judges.

It is Not the Job of a Federal Court to Stop Votes From Being Counted

By stopping the recount in the middle, the five justices acted to suppress the facts. Justice Scalia argued that the justices had to interfere even before the Supreme Court heard the Bush team's arguments because the recount might "cast a cloud upon what [Bush] claims to be the legitimacy of his election." In other words, the conservative justices moved to avoid the "threat" that Americans might learn that in the recount, Gore got more votes than Bush. This is presumably "irreparable" harm because if the recount proceeded and the truth once became known, it would never again be possible to completely obscure the facts. But it is not the job of the courts to polish the image of legitimacy of the Bush presidency by preventing disturbing facts from being confirmed. Suppressing the facts to make the Bush government seem more legitimate is the job of propagandists, not judges.

By taking power from the voters, the Supreme Court has tarnished its own legitimacy. As teachers whose lives have been dedicated to the rule of law, we protest.

articles on February 19, 2001, that documented the anger of black voters, more than 80 percent of which complained that blacks' ballots were disproportionately rejected or not counted during the election; one in three claimed that they or someone they know personally was denied fair access to voting. Many believed that "it was Jeb Bush and his cronies" who denied their vote and vowed to help defeat him in coming elections. A *Miami Herald* article (February 18, 2001) likewise reported that Democrats are "still bitter" and "irate" over the vote and "leaders hope they can turn feelings into power at the polls."

Third, it was the Bush dynasty that was behind, led, and fueled with cash and raw power the Republican coup d'état. Bush senior cronies and partners in crime James Baker and Dick Cheney, and their armies of political operatives and lawyers, engineered the strategy and tactics in the pilfering of the presidency, the Bush machine raised the money to finance the coup, and the Bush family was able to establish itself as one of the premier political dynasties in U.S. history. The theft of the 2000 election revealed the Bush dynasty to be utterly ruthless, amoral, mendacious, and Machiavellian. As noted in this study, the Bush machine effectively organized its constituencies, ranging from group troops in Florida and elsewhere to high-powered lawyers and partisan Supreme Court justices, to grab state power in a coup as ruthless as that of the Bolsheviks.

In fact, the villainies just cited are overlapping, held together by the money and influence of the Bush machine, which had at its disposal conservative judges, the Florida state apparatus, vast legal resources, political operatives, an aggressive punditocracy, and compliant media institutions. Grand Theft 2000 was highly daring but also risky for the Bush machine, whose brazen seizure of state power opens the possibility that Bush family members will be rewarded for their endeavors by thorough investigation of the family history, the full range of scandals that family members have been involved in, and their checkered personal, political, and economic past—as well as whatever present scandals they are involved in.

Previously, George Bush senior and Lucky Junior had truly been Teflon politicians with the media going down "on bended knee" to avoid embarrassing them. Now books, articles, and Web sites have copious information on the Bush family that could lead to their thorough vilification and downfall.[15] It is a mark of the family hubris, and perhaps the drive and ambition of George Bush senior, that the Bush dynasty took the risk of exposure and its consequences by pushing the obviously unqualified W. the Shrub to seek and steal the presidency. In a media and Internet society, information is not as easily controlled as in previous generations. Many politicians have been brought down by the media in recent years, and Bill Clinton has been—and continues to be—subject to perhaps the most sustained media scrutiny and assault of any president in history, creating the precedent that presidents and ex-presidents are fair game for political blood sport.

Thus, while the mainstream media has so far taken a dive on critically examining W. and the powers behind the throne, the alternative press and Internet sources are diligently amassing information on the Bush dynasty. Robert Parry, an investigative reporter who broke crucial Iran-Contra stories documenting Bush senior's involvement in the affair, criticized the Democrats and corporate media in the 1990s for not pursuing the multifarious scandals involving George Bush senior, who had been under investigation for some of the greatest political scandals in U.S. history. The Bush scandals included the "October Surprise," in which the Reagan–Bush team allegedly negotiated a deal with the Iranians in 1980 to prevent release of the U.S. hostages and a triumphant return that might have boosted Jimmy Carter's presidential hopes; instead, Carter undertook a failed rescue attempt that many believe was sabotaged by U.S. operatives connected to the Bush clique.

Parry argues that the Iran-Contra operation, in which arms were funneled to the Iranians later in the 1980s, was a payoff for this deal. He claims that information was uncovered from French and Russian intelligence sources that placed officials of the Reagan–Bush ticket in Paris during the alleged negotiations with Iranians to hold the Americans hostage until after the 1980 election, and there have been persistent reports that Bush himself was involved in the deal. There has also been a wealth of evidence that George H. W. Bush was centrally involved in the Iran-Contra affair, but this information has been largely ignored by the mainstream media.[16]

Moreover, upon concluding his presidency in 1992 after his defeat by Clinton, Bush senior pardoned members of the Reagan administration who had been accused of crimes in Iran-Contra, including Secretary of Defense Caspar Weinberger and others, infuriating special prosecutor Lawrence Walsh, who wanted to question these men concerning George Bush's involvement.[17] The Democrats, in turn, did not investigate these pardons and failed to follow up on scrutiny of Reagan–Bush era crimes, with George Bush allegedly at the center, thus opening the way for the later comeback and ascent to power of Bush's son.

The Democrats and a complicit media have a history of letting the Bush family off the hook for investigations and failing to pursue their many scandalous activities. There was no Democratic uproar over George Bush senior's pardons of Iran-Contra criminals, or of other disgraceful pardons noted below. Similarly, after Election 2000 there have been no Democratic Party hearings concerning the theft of the election in Florida, the many irregularities in the election, and the civil rights violations of those denied their votes. The Republicans, by contrast, held Congressional hearings, taking the media to task for calling Florida for Gore early in the evening and other alleged mistakes and miscalls that allegedly benefited the Democrats (though there was not a Republican peep about the scandal of calling the election prematurely for Bush, thus making him the presumed winner whose victory was being plundered in the postelection struggles). Moreover, the Republicans are holding hearings on the Clinton pardons, pursuing his every misdeed, even after he has left office, while the Democrats in 1993 let Big Bush I off the hook, preparing the way for Little Bush II.

Criticizing Bush senior's presidential pardons upon leaving office, Joe Conason noted in a February 27, 2001, *Salon* article that not only did Bush pardon a series of Iran-Contra criminals who could have implicated him in high state crimes and treason, but he also pardoned a Pakistani heroin trafficker; oilman Armand Hammer, who had contributed heavily to his campaign; and Orlando Bosch, a notorious anti-Castro terrorist who was serving jail time for having entered the United States illegally and who many believed was guilty of many terrorist crimes, including a 1976 explosion of a Cuban airliner that killed all seventy-six civilians aboard. Conason noted that these shocking pardons hardly received any press coverage or political discussion, a sharp comparison to the avalanche of coverage of and congressional hearings over Clinton's highly problematic pardons.[18]

It is indeed one of the scandals of U.S. journalism and scholarship that there have not been more investigative reports and exposés of Bush family financial shenanigans, political misdeeds, and generations of outrageous behavior, going back to Prescott Bush's support of the Nazis and his fortune from investment in a bank that did business throughout World War II with the German fascist regime (see note 1 in chapter 5). The presidency of George W. Bush provides an excellent occasion for research into the history and crimes of the Bush dynasty, and a key challenge for American democracy is getting the media and those concerned to take up this long overdue task.

NOTES

1. For a typical ripe rightwing account of these stories, see Deroy Murdock, "Scamalot: Waiting in Vain for the Clintons' Final Insult," *National Review Online*

(Jan. 31, 2001; www.nationalreview.com/murdock/murdock013101.shtml). Within days, these rumors of the Clinton team trashing the White House and stealing from Air Force One presented by the right as news were exposed as mere disinformation by the Bush propaganda ministry. *Fox News* was especially egregious in spreading the disinformation. Dubiously truthful and rarely balanced or fair, Brit Hume described the "looting" of Air Force One as a "raid" on the plane. His *Fox News* partner-in-lies, Tony Snow, a syndicated columnist and former presidential speechwriter for W.'s father, wrote that the White House "was a wreck." He claimed that Air Force One, after taking Clinton and some aides to New York following the inauguration, "looked as if it had been stripped by a skilled band of thieves—or perhaps wrecked by a trailer park twister." After listing missing items, including "silverware, porcelain dishes with the presidential seal, and even candy," Snow fumed. One story, however, published by David Goldstein in the *Kansas City Star* (May 17, 2001), "No Truth in White House Vandal Scandal," indicated that a report by the General Service Administration (GSA) concluded that none of these reports, leaked by the Bush White House, had any basis in fact.

2. Curiously, Bill Gates Sr. and a group of 120 mostly Republican and conservative billionaires signed a petition opposing the excesses of Bush's tax-cut program. See Joan Walsh, "Plucrats to the rescue!" (*Salon*, Feb. 15, 2001). Joshua Micah Marshall suggested in an *American Prospect* note (Feb. 12, 2001) titled "Shameless, Brazen and Disgusting" that the words applied to Clinton's behavior during his last days in the White House could usefully be applied to Bush's tax-cut proposals.

3. The Stockman quote was in a much-discussed interview with William Greider, "The Education of David Stockman," which recorded Reagan's budget director's disillusionment with "supply-side economics" and the Reagan administration's compromises with corporate forces. See the discussion in the Walsh article cited in note 2 above. In an article on Bush's tax "plan," Bob Herbert ("Voodoo Redux," *New York Times*, Mar. 1, 2001) recalls that in Lou Cannon's biography of Reagan, James Baker, then Reagan's secretary of treasury, regretted that budget deficits had "gotten away" from the Reagan administration and that he wished "he had paid more attention to the consequences of the tax cuts." In fact, the Reagan administration doubled the previous national debt, while Bush senior in his four disgraceful years doubled Reagan's doubling. As Yogi Berra would say, it's déjà vu all over again.

4. *Wag the Dog* was a 1998 film in which a president, resembling Bill Clinton, was involved in a sex scandal with a young intern and constructed a mythical Albanian enemy to undertake military action against during the closing days of an election campaign in order to distract the press and public—action that Clinton himself arguably undertook upon occasion. The phrase "wagging the dog" thus became a code word for military action to sidetrack attention from political embarrassment and to mobilize the public into patriotic support of the president—a political strategy, one might note, that Ronald Reagan also successfully employed with his Grenada invasion, Libyan bombing, and other well-publicized military actions that distracted the public from domestic or other political problems.

5. The China flip-flopping incurred the wrath of the ultrahard lunatic right, which deplored that China had "brought the United States to one knee." But others in the Bush administration had a different perspective on China. For instance, W.'s uncle Prescott Bush, head of the U.S. Chinese Chamber of Commerce, might have reminded W. of the multibillions to be made in business deals with the Chinese if Strangelove could be refrained from going to war with them; Prescott Bush is the son of the Bush family scion Prescott Bush, H. W.'s father and W.'s grandfather, who amassed the family fortune with the bank that financed and laundered money for National Socialism (see chapter 1).

It also came out that Bush's Secretary of Labor Elaine Chao is a China supporter. As head of the Heritage Foundation, Chao was allegedly involved in firing a research analyst, Rick Fisher, who had published studies harshly critical of China when Heritage Foundation donor Maurice "Hank" Greenberg, a pro-China lobbyist, complained. Chao's father is Chinese-born, on friendly terms with the current regime, and owner of a shipping firm that does business with China. In addition, Chao is married to rightwing Senator Mitch McConnell (R-Ky.), who had received thousands of dollars in campaign donations from Greenberg and who is himself a member of the China lobby (see http://www.worldnetdaily.com/news/article.asp?AERTICLE_ID=21 359). In addition, Lawrence Kaplan notes that many prominent members of the Republican establishment, including former National Security Advisers Brent Scowcroft and Henry Kissinger, both of whom represented companies eager to do business with China, were looking to profit from Chinese markets, like Uncle Prescott, and were not seeking war (see "Sorry. Behind the Administration's China Cave," *The New Republic*, April 23, 2001). A week later, Kaplan reported that most of the U.S. rightists, who would have gone ballistic if Clinton twice apologized to the Chinese, praised Bush's "diplomacy" because they recognized that Bush was largely promoting a hardright agenda and thus should be supported (see "Cavemen. Why the Right Backed Bush on China," *The New Republic*, April 30, 2001). In any case, there are deep divisions in the Bush administration between those who want to maintain an extremely belligerent posture toward China to legitimate proliferating defense expenditures and those who want to profit from its gigantic potential markets.

6. For a critique of Hoff Sommers and the organized rightwing attack on feminism, see Hammer, forthcoming.

7. As the stock market tanked in mid-March, worry circulated about the possibility of Bush's policies destroying the progress of the previous eight years. See Joan Walsh, "Dubya's Mad-Dog Economics: Who Says This Surplus-Squandering Hothead Is Conservative?" (http://www.salon.com/politics/feature/2001/03/16/bush/index.html, March 16, 2001), and Herman M. Schwartz and Aida A. Hozic, "Who Needs the New Economy? Bush's Bias toward Industrial Dinosaurs Is Strangling America's High-Tech-Driven Growth" (http://www.salon.com/tech/feature/2001/03/16/schwartz/index.html, March 16, 2001). While some worried that Bush's own loose talk about "recession" and a "sputtering" economy was sending out messages that were contributing to lack

of investor confidence in Bush and his economic policies, there were plenty of reasons to worry about Bush and the economy: (1) Bush is a most inexperienced economic manager, with serious deficiencies in understanding the global economy; (2) members of the Bush–Cheney gang immediately revealed that they were going to give their favored contributors whatever benefits they desired, independent of the benefits or costs for the economy as a whole; (3) Cheney's weak heart could go out at any time, creating chaos in the Cheney–Bush administration; and (4) the tax cut that is at the center of Bushnomics is perhaps the riskiest and most reckless "plan" proposed in modern history. Good reasons to worry.

8. See Paul Krugman, "Going for Broke: The Bush Tax Cut Is a Lie," *The New Republic* (May 21, 2001); Krugman expanded his argument in a book *Fuzzy Math* (2001). See also Jonathan Chalt who argued: "The debate over the Bush tax cut has been shrouded in a fog of cant and untruth. . . . The tax cut's advocates have produced a series of distortions, misrepresentations, and outright lies intended to convince Americans that the tax cut primarily benefits the poor and the middle class, or at least to demonize those who would suggest otherwise. "Going for Gold," *The New Republic* (May 21, 2001).

9. For documentation of the horrors of Bush's first hundred days, see http://members.aol.com/kgar41/horror.html; for daily documentation of the atrocities of the Bush administration, see the Web sites listed in Introduction, note 3. As the dialectic moves forward, new Web sites worth checking out to chart the antics of the Bush administration are appearing such as http://www.smirkingchimp.com/ with the telling motto: "Ask not at whom the chimp smirks, he smirks at you." There are also a variety of sites that compile humor, including cartoons, animation, and other cultural forms ridiculing Bush and his cronies; two sites posit links to a wealth of Bush satire material: www.allhatnocattle.net/cream_of_the_crop_links.htm and www.linkcrusader.com/anti-bush.htm media.

10. See Sharman Braff, "The Florida Overvote: Tragic Mistake, or Katherine Harris with Tweezers?" (www.democrats.com/view.cfm?id = 1730). This article indicates that study of the pattern of overvotes shows suspiciously high numbers of overvotes in five counties, with a large number of Gore–Bush double votes that would be hard to explain without the hypothesis of machine tampering whereby votes are run through machines a second time, which double-vote to eliminate votes. Double votes were especially high in Duval County, a Republican stronghold with large numbers of black precincts in which there were many reports of African American voter harassment on election day and many double votes that had appeared. Suspiciously, Duval initially resisted the request of independent groups to study the ballots.

11. The Bush administration made the *Miami Herald* tabulation of the undervotes appear to suggest that Bush legitimately won the Florida vote, and many newspapers and conservative sources repeated the spin. Of course, it was the manual recount of the entirety of Florida's undervotes that the U.S. Supreme Court halted, and most evidence so far suggests that Gore would have won handily had all undervotes been

counted and that if overvotes were inspected that had evidence of the voter indeed choosing Gore (by writing in his name, for instance), Gore's lead would have soared.

12. On February 23, 2001, Jeb Bush released a fifty-four-page advisory report that recommended replacement of punch-card ballots with optical scanners, but the report did not address the failure of optical scanners in producing overvotes, or the need for voter literacy. The Florida legislature did pass a voting overhaul bill on May 4, 2001, calling for the elimination of punch-card ballot machines and their replacement by optical scan machines, and the Georgia governor signed an election reform package that requires touch-screen voting in the state by the 2004 presidential election. Greg Palast warns, however, that many states undertaking voting-reform projects are repeating the disastrous mistake of Florida, which hired a company to undertake computer-aided purging of centralized voter files to eliminate dead voters, felons, and others. Palast argues that "the likely result will be the elimination of a lot of legitimate voters and an increased potential for political mischief," urging that local precincts take charge of the updating of their list, and not the state. See "The Wrong Way to Fix the Vote," *Washington Post* (June 11, 2001). *The Nation* established a Web page with links to voter reform efforts and stories concerning the need for reform (see http://www.thenation.com/special/2001electoralreform.mhtml).

13. Jake Tapper alleges (2001: 404ff.) that Al Gore himself was pushing the rumor that voting machines could be programmed to eliminate one out of ten votes for him, an irregularity that allegedly surfaced in the 1988 Florida Senatorial election (see chapter 3, note 3). Tapper completely dismisses the possibility, however, suggesting that Gore was going over the top—*X-Files* conspiracy whacko—by suggesting such a thing. However, experts have been long aware of the possibility of rigging Votomatic counting machines. In 1988, Ronnie Dugger published an article in *The New Yorker* (Nov. 7, 1988) about the potential for fraud, citing many proofs of error in computer voting systems. He noted that in the 1988 Senate election in Florida between Republican Connie Mack and Democrat Buddy McKay, that in McKay's four Democratic stronghold counties, there were 210,000 people who voted for president but did not vote in the U.S. Senate race. In a comparable U.S. Senate race in 1980, three of every 1000 presidential voters did not vote for senator whereas in the disputed 1988 election, 14 out of every 1000 did not vote for senator (Tapper explains this by noting that the Senate election that year was placed at the bottom of the ballot [405], a not totally convincing explanation).

Interestingly, Dugger published an article titled "Rage against the Machine. How Safe Are Our Voting Machines?" in *The New Republic* (December 4, 2001) that argued again that there are copious examples of serious voting machine errors and the potential for fraud. He cited many voting machine experts who acknowledged the problem and such reports circulated through the Internet during the Battle for the White House, such as a study by Jonathan Vankin, "Vote of No Confidence" (www.conspire.com/votefraud.html). Hence, there is clearly the possibility that Votomatic and other computer tabulating systems could be rigged, there are examples of fishy tabulation throughout recent history, and many experts kicked in during the Election 2000 debates indicating the possibility of fraudulent rigging of computerized voting machines. Thus, this is a significant issue that should have been investigated as to whether there might have been computer fraud in the Florida tabulation wars.

14. See the collection of key legal documents in a Brookings Institution Web site (http://www.brookings.edu/bushvgore/) and an accompanying book (2001), which provides context and legal commentary. I have drawn upon published commentary on the controversial Supreme Court ruling and have found the sharp criticisms of the decision by Ronald Dworkin, Vincent Bugliosi, and Bruce Ackerman especially helpful and convincing.

15. On Bush senior, see the appendix and sources in Kellner 1990; on Bush junior, see note 4 and the material assembled in www.bushwatch.com, www.consortium.com, and www.moldea.com. There is enough material in the background of the Bush dynasty for ten Watergates.

16. This information is archived in Robert Parry's Web site, www.consortium.com, and many more investigative reports critical of the Bush family are found in sources cited in note 15 above. In my 1990 book, *Television and the Crisis of Democracy,* I include in my appendix references to investigative reports and books on Bush's involvement in the October Surprise, the Iran-Contra affair, and other scandals that were documented and discussed in the alternative media, but with few exceptions these were ignored in the mainstream media during the 1988 campaign in which Bush won the presidency. In my 1992 book, *The Persian Gulf TV War,* I document Bush senior's role in arming the Iraqi military in the 1980s and his support for the Iraqi regime up to the eve of Iraq's invasion of Kuwait; earlier, Bush had been a supporter of Manuel Noriega in Panama, until, evidently, Noriega crossed him, and the 1990 Panama invasion followed. As I have argued in this book, George W. Bush likewise received a pass for his and his family's misdeeds during the 2000 election. Were the mainstream media to discuss Bush family scandals with a fraction of the attention lavished on the Clintons, it is conceivable that the dynasty's rule would come to an abrupt end, and they would be forced to seek asylum in Kuwait or Panama.

17. James Ridgeway in the *Village Voice* (Feb. 27, 2001) also criticized Bush senior's last-minute pardons of Iran-Contra criminals, noting that they included:

- Weinberger, who faced an impending trial on five criminal charges of lying in testimony before Congress and in criminal investigations.
- Duane Clarridge, formerly in charge of European covert operations for the CIA, who faced seven charges of lying to congressional investigators and the White House Tower Commission about shipping U.S. missiles from Israel to Iran in November 1985.
- Elliott Abrams, a former assistant secretary of state, who pleaded guilty to twice withholding information from Congress in the midst of the scandal.
- Robert McFarlane, former national security adviser, who pleaded guilty to cover-ups on four misdemeanor charges.

- Clair George, former CIA deputy director of covert ops, who was convicted on criminal charges of lying to Congress. (http://www.villagevoice.com/issues/0109/ridgeway.shtml)

The full text of Bush's pardon is found on http://news.findlaw.com/cnn/docs/pardons/bush/bushironcontraprdns.pdf; for an account of the "serial terrorist" Orlando Bosch, who Bush pardoned, see http://onlinejournal.com/Special_Reports/Smith030101/smith030101.html.

18. In a March 4, 2001, *New York Observer* article, Joe Conason adds that Bush senior also pardoned three of his Texas oil industry and corporate buddies, who had committed bank fraud, tax evasion, and other corporate crimes.

REFERENCES

A note on references. Most of my sources were Internet, newspaper, and journal articles that I cited in the text or notes. The following is a list of some books that I consulted and drew upon.

Adorno, T. W. (1994) *The Stars Down to Earth and Other Essays on the Irrational in Culture*. London: Routledge.

Adorno, T. W. et al. (1950) *The Authoritarian Personality*. New York: Norton.

Altermann, Eric (2000) *Sound and Fury. The Making of the Punditocracy*. Ithaca, N.Y.: Cornell University Press.

Beard, Charles (1986 [1916]) *An Economic Interpretation of the Constitution of the United States*. New York: Free Press.

Begala, Paul (2000) *Is Our Children Learning? The Case against George W. Bush*. New York: Simon and Schuster.

Best, Steven, and Douglas Kellner (1991) *Postmodern Theory: Critical Interrogations*. London and New York: Macmillan and Guilford Press.

Best, Steven, and Douglas Kellner (1997) *The Postmodern Turn*. London and New York: Routledge and Guilford Press.

Best, Steven, and Douglas Kellner (2001) *The Postmodern Adventure: Science, Technology, and Cultural Studies at the Third Millennium*. London and New York: Routledge and Guilford Press.

Boggs, Carl (2000) *The End of Politics*. New York: Guilford Press.

Bugliosi, Vincent (2001) *The Betrayal of America: How the Supreme Court Undermined the Constitution and Chose Our President*. New York: Thunder's Mouth Press/ Nation Books.

Brewton, Pete (1992) *The Mafia, CIA & George Bush*. New York: SPI Books.

Correspondents of the *New York Times* (2001) *36 Days*. New York: Times Books.

Dershowitz, Alan (2001) *Supreme Injustice: How the High Court Hijacked Election 2000*. New York: Oxford University Press.

Dewey, John (1997 [1919]) *Democracy and Education*. New York: Simon and Schuster.

Dionne, E. J. Jr., and William Kristol, eds. (2001). *BUSH v. GORE: The Court Cases and the Commentary*. Washington, D.C.: Brookings Institution.

Gabler, Neil (1998) *Life the Movie: How Entertainment Conquered Reality*. New York: Alfred A. Knopf.

Greenfield, Jeff (2001) *Oh Wait! One Order of Crow: Inside the Srtangest Presidential Election Finish in American History*. New York: Putnam.

Hacking, Ian (1981) "How Should We Do the History of Statistics?" *Ideology and Consciousness* 8, 15–26.

Hammer, Rhonda (2001) *Anti-Feminism and Family Terrorism: A Critical Feminist Perspective*. Lanham, Md.: Rowman & Littlefield.

Hatfield, J. H. (2000) *Fortunate Son: George W. Bush and the Making of An American President*. New York: Soft Skull Press.

Herman, Edward, and Noam Chomsky (1988) *Manufacturing Consent: The Political Economy of the Mass Media*. New York: Pantheon.

Hertsgaard, Mark (1988) *On Bended Knee*. New York: Farrar, Straus, and Giroux.

Hofstadter, Richard (1996) *The Paranoid Style in American Politics and Other Essays*. Cambridge, Mass.: Harvard University Press.

Ivins, Molly, and Lou Dubose (2000) *Shrub: The Short but Happy Political Life of George W. Bush*. New York: Random House.

Kellner, Douglas (1979) "TV, Ideology and Emancipatory Popular Culture," *Socialist Review* 45 (May–June): 13–53.

Kellner, Douglas (1989) *Critical Theory, Marxism, and Modernity*. Cambridge and Baltimore: Polity Press and Johns Hopkins University Press.

Kellner, Douglas (1990) *Television and the Crisis of Democracy*. Boulder: Westview Press.

Kellner, Douglas (1992) *The Persian Gulf TV War*. Boulder: Westview Press.

Kellner, Douglas (1995) *Media Culture: Cultural Studies, Identity and Politics between the Modern and the Postmodern*. London and New York: Routledge.

Kellner, Douglas (1999) "Globalization from Below? Toward a Radical Democratic Technopolitics," *Angelaki* 4:2: 101–13.

Kellner, Douglas (2000) "New Technologies/New Literacies: Reconstructing Education for the New Millennium," *Teaching Education*, Vol. 11, No. 3: 245–65.

Kellner, Douglas (forthcoming) *Media Spectacle*. London and New York: Routledge.

Kellner, Douglas, and Michael Ryan (1988) *Camera Politica: The Politics and Ideology of Contemporary Hollywood Film*. Bloomington: Indiana University Press.

Kloppenberg, James T. (1986) *Uncertain Victory: Social Democracy and Progressivism in European and American Thought, 1870–1920*. New York and Oxford: Oxford University Press.

Krugman, Paul R. (2001) *Fuzzy Math. The Essential Guide to the Bush Tax Plan*. New York: Norton.

Marcuse, Herbert (2001) "The Dilemmas of Bourgeois Democracy." In *Herbert Marcuse: Toward a Critical Theory of Society*, edited by Douglas Kellner. London and New York: Routledge.

McChesney, Robert (1995) *Telecommunications, Mass Media, and Democracy: The Battle for the Control of U.S. Broadcasting, 1928–1935*. New York and Oxford: Oxford University Press.

McChesney, Robert (1997) *Corporate Media and the Threat to Democracy*. New York: Seven Stories Press.

Milbank, Dana (2001) *Smashmouth*. New York: Basic Books.

Miller, Mark Crispin (2001) *The Bush Dyslexicon*. New York: Norton.

Mitchell, Elizabeth (2000) *Revenge of the Bush Dynasty*. New York: Hyperion.

Orwell, George (1961 [1948]) *1984*. New York: Signet.

Political Staff of *The Washington Post* (2001) *Deadlock: The Inside Story of America's Closest Election*. New York: Public Affairs.

Rose, Nicholas (1999) *Powers of Freedom*. Cambridge: Cambridge University Press.

Ryan, Alan (1996) *John Dewey and the High Tide of American Liberalism*. New York: Norton.

Sammon, Bill (2001) *At Any Cost: How Al Gore Tried to Steal the Election*. Washington, D.C.: Regnery Publishing.

Schechter, Danny (2001) *Mediocracy 2000—Hail to the Thief: How the Media Stole the U.S. Presidential Election*. Electronic book available at www.mediachannel.org.

Schiller, Dan (1981) *Objectivity and the News*. Philadelphia: University of Pennsylvania Press.

Schiller, Dan (1999) *Digital Capitalism*. Cambridge, Mass.: MIT Press.

Sussman, Warren (1984) *Culture as History: The Transformation of American Society in the Twentieth Century*. New York: Pantheon.

Tapper, Jake (2001) *Down & Dirty: The Plot to Steal the Presidency*. Boston and New York: Little, Brown.

Tarpley, Webster Griffin, and Anton Chaitkin (1992) *George Bush. The Unauthorized Biography*. Washington, D.C.: Executive Intelligence Review.

West, Darrell M. (2001) *The Rise and Fall of the Media Establishment*. Boston and New York: Bedford/St. Martin's.

Westbrook, Robert B. (1991) *John Dewey and American Democracy*. Ithaca, N.Y.: Cornell University Press.

Zinn, Howard (1995) *A People's History of the United States: 1492–Present*. New York: Harperperennial Library.

INDEX

Jeffords, Jim, 198, 199
Jennings, Peter, 73, 101
Jensen, Elizabeth, 132n3
Jews, in Florida, 32
Johnson, Steven, 183n17
Jones, Tommy Lee, 7
Judd, Jackie, 101
Judicial Watch, 204

Kaletsky, Anatole, 196
Kamiya, Gary, 99, 116n9
Kansas City Star, 215n1
Kaplan, Lawrence, 216n5
Kaus, Mickey, 204
Kelly, Michael, 63n4
Kennedy, Anthony, 114n1, 175
Kerrey, Bob, 190
Keyes, Alan, 86
Keyssar, Alex, 161
Kinsley, Michael, 143–44
Kissinger, Henry, 216n5
Klain, Ron, 49n12, 146
Klein, Robert, 139
Kovach, Bill, 19n9
Kranish, Michael, 14
Kroch, Joe, 93
Krugman, Paul, 199–200, 217n8
Kurtz, Howard, 12, 17nn1–2, 51, 66, 97n7, 124, 180–81n6
Kyoto Treaty, 197

"585 Law Professors Say," *211*
la Barga, Jorge, 41
Ladumia, Gloria, 134n9
Lake County, 89–90, 203
Lane, Charles, 88
Laney, Pete, 110
Lantigua, John, 79n5, 182n11
LaRouche, Lyndon, 15
L.A. Weekly, 115n6
Leach, Howard, 191
Lee, Martin A., 20n12

Lehrer, Jim, 3
Leno, Jay, 9, 17n3, 196
Lewis and Clark rulings, 71
Lewis, Anthony, 79n6
Lewis, Charles, 181n7
Lewis, Terry, 70, 72–73, 75, 146
liar: Bush, George W., 5, 9, 13; Gore, Al, 4–5, 11, 13, 19n11. *See also* lies
Lieberman, Joseph, 57, 59, 74, 178, 183n18
lies, 98n9, 108, 135, 142–43, 198–200, 202
Limbaugh, Rush, 10, 126; coverage on NBC, 123; hardball tactics, 53, 63n4; popularity, 18–19n8; voter illiteracy, 145
Lincoln, Abraham, 81
Loftus, John, 14
logging, 193
Los Angeles municipal elections, 156
Los Angeles Times, 91, 105, 190; Bush's luck, 114n5; e-mail, 132n3; Gore's errors, 181n9; international boycotts, 197; Los Angeles municipal elections, 156; results of election, 116n9; voting machines, 180n3
Lott, Trent, 196
"lucky breaks" for Bush, 106–8, 114–15n5
Luntz, Frank, 13

machines, voting. *See* voting machines
Mack, Connie, 46n3, 218n13
Madison, James, 162
managed politicians, xiv, 177
manual recounts. *See* recounts
maps, color-coded, 26, 152
Marcus, Ruth, xixn2
Marcuse, Herbert, 172
Marshall, Joshua Micah, 215n2
Martin County, 39, 48n7, 69–71
Marx, Karl, 81